Luke's Jesus in the Roman Empire and the Emperor in the Gospel of Luke

Luke's Jesus in the Roman Empire and the Emperor in the Gospel of Luke

Pyung Soo Seo

☙PICKWICK *Publications* · Eugene, Oregon

LUKE'S JESUS IN THE ROMAN EMPIRE AND THE EMPEROR
IN THE GOSPEL OF LUKE

Copyright © 2015 Pyung Soo Seo. All rights reserved. Except for brief quotations in critical publications or reviews, no part of this book may be reproduced in any manner without prior written permission from the publisher. Write: Permissions. Wipf and Stock Publishers, 199 W. 8th Ave., Suite 3, Eugene, OR 97401.

Pickwick Publications
An Imprint of Wipf and Stock Publishers
199 W. 8th Ave., Suite 3
Eugene, OR 97401

www.wipfandstock.com

ISBN 13: 978-1-4982-0054-7

Cataloguing-in-Publication Data

Seo, Pyung Soo

Luke's Jesus in the Roman empire and the emperor in the Gospel of Luke / Pyung Soo Seo.

xiv + 194 p. ; 23 cm. Includes bibliographical references.

ISBN 13: 978-1-4982-0054-7

1. Bible. Luke—Criticism, interpretation, etc. I. Title.

BS2595.2 S48 2015

Manufactured in the U.S.A.   03/09/2015

Contents

Acknowledgments | vii
Abbreviations of Periodicals, Reference Works | ix
Ancient Sources: Editions and Abbreviations | xi

Introduction | 1

1   Jesus' Birth and Trial in Relation to the Issue of Authority | 21
    Jesus' Birth: Charismatic Authority | 22
    Jesus' Trial: Traditional Authority and Bureaucratic Authority | 30
        Hearing before the Jewish Assembly (Lk. 22:66–71) | 31
        Initial Trial before Pilate (Lk. 23:1–5) | 34
        Charges | 36
            Perverting the Nation | 37
            Tribute | 38
            Kingship | 38
        Trial before Herod (Lk. 23:6–12) | 41
            Pilate's Reasons for Sending Jesus over to Herod (Luke 23:7) | 42
            Herod as Fox in Lk. 13:31 | 44
            Friendship in Lk. 23:12 | 45
        Second Trial before Pilate (Luke 23:13–25) | 47
    Summary | 51

2   Census, Tribute, and Tax Collectors | 53
    Census and Tribute | 54
        Identification of Denarius and Authority of Coin-Mint | 57
        Revolt in Relation to Religious Reasons | 61
        Jesus' Response | 62
    Various Taxes | 64
    Tax Collectors | 68

Emperor's *Imperium* and *Auctoritas* | 72
    Imperium | 73
    Auctoritas | 75
Levi (Luke 5:27–32) | 81
Zacchaeus (Luke 19:1–10) | 86
Summary | 94

3 Benefactor: Who is Greater? | 96
    The Identity of the Kings of the Gentiles | 97
    Luke's Understanding of the Title "Benefactor" | 101
    Benefactor and Savior | 112
    Summary | 114

4 Savior: Victory-Peace-Salvation | 116
    Augustus as Savior | 117
    Augustus' Victory and Peace Based upon His Military *Imperium* | 119
    Two Theories | 124
        Assimilation and Acculturation | 124
        Contra-culture theory | 128
    Jesus as Victor: His Victory over His Enemies | 130
        Non-Human Being: Satan and His relationship with the Roman Empire | 131
        Human Being | 137
    Jesus as Peace-Bringer | 139
        Sword/Violence | 141
            Jesus' Rejection of the Use of Sword (Luke 22:35–38 and Luke 22:47–53) | 141
            The Cleansing of the Temple (Luke 19:45–48) | 144
            Love Your Enemies (Luke 6:27–38) | 147
    Jesus as Savior | 155
        Jesus' Saving Activities in Relation to Tax Collectors | 157
    Zechariah's Praise | 164
        Enemy | 167
        Peace and Salvation | 174
    Summary | 176

5 Conclusion | 177

Bibliography | 181

Acknowledgments

THANKS ARE DUE TO many people for making this book possible. In particular, my deepest gratitude is for Peter Oakes, George Brooke, and Todd Klutz (University of Manchester). Their help in criticizing and examining the entire draft has been indispensable to my thesis. I am also grateful to my mother for her love and support.

Abbreviations of Periodicals, Reference Works

ABD	*Anchor Bible Dictionary*, edited by David Noel Freedman. 6 vols. New York: Doubleday, 1992
BBR	*Bulletin for Biblical Research*
BTB	*Biblical Theology Bulletin*
CBQ	*Catholic Biblical Quarterly*
CThM	*Currents in Theology and Mission*
Exp	*The Expositor*
ERS	*Ethnic and Radical Studies*
JAAR	*Journal of the American Academy of Religion*
JBL	*Journal of Biblical Literature*
JCS	*Journal of Classical Sociology*
JETS	*Journal of the Evangelical Theological Society*
JHS	*Journal of Hellenic Studies*
JRE	*Journal of Religious Ethics*
JRS	*The Journal of Roman Studies*
JSNT	*Journal for the Study of the New Testament*
JSNTSup	*Journal for the Study of the New Testament Supplements*
JTS	*The Journal of Theological Studies*
LThQ	*Lexington Theological Quarterly*
NTS	*New Testament Studies*

NovT	*Nouum Testamentum*
PW	A. F. Pauly, *Realencyclopadie der classischen Altertumswissenschaft*. New Edition by G. Wissowa. 49 vols. Munich: Druckenmuller, 1980
RQ	*Restoration Quarterly*
SNTSMS	Society for New Testament Studies Monograph Series
TDNT	*Theological Dictionary of the New Testament*. 10 vols. Edited by Gerhard Kittel and Gerhard Friedrich. Translated by Geoffrey W. Bromiley. Grand Rapids: Eerdmans, 1964–76
ZNW	*Zeitschrift fur die neutestamentliche Wissenschaft*

Ancient Sources: Editions and Abbreviations

Aen.	*Aeneid* (Virgil)
Ann.	*Annals* (Tacitus)
Ant.	*Antiquities of the Jews* (Josephus)
Antony	*The Life of Antony* (Plutarch)
Aug.	*Augustus* (Suetonius)
BMC	*British Museum Catalogues*
Carm.	*Carmen Saeculare* (Horace)
CIL	*Corpus Inscriptionum Graecarum*
Clem.	*De Clementia* (Seneca)
Dec.	*Decalogue* (Philo)
de Leg.	*De Legibus* (Cicero)
Ecl.	*Eclogues* (Virgil)
EJV	Victor Ehrenberg and A. H. M. Jones. *Documents Illustrating the Reigns of Augustus and Tiberius*. 2nd ed. Oxford: Clarendon, 1955
Ep.	*Epistles* (Seneca)
Eth. nic.	*Nicomachean Ethics* (Aristotle)
Fug.	*De Fuga et Inventione* (Philo)
Hist.	*Histories* (Polybius)

ILS	*Inscriptiones Latinae Selectae*. Edited by H. Dessau. Berlin: Weidmann, 1892–1916
IPriene	*Inschriften von Priene*. Edited by Friedrich Hiller von Gaertringen et. al. Berlin: Reimer, 1906
Leg. All.	*Legum allegoriae* (Philo)
Leg. Gai.	*Legatio ad Gaium* (Philo)
LXX	*The Septuagint*
MM	James Hope Moulton and George Milligan. *The Vocabulary of the Greek Testament: Illustrated from the Papyri and Other Non-Literary Sources*. 1930. Reprinted, Peabody, MA: Hendrickson, 1997.
Mor.	*Moralia* (Plutarch)
NH	*Natural History* (Pliny)
OGIS	*Orientis Graeci Inscriptiones Selectae*. 2 vols. Edited by W. Dittenberger. Leipzig: S. Hirzel, 1903–1905
Or.	*Orations* (Dio Chrysostom)
Physiogn.	*Physiognomonica* (Pseudo Aristotle)
PIR2	*Prosopographia Imperii Romani* Saec II. Edited by Hermannvs Dessav. Berlin: Reimer, 1897–98.
Plant.	*De Plantatione* (Philo)
POxy.	*The Oxyrhynchus Papyri*. Edited by B. P. Grenfell, A. S. Hunt et at. London: Egypt Exploration Fund, 1898–1981
RAI	Michael Grant. *Roman Anniversary Issues: An Exploratory Study of the Numismatic and Medallic Commemoration of Anniversary Years 49 B.C.—A.D. 375*. Cambridge: Cambridge University Press, 1950
RIC	*The Roman Imperial Coinage*. Edited by H. Mattingly et. al. London: Spink, 1923–1966
RPC	*Roman Provincial Coinage*. Edited by A. Burnett et. al. London: British Museum, 1999

Pyrrh.	*Pyrrhus* (Plutarch)
RG	*Res Gestae*
Rep.	*De Republica* (Cicero)
SEG	*Supplementum Ephigraphicum Graecum.* Edited by J. J. E. Hondius et al. Leiden: Brill, 1923–
Silv	*Silvae* (Statius)
Spec. Leg.	*De Specialibus Legibus* (Philo)
Suas.	*Suasoriae* (Seneca)
*Syll*³	*Sylloge Inscriptionum Graecarum.* 4 vols. Edited by W. Dittenberg et. al. 1915. Reprinted, Hildesheim: Olms, 1960
Tib.	*Tiberius* (Suetonius)
War	*War of the Jews* (Josephus)

Abbreviations for biblical writings and numerous other ancient sources either are explained in context or should be recognizable to most readers, and are therefore not listed here.

Introduction

RECENT SCHOLARSHIP HAS DRAWN particular attention to several issues relating to politics, imperial cults, and imperial propaganda in New Testament studies. For instance, Pauline scholarship, acknowledging the importance of the imperial background, has suggested that the ideology of the imperial cult influenced, at least, to some extent Paul's writings.[1] This intriguing phenomenon is also evident in Lukan scholarship, attempting to depict Luke's attitude towards the Jewish and the Roman authorities.[2] In this respect, Lukan scholars, stressing the political aspects in Luke–Acts, have dealt with the imperial context more seriously in relation to Luke's appreciation of the imperial cults or the imperial propaganda. Regardless of the position one takes about Luke's depiction of the Roman Empire, it is very unlikely that Luke is not interested in politics. It is almost impossible to comprehend Luke's writing in isolation from its historical setting, the empire.[3]

One of the main reasons for modern scholars' greater attention to Luke's Gospel in connection with the imperial background than to other Synoptic Gospels is that there is a significant difference between them. While Matthew and Mark pay little attention to secular history, Luke

---

1. E.g., Jewett, *Romans*, 48; also see White, *Apostle of God*, esp. 124–29, who links the Roman background to Paul's images of Christ's lordship and his family metaphor; Horsley's three edited books, *Paul and Empire*, where various scholars maintain that the Roman Empire was an important background for Christianity; *Paul and Politics*, and *Paul and the Roman Imperial Order*; Blumenfeld, *Political Paul*, who defines Paul as a political thinker; Wright, "Paul and Caesar," 173–93; Harrison, "Paul and Imperial Gospel," 71–96; Crossan and Reed, *In Search of Paul*.

2. For the bibliography, see the discussion below. With respect to the Gospel of Matthew, see Carter, *Matthew and Empire*; Riches and Sim, eds., *Matthew*; in particular, Oakes, "A State of Tension," 75–90, where he summarizes the relationship between Rome and NT writers.

3. Even the literary critics are well aware that the text is not isolated from the reality. E.g., Powell, *What Is Narrative Criticism?*, 97; for the focus on the historical environment in Luke–Acts, see Darr, *Herod the Fox*, 62, who defines it as "extra-text"; more recently, Yamazaki-Ransom, *Roman Empire*, 6.

does not distance himself from the reality of the Roman Empire. In this respect, it can be said that Luke is more concerned with political figures and situations than Matthew and Mark are. For example, by setting his narrative within imperial history (Luke 2:1–2; 3:1; Acts 11:28; 18:2), Luke emphasizes the importance of the Roman context. What is more, he is the only Gospel writer who refers to the emperor, sometimes, by name.[4] As Yamazaki-Ransom rightly states, "it cannot be said that Luke was viewing the empire as merely a stage for the early Christian drama."[5] It is therefore essential to consider Luke's political background, the Roman Empire, in order to draw a clear picture of his writings. As will be discussed, the question as to why Luke is deeply interested in the religio-political situation of the empire will provide us with a valuable clue to the issue of his concept of Jesus' authority in comparison with the emperor's authority.

Although many scholars are interested in the imperial background, it is wrong to assume that there is a scholarly consensus on Luke's attitude towards the Roman Empire or on his understanding of the Roman political authorities. I shall briefly outline major scholarly views on the relations between Luke–Acts and the Roman Empire. A good example would be an apologetic reading which has made a significant contribution to a scholarly interest in the political aspect of Luke–Acts. It is worth looking into the apologetic positions. In general, they can be divided into two different positions, an apologia *pro ecclesia* and an apologia *pro imperio*.

Let us start by taking a quick look at the political apologetic position. Those who take that position tend to underline that one of the Lukan purposes in his two volumes is to defend or justify Christianity before the Roman political authorities. Among them, Cadbury argues that Luke composed his two-volume work as an apology for Christianity addressed to a Roman magistrate, Theophilus.[6] According to him, the purpose of Luke–Acts is to argue that Christianity was a genuine branch of Judaism, which enjoyed a status of *religio licita*.[7] Cadbury, acknowledging the

---

4. See Luke 2:1 (Augustus: according to Yamazaki-Ransom, *Roman Empire*, 70, n.1, it is possible that Αὐγοῦστος is "a title rather than a proper name"), 3:1 (Tiberius), and Acts 11:28; 18:2 (Claudius). Also, Nero, although Luke does not refer to him by name, appears in Acts 25:8, 10–12, 21, 25; 26:32; 27:24; 28:19.

5. Yamazaki-Ransom, *Roman Empire*, 3 and 70–79.

6. Cadbury, *Making*, 5–7; this view is still supported by several scholars: for example, Fitzmyer, *Luke*, 1:10 and Evans, *Luke*, 108–11; for a history of research into Luke's political apologetic position, see Walaskay, *"And so We Came,"* 1–14.

7. Cadbury, *Making*, esp. 299–316; Fitzmyer, *Luke*, 1:10; also see Haenchen, *Acts*, 102, 630–31, 691–64. But the main difference between Cadbury and Haenchen is that,

political aspects of Luke's writing, has made an important contribution to the continuity between Judaism and Christianity. However, his use of the category *religio licita* is problematic. According to many interpreters, it is very doubtful that such *religio licita* even existed at the time of Luke's writing.[8] If we date Luke's work after the Jewish revolt of AD 66–73, it is hard to claim that Luke attempted to obtain a legal license from Rome by linking it directly to Judaism.[9]

Another influential proponent of the political *apologia pro ecclesia* position, Conzelmann, asserts that Luke depicts Jesus and his followers as accommodating to the empire, which was in turn favorable to the church on the assumption that his theology was developed as a response to "the situation in which the church finds herself by the delay of the *parousia* and her existence in secular history."[10] For him, Luke attempts to minimize the political elements in Christianity in order to show that Christianity is politically harmless.[11] In other words, for him Luke does not react against the Roman Empire. Rather, Luke strives to eliminate the possible conflict

---

while the former uses the term *religio licita*, the latter uses a more general form of tolerance, *religio quasi licita* (*Acts*, 630–31); for more reading lists of that position, see Neagoe, *Trial of the Gospel*, 9 n28.

8. See, for example, Maddox, *Purpose of Luke-Acts*, 91–93; Neagoe, *Trial of the Gospel*, 10; Walton, "State They Were In," 30.

9. Although it is uncertain, several scholars suggest that Luke–Acts is dated to the early 60s because Luke does not know the result of Paul's trial in Rome: e.g., Hemer, *Acts*, esp. 365–410; see 367–70 for a list of scholars and their suggested dates from AD 57 to 135; Robinson, *Re-dating the New Testament*; Morris, *Luke*, 26. But it is hard to accept that Luke–Acts was composed under the reign of Nero, first, because it was probably very dangerous for Luke to write openly against the emperor, and second, because Luke presupposed the fall of Jerusalem in Luke 21:20–24. Thus, a late date of composition is more plausible. In spite of some differences, the usual scholarly consensus on a post-70 and post Markan date is more conceivable. Both Marshall, *Luke*, 35, and Ellis, *Luke*, suggest not long after AD 70; Hays, *Luke's Wealth Ethics*, 77, dates Luke's writing to AD 70–90; Burridge, *Imitating Jesus*, 227, dates it around the same period of the 80s; for the dating after Nero, but before Domitian, of about AD 85, see Brent, *Imperial Cult*, 73 and Esler, *Community and Gospel*, 27–30; Rowe, "Luke-Acts," 294, and Bond, *Pontius Pilate*, 139, date it most likely to Domitian; Fitzmyer (*Luke*, 1:53–7) puts it slightly later at 80–85. Therefore, the most that can be said with certainty is that Luke wrote his two books for both Jews and a majority of Gentiles who were living in the Roman Empire and were familiar with the imperial cults in the second half of the first century (after 70s).

10. Conzelmann, *Theology*, 14.

11. Ibid., 139; he further argues that "to confess oneself to be a Christian implies no crime against Roman law," 140. Even though Conzelmann argues that Christianity is politically harmless, his claim still includes the political aspect of Christianity.

between Christianity and Rome with the modification of the "original eschatological perspective" in two ways, in time and in space.[12]

Differently, P. W. Walaskay, an advocate of an apologia *pro imperio*, maintains that Luke–Acts is not an apology for the church but an apology for Rome directed at Luke's own community, stating:

> Far from supporting the view that Luke was defending the church to a Roman magistrate, the evidence points us in the other direction. Throughout his writings Luke has carefully, consistently, and consciously presented an *apologia pro imperio* to his church.[13]

According to Walaskay, Luke aims to persuade his readers that "the institutions of the church and empire are coeval and complementary" and that "the Christian church and the Roman Empire need not fear nor suspect each other, for God stands behind both institutions giving to each the power and the authority to carry out his will."[14] On the basis of Luke's account of the trials of Jesus and Paul, in particular, Walaskay argues that the Roman system and the Roman representatives were viewed as uniformly favorable. For example, he suggests that Luke highlights Pilate's fair trial with the focus on his three-fold declaration of Jesus' innocence, while emphasizing Jewish leaders' responsibility for injustice.[15]

What is interesting is that, according to Conzelmann's and Walaskay's views (both apologetic positions), Luke's work has been considered pro-Roman. Let us briefly critique such a pro-Roman position. It is quite doubtful that Luke portrays Jesus and his followers as law-abiding or politically harmless, or that he describes Rome favorably. Walaskay's claim that Luke appears to be in favor of a degree of openness towards Rome is erroneous. As will be seen in the subsequent chapters (Jesus' trial and Luke's use of the emperor's existing titles), it is very unlikely that Luke is

---

12. Ibid., 138; for a detailed criticism of Conzelmann's view, see Cassidy, *Society and Politics*, 148–55, and his *Jesus, Politics, and Society*, 7–9 and 128–30; Maddox, *Purpose*, 96–97; Walaskay, "And so We Came," 15–22; Barrett, *Luke the Historian*, 63; Ahn, *Reign of God*, 52; Green, *Luke*, 798.

13. Walaskay, "And so We Came," 64; also see Maddox, *Purpose of Luke-Acts*, 96–97; Robbins, "Luke–Acts," 201–21, stressing a symbiotic relationship between the empire and Christianity.

14. Walaskay, "And so We Came," IX–X.

15. Ibid., 39–63; for a detailed criticism of Walaskay, see the following chapters; also see Bond, *Pontius Pilate*, 161; see Weatherly, *Jewish Responsibility*, 92–97; Neagoe, *Trial*, 12; Walton, "State," 29–30.

favorable toward Rome. For example, Walaskay's view that Luke shows Pilate's gentleness and justice in Jesus' trial[16] cannot be accepted. In contrast to his view, the trial scene functions as heightening not only Jewish leaders' responsibility for injustice but also Pilate's injustice.[17] Moreover, when Luke compares Jesus as victor/peace-bringer/savior with the emperor, the emperor's claim to such titles is questioned in Luke's writings.[18] Put briefly, Luke's description of peace is quite different from that of *Pax Romana*. In this respect, it is likely that peace and order established by Luke's Jesus were "critical to the continuance of Roman rule."[19] As Gilbert rightly suggests, Luke–Acts "generates a vigorous critique of Rome and its claims to universal authority and dominion" by using terms or images often associated with Roman power.[20] Luke neither depicts Christianity as politically harmless nor as pro-Roman.

Furthermore, although Conzelmann recognizes that Luke takes into account the situation of Christianity within the context of the Roman Empire, his misconception of a binary division between religion and politics is flawed. As a result, he fails to draw a vivid picture of the characterization of the ancient religion. In order to fully scrutinize the relations between Luke's Gospel and the Roman emperor, we need first to answer several questions: Was there any sharp distinction between religion and politics in the first-century world? What were the characteristics of ancient religion, in particular, the imperial cults? Or, if politics was associated closely with religion, how far did this relationship influence Luke's writing? These questions will aid us to answer the issue as to how Luke portrays Jewish leaders, Roman authorities, and finally the emperor in his writings. Again, we should not downplay the fact that Luke's writings were written in the context of the Roman Empire. With the help of a general picture of first-century religion, we can analyze how Luke uses the imperial images to his own advantage.

It has been questioned whether religion was separated from politics in the Roman Empire. Some would claim that the demarcation between religion and politics had been found in the ancient world. Prior to the discussion of the relationship between them in the Roman Empire,

---

16. Walaskay, *"And so We Came,"* 48–49.
17. See Ch. 2.
18. See Ch. 4.
19. Cassidy, *Society and Politics*, 148–49.
20. Gilbert, "Roman Propaganda," 242.

it is necessary to consider that in Republican Rome in general. Given the assumption that concepts of divine beings in the empire were not completely new or different from that of the Republic, an understanding of the relationship between religion and politics during that period may help us describe the characteristics of the imperial cults. J. A. North holds that the close association of religion and politics was already found in the Republic.[21] He further states: "It would not be an exaggeration to say that the competition between the political leaders of the late Republic was fought out to a significant extent in the language of religion."[22] If his argument is right, this evidences that the political leaders of the Republic were associated considerably with religions or religious activities. That is, the political leaders in that period attempted to connect their power or authority with divine beings in order to ensure success or to strengthen their power. As North observes, ancient materials illustrate that "politically active Romans of this period (late Republic) had to reckon with religion and the gods as important factors in determining events and in expressing their claims to authority and command."[23] Thus, it is almost impossible to separate religion from politics. This kind of phenomenon did also happen in the Roman Empire.

In many cases, the holders of the political power were identified with the holders of the religious influence in the empire. Most scholars agree that religion and politics were frequently interconnected and overlapped in the time of the Roman Empire.[24] In order to detail the relationship between religion and politics in the empire, let us look at the imperial cult in terms of its religiosity.[25] This might be very helpful in challenging two views, first, that religion was separated from politics, and, second, that the imperial cult was purely political, lacking any genuineness of religion or the importance of the religious life among the populace. These two views are intertwined and interconnected. All too often, when some scholars, stressing the sharp demarcation between them, explore

---

21. North, *Roman Religion*, 22; also his Table 1 at 23–24.

22. Ibid., 32.

23. Ibid., 33; e.g., see Cicero, *On the Command of Pompey*, 47.

24. Harland, *Associations*, 120; Horsley, *Jesus and Empire*, 5–12; Wright, "God and Caesar," 157; Ahn, *Reign of God*; Yamazaki-Ransom, *Roman Empire*.

25. The apologetic positions, although acknowledging both historical and political backgrounds, do not draw attention to the importance of the imperial cults. That is why they tend to ignore the close relationship between politics and religion of the empire.

the relationship between religion and politics in the Roman Empire, they tend to define the imperial cult as solely a political phenomenon.[26] Among them, Kurt Latte, when discussing the concepts of the imperial cult, stresses that emperor worship played a minor role and was not really a religious phenomenon at all.[27]

In a quite similar vein, other scholars, namely, Arthur D. Nock, Martin P. Nilsson, and Nicholas Fisher, strongly assert that imperial cults were mainly political, and insufficiently religious.[28] For instance, Nilsson, highlighting the imperial cult's lack of "all genuine religious content,"[29] argues that "[the cult's] meaning lay far more in state and social realms, where it served both to express loyalty to the rule of Roma and the emperor and to satisfy the ambition of the leading families."[30] His view focuses only on the aspect of the political role of the imperial cult. Likewise, Fisher asserts: "although the *collegia* had religious functions, they were above all concerned with status, solidarity, sociability, and aspects of social security."[31]

Fisher is correct in arguing that the *collegia* and the imperial cult were related to the socio-political realms. However, he fails to recognize the relationship between religion and society in antiquity, for his term "social" leads to a serious problem.[32] According to his argument, religious functions connected with social concerns are not sufficiently religious, since they are devoid of feelings or personal experience. It is wrong,

---

26. E.g., see Latte, *Romische Religionsgeschichte*; Nilsson, *History*, 384–94; and Bowersock, *Augustus and the Greek World*, 112–21. Along with their characterization of religion as solely political, their argument is based upon two other misconceptions: first, they tend to understand religion (the imperial cult) primarily as public, neglecting any significance of private activities; and, second, they neglect or, at least, downplay the role of rituals in the religious activities of first-century people.

27. Latte, *Romische Religionsgeschichte*, 326, asserts: "Der Kaiserkult blieb . . . die Anerkennung des romischen Weltreichs, in seiner gegenwartigen Form, eine konventionelle Geiste." He also emphasizes the increasing centrality of the imperial cult to Roman religion, particularly through its ability to synthesize itself with traditional pagan cults in various subtle ways. The imperial cult was "une invention des pères de l'Eglise," quoted in Alföldy, "Subject and Ruler," 254.

28. Nock, *Essays on Religion*; Nilsson, *Greek Piety*; and Fisher, "Roman Associations."

29. Nilsson, *Greek Piety*, 178.

30. Nilsson, *History*, 385; cf. de Ste. Croix, *Class Struggle*, 394–95.

31. Fisher, "Roman Associations," 1222–23; also see MacMullen, *Roman Social Relations*.

32. See Harland, *Associations*, 60; Brent, *Imperial Cult*.

however, to claim that only individual feelings can define a religion in the ancient world. Other aspects should be taken into account to avoid anachronistic analysis of ancient religion. That is, first-century people's personality should be carefully considered. In the Roman Empire, group identity was viewed as more important than individual identity. According to cultural anthropologists, such as Bruce Malina and Jerome Neyrey, first-century people "did not comprehend the idea of an individual person in his or her uniqueness."[33] By the application of their notion to the imperial cult, it is "important *not* to consider them as individualistic"; that is, their "dyadic" or group-oriented personality should be emphasized.[34] All too often, their identity was determined by the group which they belonged to.

The way of thinking themselves in antiquity is very different from that of thinking ourselves in modern times. As Gerd Theissen strongly maintains, the separation between religion and politics "manifested itself only in modern times" and that "in antiquity, nobody could imagine politics without religion, and neither did Israelite or early Jesus groups."[35] To put it differently, the imposition of modern notions and assumptions has caused a distinct separation between religion and politics in the Roman Empire.[36] The modern distinction between them fails to draw a clear picture of the characteristics of religion, associated with various activities, such as political, social, and economic activities. Given that the group-oriented personality was stressed in the first century world in contrast to today's individualistic personality, Fisher's argument is flawed. He does not consider how religious activities were interconnected deeply with the social life of the populace through various religious activities. The social concerns were not separable from their religio-political life.

---

33. Malina and Neyrey, "First-Century Personality," 72.

34. Ibid.; italics original.

35. Theissen, "Political Dimension," 226. However, the fact that politics was not separated from religion does not necessarily mean that politics and religion were regarded as one realm. It seems to me that their boundaries were not as clear as the distinction between religion and politics in modern times. In fact, at times they overlapped. Even though Theissen's argument is not completely wrong, it is dangerous to claim that religion and politics were regarded as one sphere. Rather, I wish to emphasize the strong cohesion between two realms. Based upon such a strong relationship, we can analyze the concepts or characteristics of ancient politics and religion.

36. Wright, "God and Caesar," 157 and 161, argues that the modern notion of the separation between religion and politics, between church and state, is a product of the Enlightenment, and cannot be found in Judaism or early Christianity.

In this regard, it is wrong to claim that the social realm is equated purely with the political realm. That is, by relating religious functions to social activities, first-century people's worldview or their way of religious life was expressed and enhanced by means of group-oriented personality based upon social concerns. It is also expressed through various forms of group rituals in ways that ensured the safety and the identity of the members.[37] That is why first century people's piety and honor towards their gods and goddesses as well as the emperors were expressed within group settings rather than within personal settings. As Harland rightly asserts, "the forms that such cultic honors (or 'worship' to use a more modern term) could take do not necessarily coincide with modern or Western preconceptions of what being religious should mean."[38]

Many scholars have emphasized the importance of the integration of imperial cults within civic life in Asia Minor, along with political, social, and religious significance for various social strata of the population.[39] They strongly argue that, in contrast to the traditional view, a variety of evidence of imperial rituals within civic life indicates the genuine significance of the imperial gods within religious life at the local level. In this regard, Harland states:

> Far from being solely political with no religious significance for the populace, imperial cults and the gods they honored were thoroughly integrated at various levels within society.[40]

Therefore, the imperial cults should be understood as both a political and religious phenomenon.

Let us look into the Augustan cult, in particular. In the beginning of the empire, the Augustan revolution was as much religious as it was political. Brent asserts:

> Divination and the rites of the augur were constitutional as well as religious necessities in a society in which both religion and politics were intertwined. The [Augustan] imperial cult

---

37. On the discussions of the significance of rituals, see Bourque, "Anthropologist's View of Ritual," 19–33; Kertzer, *Rituals, Politics and Power*, 8, who describes ritual as "action wrapped in a web of symbolism"; Bell, *Ritual*.

38. Harland, *Associations*, 61.

39. E.g., Price, *Rituals and Power*; Friesen, *Twice Neokoros*; Mitchell, *Anatolia*, 1:100–17; Harland, *Associations*; Gradel, *Emperor Worship*.

40. Harland, *Associations*, 266–67.

represents therefore both a constitutional revolution and a religious reformation.[41]

There are many examples which signify a strong link between religion and politics in the Augustan cult. At times, the performance of Augustus' religious role was used for highlighting the association between religion and politics in the Roman Empire. For example, in *Res Gestae*, it is reported:

> The altar of peace of Augustus the Senate, in thanks for my return ordered to be consecrated in the Campus Martius, in which it ordered that magistrates and priests (*magistratus et sacerdotes*) and Vestal Virgins should make an annual sacrifice . . . The temple of Janus on the Quirinal, which our ancestors wished to remain shut, when peace had been secured by victories throughout the whole Roman Empire, by land and by sea . . .[42]

Two things are important here. First, the cult sites were not simply added to temples of the local pantheon but were located at the centers of the new Augustan cities.[43] In doing so, Augustus, not only as a political leader but also as a divine-being, attempted to enhance his power and authority. Mitchell states:

> This was one reason why the cult became central in the minds of its citizens. Emperor worship was not a political subterfuge, designed to elicit the loyalty of un-tutored provincials, but was one of the ways in which Romans themselves and provincials alongside them defined their own relationship with a new political phenomenon, an emperor whose powers and charisma were so transcendent that he appeared to them as both man and god.[44]

As Mitchell stresses, it is evident that the Augustan cult had a religious significance.

Second, it is said that both magistrates and priests, political and religious leaders, played an active role in making an annual sacrifice. Their cooperation hints at crossovers between religion and politics. The fact that sacrifice, one of the most important religious activities, was

---

41. Brent, *Imperial Cult*, 17.

42. *RG* 12–13; for Brent, *Imperial Cult*, 35, this passage clearly "connects the annual sacrifices at the Ara Pacis with augury and *pax deorum* and also with the Temple of Janus."

43. Winter, "Acts and Roman Religion," 96; also see Fishwick, *Imperial Cult*.

44. Mitchell, *Anatolia I*, 103.

performed by both implies that the boundaries between the two were not very clear.[45]

A weak distinction between religion and politics is also found in the emperor's title. Augustus himself became a member of all the colleges of priests; he also assumed the high priestly office of *pontifex maximus* in 12 BC, which signified "divine hero, with honorific symbols and piety," although he delayed for reasons of propriety.[46] In temples and house shrines, the genius of Augustus wears the veil as a symbol of traditional Roman *pietas*. Also, when religious laws were to be decided, it was the emperor himself, as a *pontifex maximus*, who was very influential over the senate.[47] Augustus, a political ruler, was frequently viewed as a divine being or, at least, as the most important priest having the high priestly office of *pontifex maximus* and conducting *lustrum* during census.[48]

What is more, when the provincial council decreed a competition in order to honor Augustus around 9 B.C, the winning proposal was suggested by the proconsul of the province, Paullus Fabius Maximus. His edict of Asia Minor, heightening Augustus' religious role, shows how it established a new calendar year beginning on Augustus' birthday, 23 September and how Augustus' birthday was celebrated as the beginning of the Golden Age.[49]

> [It is difficult to know whether?] the birthday of the most divine Caesar is a matter of greater pleasure or greater benefit. We could justly consider that day to be equal to the beginning of all things. He restored the form of all things to usefulness, if not to

---

45. Brent, *Imperial Cult*, 76, holds that in the Roman Empire magistrates often held cultic priesthoods.

46. Jewett, *Romans*, 48; also see North, *Roman Religion*, 33.

47. North, *Roman Religion*, 34, here North describes this phenomenon as "the new house of the emperor-priest"; see also Tacitus, *Ann.* 3.58–59, 71.

48. On the discussion of relations between *lustrum* and religious significance, see Brent, *Imperial Cult*, 84, where he claims that the *lustrum* had "a religious dimension in acts of census on the basis of Livy's work's account of Servius," one of the legendary founders of the Roman constitution (534 BC). He further claims that "the *lustrum* here refers to the 'purification' of the citizen body after its members had been determined (*censu perfecto*), and the capacity of each person in the rank now allotted them to contribute to the cost of the war against the Vei. The ceremony (*suovetaurilia*) was performed in the Campus Martius where a pig, sheep, and bull were sacrificed (Livy 1.44.2)." Brent, *Imperial Cult*, 84; also see Plate 6; Livy 39.22.4–5; 42.20; *Julius Obsequ.* 13, 44, 46, 49, 52, 63.

49. The beginning of the proconsul's edict had been lost. See Price's book, *Rituals and Power*.

their natural state, since it had deteriorated and suffered misfortune. He gave a new appearance to the whole world, which would gladly have accepted its own destruction had Caesar not been born for the common good fortune of all. Thus a person could justly consider this to be the beginning of life and of existence, and the end of regrets about having been born. Since on no (other) day could each one receive a starting point more beneficial for corporate and personal improvement than the day that has been beneficial to all; And since it happens that all the cities of Asia have the same date for entrance into local office, which is an arrangement that has clearly been formed according to some divine counsel in order that it might be the starting point of honors to Augustus; And since it is difficult to give thanks equal to such benefactions as his unless we devise some new manner of reciprocation for each of them; And since people could celebrate more gladly the birthday common to all because some personal pleasure had been brought to them through (his) rule; Therefore, it seems proper to me that the birthday of the most divine Caesar be the one, uniform New Year's day for all the polities. On that day all will take up their local offices, that is, on the ninth day before the Kalends of October, in order that he might be honored far beyond any ceremonies performed for him and that he might rather be distinguished by all, which I consider to be the greatest service rendered by the province. A decree of the koinon of Asia should be written encompassing all his virtues, so that the action devised by us for the honor of Augustus should endure forever. I will command that the decree, engraved on a stele, be set up in the temple, having arranged for the edict to be written in both languages.[50]

Also, let us take a look at the decree of the provincial council which explains the reasons to honor Augustus. It was inscribed along with Fabius' decree.

> A decision of the Hellenes in Asia; proposed by the high priest Apollonios son of Menophilos of Aizanoi. Whereas the providence that ordains our whole life has established with zeal and distinction that which is most perfect in our life by bringing

---

50. *OGIS* 458.1.3–30 = *IPriene* 105; Friesen's translation, *Imperial Cults*, 33. Also see Price's translation, *Rituals and Power*, 55. The Greek text is cited from Ehrenberg and Jones (EJ), *Documents*, no. 98, lines 32–41 (p. 82); also see, Klauck, *Religious Context*, 297–98. This is an important text which will be used as evidence signifying Augustus' authority (or his superiority) and his benefaction in Ch.3 and in the victor/peace-bringer/savior chapter in comparison with Jesus' authority.

> Augustus, whom she filled with virtue as a benefaction to all humanity; sending to us and to those after us a savior who put an end to war and brought order to all things; and Caesar, when he appeared, the hopes of those who preceded [. . .] placed, not only surpassing those benefactors who had come before but also leaving to those who shall come no hope of surpassing (him); and the birth of the god was the beginning of good tidings to the world through him . . .[51]

Both Fabius' decree and the decree of the provincial council are good examples of the religiosity of the early imperial/Augustan cult, fuelled by relief at the end of the civil wars. From Fabius' decree, it is shown that Augustus' birthday, stressing the good news and his salvific and beneficial activity, is considered as the beginning of everything, since it was the end of an individual's regret that he had been born.[52] Augustus is depicted as "one of the divinities by which the people took the oath"[53] by heightening his religious aspects in connection with his political power. In other words, the characterization of the Augustan cult is explicitly expressed in the decree, showing that his political status is not isolated from his religious significance. It is almost impossible to separate religion from politics, and, finally, to 'depoliticize' Jesus or Christianity.[54] Therefore, in order to understand early Christianity, it is crucial to consider its political environment, the Roman Empire, and the emperor.[55] Apologetic studies, based upon a simple demarcation between the Romans and the Jews or between the political and the religious, ignore characteristics of first-century religion.[56]

Let us briefly see a more recent study on Luke and the empire. S. Kim's book, *Christ and Caesar*, provides an analysis and assessment of the relationship between Jesus and the emperor in the writings of Luke and Paul. His book is divided into two parts: one for Paul and another for Luke. Kim argues that both Luke's and Paul's writings are not in opposition to

---

51. *OGIS* 458.1.30–71; Friesen's translation, *Imperial Cults*, 34.

52. See Lintott, *Imperium Romanum*, 182–83; Price, *Rituals and Power*, 54–5; EJ, 98.

53. Lintott, *Imperium Romanum*, 183.

54. See Horsley, *Jesus and Empire*, 5–12.

55. See Yamazaki-Ransom, *Roman Empire*, 2.

56. See Horsley, *Paul and Roman Imperial Order*, 5. As Bryan, *Render to Caesar*, 6, rightly stresses, we have to attempt to move beyond the simple dichotomy of good and evil.

Caesar. Rejecting both Richard Horsley's and N. T. Wright's views that Jesus is proclaiming a political kingdom as opposition to the Roman Empire, Kim argues that both Luke and Paul seem favorable towards the Roman empire, and that the church in both writings is aided by Roman power in the spread of the gospel.[57] He further asserts that, for Luke, the redemption Jesus brought has nothing to do with the overthrowing of the Roman Empire or replacing it with a politically independent government.[58] For him, redemption or salvation in Luke is a deliverance from the kingdom of Satan, not from the kingdom of the emperor. Thus, he strongly argues that Jesus' redemptive work in Luke has nothing to do with altering the political, economic, and social structures to bring Israel political freedom and social justice.[59] Thus, he claims that Luke's purpose in writing is to show the gospel as not threatening to the Roman Empire. In this regard, he seems to stress that we must see Luke's writings as religious rather than political, for he continuously maintain that neither Jesus nor Christianity were against the imperial Roman order, but rather sin, death, Satan, and other spiritual evils.

There is, however, a serious problem with Kim's argument. Like the apologetic positions, Kim's view that Luke (or Paul) focuses mainly on spiritual, not on socio-political realities, is inconceivable. Neglecting that the socio-political aspects influenced Luke's writings, Kim consistently denies other aspects, such as politics and socio-economic structures. As noted above, religion and politics appear to be closer related in Luke than Kim asserts. As a result, his assertion does not deal with an important question as to whether Luke wrote his book in conscious reaction to the imperial cult and ideology of Rome. As seen in Fabius' imperial decree, the contents of religion and politics, at times, overlapped each other in the empire.

Along with Kim's book, C. Kavin Rowe's monograph, *World Upside Down: Reading Acts in the Graeco-Roman Age*, has made another helpful contribution to Lukan scholarship although it deals mainly with Acts.[60] Rowe focuses on the relations between Luke and the Roman Empire by providing historical background and insight into Greco-Roman culture. He directly challenges an apologetic reading, and notes: Luke

---

57. Kim, *Christ and Caesar*, 189. He further argues that Paul and Luke had a "dialectical attitude" towards the Roman imperial order (190).

58. Ibid., 95.

59. Ibid., 147.

60. Rowe, *World Upside Down*; see also his article "Luke–Acts," 279–300, and his book *Early Narrative*.

"aims at nothing less than the construction of an alternative total way of life - a comprehensive pattern of being - one that runs counter to the life-patterns of the Graeco-Roman world."[61] In this regard, he discusses how Acts introduces a new culture of Christianity, asserting that "New culture, yes—coup, no. The tension is thus set."[62] Rowe claims that Luke's message seriously challenges the dominant culture. For him, this means that Christians do not wish to replace the emperor with Jesus, but they wish to alter the culture. In doing so, he further argues that Luke's gospel is not anti-Rome because Luke is not calling for the violent overthrow of the government.

Despite his historical and cultural context in Acts, there are several problems with Rowe's argument. First, Rowe seems to argue that Luke's depiction of Gentile culture is portrayed in a negative way, maintaining that Luke attempts to overturn Gentile culture. However, it is not just Gentile culture which rejects the gospel. As some Gentiles reject Jesus' teaching, some of the Jews in Acts do not welcome Jesus' message. Acts shows that part of Israel does not recognize Jesus as the fulfillment of God's promise.

Second, Rowe's argument is not good enough to explicate *how* Jesus is viewed as the true Lord, while it is good enough to explain *why*. That is, Rowe does not connect the title κύριος directly with Jesus' authority in comparison with that of the emperor, although he is successful in stressing Jesus' identity by using the title. In this respect, he pays little attention to the one particular issue that could move the discussion forward, namely, the closeness between Luke's stance toward the empire and his evaluation of Jesus' authority in comparison with the emperor.

More importantly, although they are right in asserting that Luke's literary agenda is not linked to an overthrowing of the Roman Empire, both Kim and Rowe seem to contradict themselves at times. Kim argues, "Luke deliberately contrasts Jesus the Messianic king/lord to Caesar Augustus, and claims that Jesus is the true *kyrios* and *soter*, the true bearer of the kingship of God and that he will bring the true *pax* on earth, replacing the false *pax* brought about by the military conquest of Caesar, a false *kyrios* and *soter*."[63] In a similar manner, Rowe maintains that Luke

---

61. Rowe, *World Upside Down*, 4 and 17.
62. Ibid., 91.
63. Kim, *Christ and Caesar*, 80–81.

stresses "the universal Lordship of God in Jesus."[64] But both refrain from calling this anti-imperial stance. Their view that Luke's gospel, because he is not calling for the violent overthrow of the empire, is not anti-Rome is wrong. In other words, a writer's anti-Roman stance is one thing, but his or her overthrowing of the Roman state is another. The two things should be dealt with separately.[65]

Both Kim and Rowe do not consider whether certain imperial titles (savior, lord, benefactor, etc) would be seen as exclusive to the emperor in certain contexts.[66] In this regard, their assertion that Luke does not aim intentionally to show competition between Jesus and Caesar[67] should be re-considered. Nor do they discuss how first-century audiences who would be familiar with these titles for Caesar would be able to detach themselves from their culture so easily. How would first-century people interpret Luke's use of the title κύριος, which was widely used for the emperor? What if they understood it as a direct/indirect competition between Jesus and Caesar? Given the importance of the emperor in the Roman world and the pervasiveness of imperial ideology throughout the empire, it is not unreasonable that Luke's use of the titles would be related implicitly to his anti-imperial messages, which encouraged his readers to be devoted to Jesus, not to the emperor.

I do agree that Jesus in Luke is not calling for the overthrow of the empire. However, it seems to me that Kim's and Rowe's view of resistance is somewhat narrow, as they do not acknowledge passive forms of resistance. Several anti-imperial aspects of Luke's message do not require that he sought the overthrow of the empire. A more rounded explanation of the socio-economic-political message of Jesus in Luke would emphasize Jesus' implicit (or, sometimes, coded) challenge to religious authority, economic exploitation, and the emperor's authority.

It is true that Luke does not highlight such a direct competition as in Revelation. But, at least, in Luke's writings there is a clue to an indirect competition between them. When Luke's narrative rejects pagan reverence/worship, Luke does not intend to remove the key function of the honor system. As the title κύριος bears its honor/authority, Luke implicitly depicts Jesus as a true κύριος in competition with the emperor.

---

64. Rowe, *World Upside Down*, 136.
65. See also Ch.3, "Benefactor: Who is Greater?"
66. See the chapters on Benefactor and Savior.
67. Rowe, *World Upside Down*, 5 and 91.

He does so by attempting to highlight Jesus' true lordship in comparison with other gods or emperors in Luke–Acts.[68]

Then, in what ways does Luke attempt implicitly to critique the Roman Empire? Many scholars have attempted to analyze several issues relating to tax collectors. They have been interested in the relationship between Jesus and the tax collectors,[69] Jesus' table fellowship with them,[70] Zacchaeus' conversion,[71] the parable of the Pharisee and the tax collector,[72] and the characterization of the tax collectors among first-century Jews.[73] Despite the scholarly interest in the tax collectors, one important aspect of the narratives has been almost entirely overlooked; that is, relations between them and the Roman power. In this study, I will argue that the tax collectors were employees of Roman power. Many scholars draw little attention to the relationship the power of the emperor and the exploitation of tax collectors, although admitting that they oppressed others. Moreover, they fail to see the implicit links between Jesus' authority and the emperor's authority through the stories about the tax collectors. For me, they seem to ignore who is ultimately responsible for their defrauding people. For example, Harrison acknowledges that repentance is one of the most important themes in tax collectors and Pharisees.[74] But he tends to neglect that repentance for Luke is something more significant than Harrison supposes. For Luke, repentance is an implicit presentation of his critique against the emperor's authority. Or, some interpreters neglect how important Lukan themes, such as repentance and Jesus' mission of seeking and saving the lost, in the story of Zacchaeus[75] are implicitly related to Luke's critique of the emperor's authority. With careful historical consideration of the characters and setting of the scene, it

---

68. In this respect, Luke strives to keep the meaningfulness of honor language of the ancient world. He does not aim to change all the things in the empire, but rather seems to question whether the emperor should be considered as the most honorable figure at that time.

69. Walker, "Jesus and Tax Collectors," 221–38.

70. Kilgallen, "Was Jesus Right?" 590–600.

71. Corbin-Reuschling, "Zacchaeus's Conversion," 67–88; Tannehill, "Story of Zacchaeus," 201–21.

72. Harrison, "Case of Pharisee and the Tax Collector," 99–111; Friedrichsen, "Temple, a Pharisee, a Tax Collector," 89–119; Doran, "Pharisee and Tax Collector," 259–70.

73. Okorie, "Characterization of Tax Collectors," 27–32.

74. Harrison, "Case of Pharisee and Tax Collector," 105.

75. Tannehill, "Story of Zacchaeus," 210.

will be explored how Luke contrast Jesus and the emperor. For me, Luke's focus on Jesus' authority through the tax-related accounts is stated in a minimal and implicit way but deepens in significance. That is, I argue that the common understanding of tax collectors among scholars can be reframed and broadened by stressing the importance of tax-related issues in Roman society and imperial ideology. Readers of Luke have long noted several issues, and those will not be rejected here. But how would a listener more attuned to imperial ideology/cult than other issues have understood the tax-related accounts? What connections and conclusions might that listener have made concerning the identity of Jesus? Reading several tax-related accounts in Luke through the lens of Roman culture and imperial ideology enables us to see Jesus' interaction with tax collectors as Luke's implicit critique of the emperor's authority on the basis of the assumption that Luke strategically characterizes Jesus in comparison with the Roman emperor, the most powerful man-god in the universe, in order to elevate Jesus' authority.

Acknowledgment that the boundary between religion and politics was very unclear in the ancient world plays a vital role in examining how political Luke was in his Gospel in response to the Jewish leaders and the emperor. Given that the emperor, as a political leader, was worshipped in various forms of imperial cult, it is very likely that Luke, as a religious writer, was involved in political activities because of the nature of ancient religion. To put it another way, as the emperor's religious role is highlighted, Luke's religious writing conveys a significant political implication. With the focus on the historical and political background of his Gospel, the goal of this study is to analyze Luke's description of Jesus' authority on the basis of his attitude towards the Roman Empire. Luke's portrayal of the empire will provide us with his basic concept of the emperor, because the emperor himself represents the empire. In achieving the goal, this study will compare Jesus' authority with the emperor's authority; that is, it will analyze in what ways Luke attempts to stress Jesus' superiority over the emperor even though their relationship is not stated directly in his writings.

Although some scholars have been aware of Luke's critique of the emperor and the Roman officials, few have attempted to examine to what degree Luke is not in favor of the emperor's power/authority in detail. Unlike previous scholarship, I will divide the emperor's power/authority into two realms, his *auctoritas* and his *imperium*, in order to analyze Luke's evaluation of the emperor's authority and his emphasis on Jesus' authority. In this respect, several questions will be answered. How does

Luke relate Jesus' authority to the emperor's authority? What is the role of tax-related issues in his writing in connection with the emperor's moral *auctoritas*? What significance does the tax collectors' immorality bear? Why are those questions so important for understanding Jesus' authority in comparison with the emperor's power? In what ways is Jesus as savior different from the emperor as savior? How does Luke interpret the emperor's *imperium* in the discussion of the title 'savior'?

Given that Luke actively engages the social, cultural, and political values of the empire, certain patterns evident in the depictions of the emperor's authority will be identified by using heuristic models for the relationship between Jesus and the emperor. Luke is not only deliberate in his development of Jesus' authority and his introduction of Roman power, but also he hints at the theme of Jesus' authority through the narrative in such a way that the uses of his different narratives are meaningfully related to each other. The intentionality with which Luke develops the significance of Jesus' authority should be emphasized. Thus, Luke's particular interest in politics (e.g. Roman power) should not be ignored in the discussion of his depiction of the emperor's authority in comparison with Jesus' authority. This study focuses on Luke's attitude toward the empire and his definition of Jesus' authority by re-defining the emperor's authority.

Outline of the Study[76]

Chapter 1, as a whole, falls into two sub-chapters: Luke's emphasis on Jesus' authority in comparison with John the Baptist at the beginning

---

76. In terms of the methodology of my study, I use various methods, rather than using a single method, in order to achieve my goal. They include literary, redactional, socio-historical, rhetorical criticism and the like. These methods will be used as complementary tools for a fuller comprehension of Luke's writing. When it comes to the descriptions of the reality of the empire, I will apply archaeology and iconography because they are very useful in describing various imperial themes and historical background. When discussing the social and cultural values of first-century people, the social-scientific method will be used since their behavior or their thoughts are not the same as ours. When necessary, several social theories will also be applied to make my argument more convincing. Moreover, I will use intertextuality when comparing one with another. In this respect, I do not limit my argument to similarities between Luke's Gospel and precursor sources; rather, I stress differences between the two. Thus, I focus on how Luke has shaped and molded the narrative to express his theological goals.

of his writing, and his blame of Jewish leaders, Herod, and the Roman governor in the account of Jesus' trial.

Chapter 2 will centre on Luke's purpose in the census and tax-related narratives. It analyses the main issue concerning taxes expressed in Luke's Gospel with the focus on the context of the Roman taxation system, because only Luke, unlike the other evangelists, associates Jesus' birth and death with tax-related issues. Also, I will answer the question as to how Luke understands Augustus' authority in terms of tax collectors.

Chapter 3 will deal with the title 'benefactor' expressed in Luke 22:24–27. It focuses on the question as to whether the grouping of 'the kings of the Gentiles' includes the Roman emperor. Also, it will argue from what perspective Luke describes such rulers in order to explore the criteria for true benefactors.

Finally, in Chapter 4, I will argue that the title, savior, cannot be explained without considering other significant titles of the emperor, mainly, victor and peace-bringer. These titles can also be applied to Jesus' identity when discussing him as savior. The similarities between Jesus and the emperor will be explained by assimilation theory; and the differences by contra-culture theory. After discussing how Augustus (or his successors) achieved peace in the Roman Empire, I also intend to relate Jesus' interaction with tax collectors to Jesus' salvation activity in Luke's Gospel. On the basis of this, I will explore the meaningfulness of Jesus' salvation which comes after his victory over tax-collectors' wrongdoings. That is, I will show in what ways Luke attempts to regard Augustus as a pseudo-savior in contrast to his description of Jesus as a true savior through the stories of tax collectors. Moreover, Zechariah's praise (Luke 1:68–79) will be analyzed in the light of the analysis of 'victor/peace-bringer/savior'.

1

Jesus' Birth and Trial in Relation to the Issue of Authority

LUKE'S GOSPEL IS THE story of Jesus, emphasizing that he, along with God, is the most important figure. An astonishing number of themes relating to Jesus are expressed in Luke–Acts. Among them, my focus is primarily on Jesus' authority in the context of the Roman Empire because my argument is that one of the main intentions in Luke's writings is to stress Jesus' authority given by God. Prior to making comparisons and contrasts between Jesus' authority and that of the emperor in detail, this chapter deals with two topics. In the first section, I will examine Luke's emphasis on Jesus' authority with the focus on his comparison between Jesus and John the Baptist in the birth narratives. This will verify that Luke has a keen interest in the theme of authority.

The second part will explore Luke's portrayal of both religious and political leaders, namely, Jewish leaders, Herod, and the Roman governor, through Jesus' trial scene on the basis of his comprehension of their authority. In order to answer the question of whether, or not, Luke depicts them in a negative sense, it is necessary to ask another significant question as to who put Jesus to death because this question will provide a clue to his understanding of the existing authorities. With the help of this question, we will examine how Luke challenges both Jewish and Roman authorities through Jesus' trial and crucifixion: Jewish leaders within a narrow Palestine context, and Pilate within a larger Roman context. More broadly, the second section aims to draw a general picture of Luke's view on the Roman Empire before talking about the emperor's authority in the later chapters.

It is necessary briefly to distinguish different types of authority found in Luke's Gospel. Max Weber presents three kinds of authority in relation to domination or power: first, charismatic authority which is accepted without force; second, traditional authority (e.g., dynastic descent) which effects acceptance of authority without force; and third, bureaucratic authority legitimized by rules.[1] On the basis of Weber's argument, charismatic leaders, dynastic rulers, and bureaucratic administrators will be discussed individually, because each of them, with some modifications, is referred to in Luke. Weber's three categories will set us looking at different types of authority figure in Luke, and set us thinking about how Jesus' authority compares to John the Baptist and how Luke is critical of the authority of Jewish leaders/Herod/Pilate.

Jesus' Birth: Charismatic Authority

Luke's interest in Jesus' authority starts at the beginning of his Gospel. Let us explore how he elevates Jesus' status in terms of Weber's categorization of charismatic authority. Weber defines "charisma" as: "[A] certain quality of an individual personality, by virtue of which he is set apart from ordinary men and treated as endowed with supernatural, superhuman, or at least specifically exceptional powers or qualities. These are such as are not accessible to the ordinary person, but are regarded as of divine origin or as exemplary, and on the basis of them the individual concerned is treated as a leader."[2] In this regard, Weber claims that charismatic authority is based upon a charismatic leader's "extraordinariness," such as performing miracles, heroic acts and the like.[3] In a very similar vein, Diana Kendall defines charismatic authority as "power legitimized on the basis of a leader's exceptional personal qualities or the demonstration of extraordinary insight and accomplishment, which inspire loyalty and obedience from followers."[4] Weber, stressing the relationship between the leader and the disciples/followers, asserts that the charismatic leader's

---

1. Weber, "Der Beruf zur Politik," 167–85; *Wirtschaft und Gesellschaft*, 822, which is also available online http://www.textlog.de/weber_wirtschaft.html), or its English version *Economy and Society; Theory of Social and Economic Organization*; along with these three kinds, he sometimes mentions a fourth form, democratic rule. For the further discussion of Weber's three types of authority, see Coser, *Masters of Sociological Thought*; and Collins, *Weberian Sociological Theory*.

2. Weber, *Wirtschaft und Gesellschaft*, Ch. 3.10, at http://www.textlog.de/7415.html; English version in *Theory of Social and Economic Organization*, 327–28.

3. Weber, *Wirtschaft und Gesellschaft*, 140 and 656.

4. Kendall, *Sociology in Our Times*, 438–39.

mission and insight inspire his followers who finally have a personal devotion to him.[5]

There are several instances indicating that Luke attempts to highlight Jesus' authority or his status by comparing with that of John the Baptist, who was often viewed as a charismatic leader among the Jews. The evidence that John the Baptist probably possessed charismatic authority is found in Luke 3:7 where many people came to him in order to be baptized. Also, Luke reports that John had his own disciples sent to Jesus in Luke 7:18–23. Besides, Luke reports Jesus' saying in the following verse (v. 28), "among those born of women no one is greater than John." It is clear that John's charismatic authority is expressed in Luke's Gospel.

Let us look into Luke's strategic comparison between Jesus and John the Baptist. Many scholars have acknowledged that Luke is deeply interested in the use of parallelism in Luke–Acts.[6] Among them, Joel B. Green claims that "all of the material in Luke 1:5—2:52 may be understood as fitting into a parallel scheme."[7] The key question is why Luke provides such a parallel in the birth narratives. The answer is that he does so in order to highlight Jesus' authority in comparison with that of John the

---

5. Weber, "Three Types," 1–11; Weber, *Wirtschaft und Gesellschaft*, 140 and 656; also see Adair-Toteff, "Max Weber's Charisma," 194.

6. E.g., Cadbury, *Making*, 231–35; Flender, *Luke*, 8–35, argues that the birth narratives display a combination of "parallelism and decisive difference" (91–92); Talbert, *Literary Pattern*, 1, asserting that Luke tends to "balance some feature of his work with another which corresponds to it or is analogous to it in some way"; Fitzmyer, *Luke*, 1:313–14, where he provides a chart of the parallels between Jesus and John; Brown, *Birth of the Messiah*, summarizing scholarly views on the parallel between Jesus and John; Clark, *Parallel Lives*, 97ff., relating the Lukan writing to Plutarch's *Lives*, argues that Luke applies "techniques of rhetoric common in the ancient world." Although the scholars mentioned above rightly discuss the importance of the parallels between Jesus and John, they pay little attention to the fact that the parallels can be explained in terms of Weber's category (esp. charismatic authority).

7. Green, *Theology*, 51 n3. Several scholars have focused their argument on the Lukan composition of Luke 1–2. For Green's analysis of material under seven headings: introduction of parents, annunciation, mother's response, birth circumcision, naming, prophetic response, growth of child, see his book at 51–54. For more discussion of Luke's composition of Luke 1–2, see Brown, *Birth of Messiah*, 251 and 339–40. Farris critiques Brown's understanding of Luke's composition in his book, *Hymns of Luke's Infancy*, 102–7. See also Nolland, *Luke*. Whatever the process of composition may have been, such discussion does not heavily influence Luke's emphasis on Jesus' authority because he intentionally arranged chapters 1 and 2 to highlight a parallel between Jesus and John the Baptist. Thus, I shall read the text as it stands. The question in this study centers on why Luke arranged Luke 1–2 in such a way.

Baptist.[8] It is interesting to note that Jesus' superiority over John starts from their mothers in Luke's Gospel, even before their birth. Several episodes play crucial roles in decoding Luke's intention of the parallel treatment of Jesus and John.

Firstly, in John's birth narrative, Luke reports that Zechariah and Elizabeth had no children, because she "was barren, and both were getting on in years (Luke 1:7; and 18)." Biologically speaking, it was very hard for them to conceive due to their old age. However, this does not necessarily mean that the couple had no sexual intercourse, because the text itself does not provide any information about this. C. Kevin Rowe states:

> There can be no doubt as to the "natural" means of John the Baptist's conception. Though Luke does not follow Zechariah and Elizabeth into their bedroom, as it were, he does provide space and time for their sexual union. Zechariah went away "into his house" (literally, 1:23), and after seemly lapse of time, it becomes clear that Elizabeth is pregnant (1:24–25).[9]

In other words, it is not completely impossible that they could have a child through sexual intercourse, even though the chances were very slim.

Luke tells us that Mary was a virgin, engaged to Joseph (Luke 1:27). It is interesting to note that Mary, in contrast to Elizabeth, did not have a husband. To put it differently, she did not have sexual intercourse with a man, as far as the word "virgin" (παρθένος)[10] was understood as a woman who had never had sexual intercourse. Mary's virginity is once more emphasized in 1:34 although the term παρθένος is not directly referred to: "How can this be, since I am a *virgin*" (literally, the Greek text [ἐπεὶ ἄνδρα οὐ γινώσκω] is interpreted as "I do not know a man"). When the angel Gabriel came to her, he said that she would "conceive in your womb and bear a son" (Luke 1:31). The angel took an example of Elizabeth's pregnancy, and said, "nothing will be impossible with God" (v. 37). It seems to me that through two different pregnancy narratives Luke aims at distinguishing Elizabeth's pregnancy from Mary's: the former was a married woman in spite of her old age, the latter a virgin. One might raise two crucial questions. First, why is two mothers' conception to be considered

---

8. Clark, *Parallel Lives*, 106.

9. Rowe, *Early Narrative Christology*, 35.

10. See Acts 21:9; 1 Cor 7:25, 28, 34, 36–38; Josephus, *War*, 4.244; 6.196; for the word παρθένια (tokens of virginity or virginity), see Deut (LXX) 22:15, 17, 20.

so important in relation to Jesus and John? Second, whose pregnancy is to be viewed as more miraculous: Elizabeth who had a husband, but was barren, or Mary who was a virgin without a husband? Let us answer the second question first. It would be true that Mary's pregnancy is considered more miraculous, since she had no sexual contact with a man. What is more, it is stressed that Mary's child, unlike Elizabeth's child, was conceived by the Holy Spirit (1:35), not by a man.[11] Here Luke tends to associate Jesus more directly with the Holy Spirit. The direct relationship between Jesus and the Holy Spirit is again stressed in John's preaching (Luke 3:15–16). When people asked whether John was the Messiah, John answered, "I baptize you with water; but one who is more powerful than I is coming; I am not worthy to untie the thong of his sandals. He [Jesus] will baptize you with the Holy Spirit and fire" (3:16). As for the first question, through the parallel of the birth narratives Luke intends to show that Jesus' birth is more miraculous than John's; that is, Jesus is superior to John even before their birth. This means that Jesus' charismatic authority should be considered superior to that of John.

Secondly, Jesus' superiority over John is also found when Mary went to the house of Zechariah and greeted Elizabeth (Luke 1:39–56). At a glance, it might be seen as a simple encounter between Mary and Elizabeth. But Luke's intention of their encounter should not be underestimated, first, because this story is found in neither Matthew nor Mark, and, second accordingly, because his parallel between John and Jesus is evident. When Mary went to Elizabeth's house, it is reported that "the child (John the Baptist) leapt in her womb" (v. 41). Again, in v. 44 Elizabeth said that when she heard Mary's greeting, the child in her womb leapt for joy (v. 44). For me, Luke intends to stress that Jesus in Mary's womb encounters John the Baptist in Elizabeth's womb, not that Mary encounters Elizabeth. Thus, it is highly likely that the actual encounter between Jesus and John implies the former's superiority over the latter by describing John's leaping for joy.

Thirdly, further evidence of Luke's attempt at showing Jesus' superiority over John is clearly found in his baptism although this account is not part of the birth narratives. Luke is probably well aware that Jesus' baptism by John could be seen as an embarrassment for some of his audience on the ground that his baptism can imply that he regarded himself

---

11. See Clark, *Parallel Lives*, 106.

as a sinner, who needed remission of his sins by John's baptism.[12] This embarrassment could result in the assumption that Jesus was subordinate to John the Baptist. In order to eliminate, or at least, minimize this embarrassment, Luke depicts the story somewhat differently. In Luke 3:21, grammatically speaking, when Jesus was baptized, the agent is omitted ("Now when all the people were baptized, and when Jesus also had been baptized . . ."). While both Mark and Matthew clearly mention that Jesus was baptized by John the Baptist (Mark 1:9; Matt 3:13), Luke does not refer to John by name. It would be true that the absence of the agent does not make it hard for Luke's audience to find out who baptized Jesus. But Luke himself strives to stress Jesus' baptism by the Holy Spirit or God[13], rather than by John (Luke 3:22). To put it differently, Luke focuses on the ultimate one (God) who baptized Jesus rather than the physical one, John. In the New Testament, it has generally been accepted that when the agent is missing in a passive sentence, the agent is normally God himself. With the help of some alterations of baptism, Luke is successful in achieving his goal in elevating Jesus' authority over John's. In other words, the new charismatic figure, Jesus, shows his superiority over the old charismatic leader, John the Baptist.[14] Accordingly, he became a new holder of charismatic authority.

What is more, Luke's conscious and articulated setting of Jesus' birth functions as heightening his charismatic authority over that of John. Although the relationship seems to become a bit more complicated due to two different settings, Luke's reference to the Augustan census (Luke 2:1–7), associated with Jesus' birth, helps us better to understand the relationship between Jesus and John the Baptist. My primary interest in the census is quite different from other scholars who have centered on several questions about chronological details of the birth narrative.[15] I

---

12. Cf. Theissen, "Political Dimension," 230; Jesus in John 1:29–34 comes to the Baptist with sin—but these sins are the sins of the world, not Jesus' sins; in Matt 3:13–17, the Baptist refuses to baptize Jesus, because he needs to be baptized by Jesus.

13. See Borgman, *Way according to Luke*, 63.

14. Jesus' increasing power is also implicitly expressed by the contrast in Luke 1:80 and 2:52.

15. Luke refers to the Augustan census in Luke 2:1–7. In this respect, his reference to it has led to several scholarly issues. The argument is focused primarily on the issue as to whether Luke's account is historical. There are several scholarly issues: the questions are about Quirinius' governorship, about whether Jesus was born *during* or *before* the census conducted by him; Luke depicts that Joseph and Mary went to Bethlehem because of the census. For various views on Luke's historical errors, see

wish to aim at identifying Luke's purpose through his two birth accounts. In other words, my study does not attempt to analyze chronological accuracy or other scholarly issues, but focuses mainly on the issue of authority, asking why Luke sets John's and Jesus' birth narratives somewhat differently. It is obvious that these two figures were both depicted in the context of the rulers of the secular world. On the one hand, the infancy narrative about John is set "in the days of King Herod of Judaea" (Luke 1:5).[16] On the other hand, Jesus' birth is associated with Quirinius' census decreed by Augustus. Even though referring to the secular rulers in both narratives, Luke clearly differentiates John's birth from Jesus' birth by associating the narratives with their power or authority. While John's birth is depicted in the context of Palestine by referring to the King of Judaea, Luke sets Jesus' birth in the wider context by linking it to the supreme authority of Augustus. Given the assumption that Luke's readers (or audience) probably knew who was more powerful between Herod and Augustus, they probably also knew whose authority was considered greater between Jesus and John. In this respect, Luke seems to compare John's authority with Jesus' authority by using the power relationship between Herod and Augustus.

To scrutinize the power relationship between Herod and Augustus, let us look at some historical points. It is correct that Herod's kingdom was not a Roman province in the time of John's birth. In this regard, it could be argued that Herod was independent from Rome. For instance, Josephus reports that Herod's reign was, to some extent, independent from Roman power. First, Antony gave the office and authority of kingship to Herod, and let him do as he saw fit (*Ant.* 15.3.8). Second, after the battle of Actium, Octavian allowed Herod to have greater freedom than he had enjoyed before (*Ant.* 15.6.7). Moreover, he permitted that Herod could determine the succession to his throne (*Ant.* 15.10.0), and he associated the procurators of Syria with him, telling them that they needed to consult Herod before doing anything (*Ant.* 15.10.3). Based upon those aspects, it has been sometimes interpreted that Herod was independent from Roman power.

Johnson, *Luke*, 49; Meier, *Marginal Jew*, 1:412 n9; Brown, *Birth of Messiah*, 547–56; Schalit, *König Herodes*, 256–97; Goulder, *Luke*, 1:246–55; Turner, *Grammatical Insights*, 23–24; Bruce, *Jesus and Christian Origins*, 192; Pearson, "Lukan Censuses,"; Hoehner, *Chronological Aspects*, 21; Smith, "Of Jesus and Quirinius," 278–93; Ramsay, "Luke's Narrative," 387.

16. The latest date for which would be the year of Herod's death was 4 BC.

Such descriptions, however, should not be over-estimated when studying the relationship between Herod and Roman power. Even though Judaea was not a Roman province at the time of John's birth (Luke 1:5), it must be highlighted that Herod's kingdom was still under the Roman power. It is very unlikely that Herod was an independent king. He was dependent considerably on Roman rule for his power, kingship, and his political influence.[17]

In order to have a better understanding of the relationship between Rome and Herod, it is essential to consider a general Roman practice concerning its client kings. First and foremost, the emperor had an active role in appointing princes who would rule in his own interest. Rome encouraged client kings "to tame and civilize their subjects until they were fit to come directly under Roman rule."[18] As E. T. Salmon aptly states, "client kings were encouraged to foster urbanization and general economic improvement (i.e., *taxation*); when their kingdoms had reached a level compatible with that generally prevailing throughout the empire, they could be and usually were incorporated so as to become provinces or parts of provinces,"[19] for Augustus "had made it unmistakably clear that client kingdoms possessed no more than an interim status: annexation was always intended as soon as they were sufficiently romanized."[20]

Second, although the kingship of Judaea had been given to Herod by Antony, there were Roman troops stationed in Palestine, and he and his family frequently made use of them.[21] Also, the right of succession conferred on Herod by Antony was later reaffirmed by Augustus. According to Josephus (*Ant.* 16.4.1), Herod retained the right, but what is more important is that Herod had to first ask Rome when he determined which of his sons would succeed in the kingship (*Ant.* 16.3.3). This clearly indicates that Herod's power was subordinate to the emperor's authority. Therefore, it is a mistake to argue that the authority of Herod's kingdom was independent.

As the historical evaluation clearly shows, Herod the Great, despite the fact that he had some freedom, was dependent, to a large extent, on

17. Pearson, "Lukan Censuses," 262–82.
18. Ibid., 267.
19. Salmon, *History of the Roman World*, 104–5.
20. Ibid., 130.
21. *Ant.* 15.3.7; *Ant.* 15.3.14, "As it was to be expected that such princes should frequently have to control their subjects' disaffection, it was a common practice to support the Roman nominee by a small detachment of Roman troops."

Roman power, particularly the emperor's power.[22] That is, Augustus' power is far greater than that of Herod. In doing so, Luke, who is well aware of such dependence, seems to link the power relations between Herod and Augustus to another power relation between John and Jesus through the two birth narratives. By setting John in the context of Herod and Jesus in the Augustan context respectively, Luke aims at highlighting the fact that Jesus is more powerful than John as Augustus is more powerful than Herod, or that John is subordinate to Jesus as Herod is dependent on Augustus.

Furthermore, their different settings of the birth narratives correspond to their different missions which govern the degree of their authority. As F. O'Fearghail, stressing the universal setting of Jesus' birth, points out, "distinctive features of the missions of the two figures also emerge from the parallel."[23] Similarly, Clark states: "John's mission is directed solely to Israel (1:16–17, 80), while Jesus is to reign over 'the house of Jacob' (1:33), and his birth signifies 'good news for all the people' (2:10), yet he is destined to be not only glory for God's people Israel, but also 'a light to lighten the Gentiles' (2:32)."[24] That is, while John's mission is limited to Israel (as Herod's influence is), Jesus' mission has a universal connotation (as the emperor's influence does).

Another question can be raised. To what extent is Jesus' charismatic authority, as Weber categorizes it, related to Jesus' power? Weber attempts to define the concept of power, arguing that power is defined as "every opportunity to realize one's will within a social relation regardless of the basis for this opportunity."[25] In this regard, Amitai Etzioni's analysis is consistent with Weber's categorization. Etzioni's theory provides three ways of realizing one's will; by use of utilitarian, coercive, or persuasive power.[26] Among them, persuasive power is helpful for understanding how Luke's Jesus achieved power through his forerunner's charismatic authority. Etzioni explains persuasive power as follows: people obey when they were convinced or persuaded. Persuasion is involved in every legitimate exercise of power, because it is characteristic of legitimate pow-

22. Pearson, "Lucan Censuses," 268.
23. O'Fearghail, *Introduction to Luke-Acts*, 18.
24. Clark, *Parallel Lives*, 106.
25. Weber, "Three Types," 7.
26. Etzioni, *Active Society*, 357–358; Etzioni's categorization of coercive power can be applied to the emperor's *imperium* in Ch. 4; Theissen also uses Etzioni's theory in his article, "Political Dimension," 225–50.

er that a ruler's authority is internally accepted by those who are ruled. This way of having effect on others is by influence. Etzioni's understanding of persuasive power is somewhat similar to Weber's categorization of charismatic authority because both stress one's influence on others. Given the assumption that John's movement was popular, or that he was an influential figure among people[27], it is very likely that Luke strives to persuade people by using an existing influential figure, John the Baptist. In this respect, John's persuasive power functions as charismatic authority. With the focus on comparison, Luke is successful in advertising Jesus' persuasive power/charismatic authority, stressing who Jesus was and in what ways John was subordinate to him. Therefore, it was possible for Jesus in Luke's Gospel to gain charismatic power and authority in a socio-political-religious sense.[28]

It is noticeable that Luke uses a method, the so-called comparison and differentiation, in Jesus' birth narrative when elevating or highlighting his status or authority. However, this does not always mean that Luke uses it purely as a rivalry-hostility relationship. Rather, he simply makes better use of the method in order to express how Jesus should be perceived by his hearers, who were probably familiar with John. With the help of the use of the existing figure, people could easily understand Jesus' authority.[29]

Jesus' Trial: Traditional Authority and Bureaucratic Authority

Let us now turn to Jesus' trial. His charisma, or his ability to attract and attach other people to himself with the help of his influence, allows them voluntarily to participate in his sovereignty.[30] However, his authority is often attacked first by the Jewish leaders, second by Herod Antipas, and

---

27. See Josephus, *Ant.* 18.117–19.

28. When Theissen discusses how Jesus exercises his power, he notes: "The most important aspect of Jesus' exercise of power is persuasion. By basing all power on the power of the kingdom of God, he based his power on the central conviction of the Israelite community- in the faith in the one and only God of Israel. All the influence he exerts on other people is legitimated by this faith" ("Political Dimension," 228).

29. This method is also to be used when Luke portrays Jesus as savior and benefactor, terms frequently used for the Roman emperors. But it is hard to assume that Luke stresses a simple relationship of *Christkult* vs. *Caesarkult* proposed by Deissmann, *Light from the Ancient East*. I shall discuss the titles in Chs. 3 and 4.

30. Theissen, "Political Dimension," 229.

third by the Roman officials. He is charged with his activities based on his authority. As a result, conflict between Jesus and them is brought about in the account of Jesus' trial.

In general, Jesus' trial scenes can be divided into four parts: the trial before the Jewish leaders, the first trial before Pilate, the trial before Herod, and finally, the second trial before Pilate. It is said that Luke's structure of the trial account is more complicated than that of Mark. Also, the former is not the same as the latter, and accordingly their intentions are sometimes very different from each other.[31] When compared with Mark's account, it becomes clear that Luke focuses more on the Roman proceedings. For example, Luke gives a lengthier description, twenty verses including the trial before Herod, while the trial before Pilate consists of only fifteen verses in Mark. As Bond aptly states, this structure in Luke "gives the impression that Jesus is in Roman hands even longer."[32] What is interesting here is that Luke's account of Jesus' trial before Herod is situated between two hearings before Pilate. Moreover, it is noticeable that the verses about the trial before the Jewish leaders in Mark (twelve verses in Mark 14:53, 55–65) are longer than those in Luke (six verses).[33] Let us consider the hearing and trials individually.

Hearing before the Jewish Assembly (Luke 22:66–71)

With the help of Weber's categorization, it would be possible to see both Jewish leaders and Herod (dynastic ruler) as holders of traditional authority.[34] At the same time, it is also possible to categorize them as holders of 'bureaucratic authority' on the grounds that their position was heavily dependent on Roman power. The chief priests were aligned with

---

31. Jesus' hearing before the Sanhedrin in Mark (Mark 14:53–64) takes place by night, at the high priest's house, with the episode of Jesus' mistreatment and Peter's denial immediately following (Mark 14:65 and 14:66–72 respectively); Luke's transposition of the incidents of Peter's denial and Jesus' mockery enables him to move from the Sanhedrin examination directly to the Roman trial (see Luke 22:54–65; Mark 14:65–72). See Neagoe, *Trial of the Gospel*, 70 n27.

32. Bond, *Pontius Pilate*, 141.

33. In this respect, Bond argues that Luke presents his audience with one trial comprising of four scenes which is why there is no Jewish condemnation in Luke 22:66–71 (ibid., 141 n16).

34. See Weber, "Three Types," 4. Unlike charismatic authority based upon extraordinariness, traditional authority is legitimated by tradition. The ability and right to rule is passed down, or given through heredity.

the Roman power, and as noted above, Herod needed Roman permission or support in order to ensure his kingship.

Given the assumption that the Jewish Assembly was the centre of Jewish society religiously, politically, and economically, the Jewish Assembly, including high priests, scribes and their allies, can be seen as the holders of authority or power within the Jewish communities.[35] Even though Palestine was, to a large extent, controlled by the Roman Empire, it is clear that there were some Jewish civic elites who were very influential among people. The local elites were probably Jewish religious leaders of the assembly. Accordingly, it can be said that they had some power over their people. Such authority enabled them to have the hearing against Jesus and to bring him to the governor (22:66—23:1). This fact is evident when Jesus' death is taken into account.

Luke highlights the Jewish leaders' active involvement in Jesus' death in cooperation with the Roman power as it is written in Luke 20:20: ". . . so as to hand him over to the jurisdiction and authority of the governor." Most scholars agree with the view that the Jewish leaders were responsible for Jesus' death. Among them, Cassidy asserts:

> Clearly, Luke goes far beyond Mark in emphasizing the persistence with which the chief priests and their accomplices pursued Jesus and the intensity of the pressure they brought to bear upon Pilate.[36]

If Cassidy's argument is right, Luke stresses that one of his concerns is to show the Jewish leaders' responsibility for Jesus' death. Several key questions are hereby raised: why did Luke attempt to heighten the Jewish

---

35. Traditional scholarship argues that the Sanhedrin (συνέδριον, Luke 22:66) which tried Jesus was a fixed judicial body, consisting of seventy or seventy-one members (scribes, elders, prominent members of high priestly families and the high priest), and functioning in much the same way as the (Great) Sanhedrin of Mishna; see, e.g., Lohse, "συνέδριον," 863–64. However, this view has been challenged by some scholars. Among them, Brown, *Death of the Messiah*, 340–43, esp. 349, asserts that the term "Sanhedrin" in first-century Judaea should be interpreted as a relatively flexible group of the Jewish leaders, such as chief priests, scribes, and influential citizens ("elders"), organized around the high priest and doing various administrative and legal tasks, rather than a group representing a fixed seventy or seventy-one members of a formal body, meeting on a regular basis. Moreover, while Evans interprets συνέδριον simply "council" (e.g., Evans, *Saint Luke*, 834); other scholars argue that it is more likely to be regarded as "council chamber" (e.g., Marshall, *Luke*, 848; Winter, *On the Trial*, 28 n4); also see Sanders, *Judaism*, 472–90.

36. Cassidy, "Luke's Audience," 147.

leaders' active involvement in Jesus' death? How did they bring a charge against Jesus by using their authority? Or, in what ways did they play the leading role in bringing about Jesus' death? Somewhat differently and concretely, did Luke intend to challenge their traditional/bureaucratic authority or power through the story of Jesus' death?

The conversation between Jesus and his opponents provides us with indications of Jesus' identity and the source of his authority. They asked whether he was "the Son of God" (22:70) right after Jesus' saying, "from now on the Son of Man shall be seated at the right hand of the power of God (τῆς δυνάμεως τοῦ θεοῦ)" in 22:69.[37] Here, as Nolland correctly notes, Luke emphasizes Jesus' future enthronement which would vindicate him over his opponents.[38] Along with Nolland's idea, I wish to add an additional point, since he does not draw attention to the question about how Jesus' future enthronement is linked directly to his authority. My reading of Luke 22:69 focuses on the term τῆς δυνάμεως τοῦ θεοῦ. It seems to me that Jesus' answer functions as a challenge to the authority of the Jewish leaders. Jesus simply says that the Son of Man shall be seated at the right hand of the power of God, rather than directly rejecting or denying the authority of the Jewish leaders. Through his answer ("You say that I am"; 22:70), Luke further stresses that Jesus' authority comes from God. In doing so, Luke seems to claim that Jesus' future enthronement is related directly to the power (or authority) of God. By linking Jesus' future enthronement to his authority, Luke implicitly criticizes the authority of the Jewish leaders abusing authority. That is, the Jewish traditional/bureaucratic authority, which denies Jesus' authority based upon God's power, actually rejects God's authority. Therefore, Luke indicates that their authority did not derive from God.

Moreover, in the trial before the Jewish leaders, it is noticeable that Luke completely omits the Jewish leaders' search for testimony against Jesus described in Mark. He also omits Mark's description of a temple-related accusation (Mark 14:55–59).[39] In addition, Luke does not describe

---

37. Neagoe, *Trial*, 66, argues that the statement in 22:69 has "a double allusion, partly to Dan 7:13–14, where 'one like a son of man' comes to the Ancient Days and receives kingly dominion, and partly to Ps 110:1, where God tells someone who was about to be enthroned on David's throne, "sit at my right hand until I make your enemies a footstool for your feet."

38. Nolland, *Luke*, 3:110; cf. Brown, *Death of the Messiah*, 1:504–5; also see the following chapters, where Luke depicts Jesus as a victor.

39. For a list of proposed explanations of this omission, see Brown, *Death of the Messiah*, 1:436–67.

that the Jewish leaders reach a verdict or that Jesus is a condemned man, in contrast to Mark who records their decision, saying that "all of them condemned him as deserving death" (Mark 14:64). Why does Luke omit such accounts? This is associated with the Jewish leaders' plot in Luke 20:20 where they attempted to pass Jesus over to Pilate's authority. It seems to me that Luke places more emphasis on the Jewish leaders' dependence on the Roman governor by omitting their ability to give their own verdict. In other words, their authority relies on the Roman power, not on the power of God. Luke further links the Jewish leaders' false charges to Pilate's false verdict in terms of the responsibility for Jesus' death in the subsequent chapter. In Luke, the only official verdict is given by Pilate (Luke 23:24), since the "sentence," in association with the Jewish leaders, is to be passed on to Pilate (Luke 23:1) who acts as a final judge. In this regard, Luke is very concerned with Pilate's authority in the trial scene.

Initial Trial before Pilate (Luke 23:1–5)

Pontius Pilate (a holder of bureaucratic authority), who was sent by Tiberius, was the fifth governor of the Roman province of Judaea for ten years (26–37 AD).[40] It is not easy to define a historical characterization of Pilate due to the lack of sources. A full discussion of the historical Pilate could be important[41], but what is more important is how far Luke's portrayal of Pilate is different from that of Mark or Matthew in this study. This difference can be analyzed through Jesus' trial before Pilate, as a literary character, in terms of the issue of authority. This section focuses more on Luke's intention than on the facts (or historical information) behind Luke's Gospel with the comparison with Mark's (or Matthew's) portrayals of Pilate (or, more broadly, the Roman Empire).[42] In other words, it explores which motives best explain the distinctiveness of Luke's

---

40. See Josephus, *Ant.* 18.32–35, 89.

41. For the analysis of historical Pilate in the ancient materials, see Winter, *On the Trial*, 70–73; Cohn, *Trial and Death*, 16; Turner, "Chronological Framework," 59–74; Smallwood, *Jews under Roman Rule*, agreed that Pilate exhibited a blatant disregard for his subjects' religious sensibilities; Bond, *Pontius Pilate*; Schwartz, "Pontius Pilate," 395–401; Carter, *Pontius Pilate*.

42. Pilate in relation to Jesus' trial is described differently among the Gospels: Luke and John deal with Pilate's threefold declaration of Jesus' innocence; Mark and John refer to his mockery; and his offer of the choice between Jesus and Barabbas in Matthew; Pilate's wife's dream or Pilate's hand-washing in Matthew and the sending of Jesus to Herod in Luke.

story in the context of the Roman Empire. It also analyses whom Luke regards as responsible for Jesus' death at the narrative level rather than at the historical level.

As a whole, Luke refers to Pilate three times in his Gospel before Jesus' trial scene: Pilate first as governor of Judaea in Luke 3:1, second as the slaughterer of the Galileans in 13:1, and third as authority of the governor in Luke 20:20c, although the name "Pilate" is not mentioned here.[43] By referring to him three times before Jesus' trial, Luke seems to give his audience some clues to his attitude towards him in advance. As a rule, Luke, with such references, does not portray Pilate in a positive tone.[44]

First, Luke refers to Pilate as one of the pagan rulers mentioned in Luke 3:1. Along with the fact that the verse could be interpreted as evidence of Luke's accuracy in his writing by providing some notable historical figures, I wish to focus on the identity of the rulers in connection with "the kings of the Gentiles" in Luke 22:25, which will be discussed later in detail. In brief, my argument is that the pagan kings, in connection with the title "benefactor," are depicted in a negative tone in 22:25, and that the verse in Luke 3:1 implicitly functions as indicating the identity of the pagan kings in 22:25. Thus, Luke's attitude towards Pilate, who can be seen as one of them, is unfavorable. The second reference in 13:1 explicitly shows that Pilate was the one who slaughtered the Galileans for some reason.[45] Third, it seems to me that the Jewish leaders thought of the governor in 20:20 as their ally. That is why the Jewish leaders wished to hand him over to Pilate, who later declared Jesus' crucifixion as they wished. In Luke, they understood Pilate as their ally rather than as their enemy even though he killed many Galileans in 13:1. Taken together, even prior to the trial scene, Luke draws a negative picture of Pilate.

When Pilate in Jesus' trial is carefully considered, it becomes more evident that Luke's stance toward him is not favorable at all. Pilate's declaration has an important role in analyzing whether Pilate is responsible for Jesus' death. His declaration of Jesus' innocence is found three times in

---

43. Other references to Pilate are found in the trial scene in 23:1–25, and he is briefly mentioned in 23:52 when Joseph of Arimathea "went to Pilate and asked for the body of Jesus." The final references to Pilate occur in Acts at 3:13; 4:27; and 13:28 in relation to Jesus' death.

44. *Contra.* Cadbury, *Making*; Conzelmann, *Theology*; Tyson, *Death of Jesus*; also see Walaskay, *"And so We Came."*

45. We do not have precise information about this incident either from biblical or from nonbiblical materials. To make matters worse, Luke refers to the incident very briefly.

Luke's Gospel: once here in the initial trial before Pilate (Luke 23:4) and twice in the second trial (Luke 23:14 and 22). Like Pilate, it is said that Herod found no crime in him (23:15).[46] Before moving on to examine his responsibility for Jesus' death, let us discuss Jesus' charges brought by the Jewish leaders because the accusation is a significant issue in the scene of Pilate's first trial where he declares Jesus' innocence.

Charges

While Mark records that the chief priests accused Jesus of "many things" (Mark 15:2–3) without specific explanations, Luke describes the charges in more detail. In Luke, the accusation consists of three clauses, introduced respectively by three Greek participles (διαστρέφοντα, κωλύοντα, and λέγοντα) and separated from each other by the conjunction καί. In terms of categorization of the charges, Cassidy regards them as three parallel charges although they can be seen as "interrelated" through the common claim that "Jesus had adopted a stance similar to the Zealots."[47] In a different vein, Neagoe argues that "the first clause of the triple construction is to be regarded as the governing charge, with the latter two as explicating of it."[48] Similarly, according to Bond, the accusation is "one general charge and two specific examples: Jesus is said to have perverted their nation, forbidden the payment of tribute to Caesar and claimed to be Christ, a king."[49] It is more probable to understand that, according to the accusation of the Jewish leaders, Jesus perverted the nation because he rejected to pay the tribute to the emperor and declared himself as the Messiah. Let us take a look at each charge individually in order to evaluate whether, or not, the accusation is right, since this is related implicitly both to the authority of the Jewish leaders and to Pilate's final verdict.

---

46. In this respect, Bond, *Pontius Pilate*, 144–45, claims that Luke describes that, although Jesus' innocence was declared by both Pilate and Herod, he was put to death "because of Jewish machinations." However, it seems to me that Luke has more than one purpose in the trial scene. I am not denying that the Jewish leaders were responsible for Jesus' death. But, along with Jewish responsibility, Luke also highlights the relationship between Pilate and Herod as a means of blaming Pilate for Jesus' death. This becomes clearer when taking into account their friendship in Luke 23:12. See below.

47. Cassidy, *Jesus, Politics*, 65 and 167.

48. Neagoe, *Trial*, 70; Brown, *Death of the Messiah*, 1:738; Nolland, *Luke*, 3:1117–18; Schneider, "Political Charge," 407–8.

49. For similar charges, see Acts 24:5–6, 12; 25:8 (Paul); and Acts 17:6–9 (Jason and other).

Perverting the Nation

As mentioned, the first charge, "perverting the nation" (διαστρέφοντα τὸ ἔθνος) in Luke 23:2, governs the following two charges. At a glance, the charge seems to indicate that Jesus is quite political against the Roman regime. Bond states:

> The verb (Luke 23:2) διαστρέφω (to pervert) can be used in a religious sense meaning "to turn away from the true faith" as in 1 Kings 18:17–18, Acts 13:8, 10, 20:30 . . . But in view of the two clearly political charges which follow, the apparently synonymous use of the more politically sounding verb ἀνασείω (to stir up) in v. 5, and the Jewish use of τὸ ἔθνος ἡμῶν before the Roman governor to denote their "nation" rather than their faith or laws, it seems best to understand the charge in a political sense: Jesus is accused of inciting his fellow countrymen to sedition.[50]

She further argues that the first charge is false since it is related to what Jesus says in 9:41 where he "describes the nation as already perverse, indicating that its perversity is not a result of Jesus' teaching."[51] At a glance, Jesus was accused of leading the Jewish people away from its submission to the emperor.[52] This charge is expressed through the lips of the Jewish leaders as if he attempted to subvert the imperial regime. But what is to be noted is that Jesus did not do what the subsequent charges indicate. Luke seems to stress here that the testimony does not look genuine since it comes from the holders of false authority, the Jewish leaders. Moreover, Luke's Jesus is far from such a political revolutionary.[53] Jesus'

---

50. Bond, *Pontius Pilate*, 145 n31; also see Evans, *Luke*, 845; Sanders, *Jews in Luke–Acts*, 7, notes that similar charges were leveled against Moses by Pharaoh (Exod 5:4) and against Elijah by Ahab (1 Kgs 18:17). Bond's argument is right that the word διαστρέφω employs a political implication in Luke 23:2 and that, accordingly, the charge is political. However, her view is partly problematic. It is not important to clearly differentiate διαστρέφω in a religious sense from ἀνασείω in a political sense. In many cases, both terms were interrelated in the first-century world. It is hard to accept that the word ἀνασείω should be considered more political. What should be highlighted in this charge is that Jesus is charged by the religious leaders in a political tone: this shows the overlap between religion and politics in the Roman Empire.

51. Bond, *Pontius Pilate*, 145.

52. Neagoe, *Trial*, 71; Fitzmyer, *Luke*, 2:1473; Nolland, *Luke*, 3:1117.

53. Fitzmyer, *Luke*, 2:1473 notes, "Jesus may indeed have subverted the nation in warning the crowds against the 'leaven of the Pharisees' (12:1), i.e. subverted it in a religious sense. But such action in a political sense has not been evident thus far in the Gospel." Also see Ch. 4.

teachings, such as moral and social visions, have nothing to do with perverting the emperor's land. Thus, the first charge is proved to be false; Jesus' teachings are concerned with correcting people's immorality,[54] not with subverting or perverting the nation.

Tribute

According to the Jewish leaders, the second charge is concerned with Jesus' forbidding the people to pay taxes to the emperor. The tax-related charge, which recalls the issue in Luke 20:20–25 where the phrase "the jurisdiction and authority of the governor" is referred to, is associated with Pilate's duties.[55] Neagoe rightly asserts that the second charge is clearly "a distortion of Jesus' answer."[56] As can be seen in 20:25, Jesus evidently did not oppose the payment of tribute to Caesar. As with the first charge, it is proved that the second charge brought by the Jewish leaders is false.

Kingship

It is said that Jesus is the Christ (Luke 2:26; 4:41; 9:20), a king of the Davidic line (e.g. Luke 1:32–33; 2:4; 3:31; 18:37; Acts 17:7), even though he does not refer to himself with such titles. Pilate asked Jesus concerning the third charge, "Are you the king of the Jews?" (23:3). Jesus ambiguously replies, "You say so (Σὺ λέγεις)." Even though his reply seems somewhat ambiguous, he, at least, does not refuse to answer Pilate's question in contrast to his reaction to Herod's question in 23:9 ("Jesus gave him no answer"). Luke also omits Mark's account of Jesus' refusal to answer Pilate (Mark 15:4–5). In this respect, Conzelmann asserts:

> He gives the information they [Roman authorities] require and so enables them to arrive at the objective legal decision, which is in fact immediately done officially. The answer he gives is no fuller than in Mark, but there is no refusal to answer.[57]

---

54. On the discussion of Jesus' correction of immorality in connection with the emperor's authority, see Ch. 2.

55. For a detailed discussion of tax-related issues in Luke's Gospel, see the next chapter.

56. Neagoe, *Trial*, 72.

57. Conzelmann, *Theology*, 86.

However, the serious problem with Conzelmann's idea is that Jesus' reply has nothing to do with any information which Pilate requires. According to the Roman criminal law, silence, in general, was considered as guilt. Luke, who probably knows some of the Roman law, highlights that Jesus did not remain silent before Pilate as opposed to Mark's account.[58] It is likely that Luke omits Mark's account of Jesus' refusal to answer Pilate (Mark 15:4–5) in order to minimize any legal image of Jesus' guiltiness.

Although he answered the governor's question, the meaning of Jesus' reply, Σὺ λέγεις, still remains ambiguous. That is, it is to be explored whether his reply indicates a denial or an admission. Why did Pilate declare that he was not guilty? R. Pesch argues that this reply needs to be regarded as a denial.[59] He goes on to assert that it is a question which amounts to a denial, and that Pilate's use of ὃν λέγετε in Mark 15:12 also suggests Jesus' denial of kingship.[60] Similarly, Bond holds that "Pilate has completely misunderstood Jesus' messiahship in terms of political or materialistic kingship," asserting that Jesus' messiahship does not have any political sense.[61] She further regards Jesus' reply as a denial, noting: ". . . otherwise his following statement is incomprehensible, 'I find no basis for an accusation against this man' (Luke 23:4)."[62]

---

58. Bond, *Pontius Pilate*, 108, argues that Jesus' silence found in Mark sometimes signifies a "sense of dignity," especially in the face of false witnesses in Mark 14:60 (the many accusations of the priests are also false). Neagoe, *Trial*, 74 n42, puts it: "Conzelmann's stress on Luke's omission of Jesus' refusal to answer Pilate (cf. Mark 15:4–5) misreads the Markan account. It is not to Pilate that Jesus refuses to respond (that happens only in John 19:9), but to the chief priests' accusations, Pilate being instead the one who wonders at the fact that Jesus made no response to their charges. Moreover, Luke also omits Jesus' parallel silence during the Sanhedrin hearing (Mark 14:61)."

59. Pesch, *Das Markusevangelium*, 456.

60. Ibid., 457.

61. Bond, *Pontius Pilate*, 107.

62. Ibid., 152; concerning 23:6 ("When Pilate heard this, he asked whether the man was a Galilean"), Bond maintains that Jesus in Luke is completely unknown to Pilate, stating that, "if Jesus was any threat whatsoever to the state, the governor must have received reports about him already" (ibid., 153). It is, however, too speculative to assert that Pilate's question about Jesus' hometown indicates that Pilate has no reports about him since he is not a threat to Rome. My first assumption is that, given the fact that Pilate, like other governors, did stay at Caesarea during most of his time, it is very likely that he had no precise reports about Jesus, since Jesus was not depicted as a political rebel. Or, if he had already heard about him, he just asked to confirm whether this man was the same person as he had already known. My second assumption is that the reference to Galilean in 23:6 can be related to the Galileans in 13:1. Perhaps, Pilate did not want to remember the event any longer. The important thing is here that

Conversely, Jesus' reply can be interpreted as a full admission, or, at least, it does not deny that he is the king of the Jews.[63] A similar answer already occurred in the previous scene. When Jesus' ambiguous answer is taken together with that in 22:70 (Ὑμεῖς λέγετε ὅτι ἐγώ εἰμι)[64], it becomes less ambiguous. The difference between the two answers is that, while they are plural in 22:70, both subject and verb are singular in 23:3. As Jesus' reply in 22:70 is viewed more as admission than as denial, his answer in 23:3 can be interpreted as admission.

What should be noted is that Jesus could be perceived as the one who distorted the nation from the perspective of the Jewish leaders or the Roman Empire, not from the perspective of God. Given that Luke acknowledges the importance of peace and security, one of the most important catchphrases in the Roman Empire, three different Greek terms (23:2 διαστρέφω, distort/pervert in 23:2, ἀνασείω, stir up in 23:5, and ἀποστρέφω, pervert in 23:14) indicate that Jesus, at least from the perspective of the Roman Empire, could be a potential threat to Rome regardless of the assumption of whether Luke's Jesus really intended to stir up the nation. But this does not mean that he was a real threat to the emperor. Luke aims to describe Jesus as the king whose authority is different from what their opponents normally argue.[65] At the same time, Pilate probably knew that Jesus' messiahship had nothing to do with "political or materialistic kingship" as opposed to his opponents' claim. As Cassidy correctly maintains, Pilate found no basis for the accusation against Jesus because he did not see him as Zealot, one of the main Roman political/social enemies.[66] In other words, Pilate did not regard Jesus' claim to messianic kingship as a claim of overturning the empire. In spite of his

---

we should not limit our interpretation of Luke 23:6 to the conclusion that Jesus was completely unknown to Pilate. We do not know whether he was unknown or known to him. Thus, it is wrong to argue that Jesus was not a threat to Rome since Pilate did not know him. The question of whether he was a threat is one thing; and the question of whether Pilate already knew him is another.

63. E.g., Piper, "God's Good News," 179; Cole, *Mark*, 233; Johnson, *Luke*, 365; Ahn, *Reign of God*, 187–94.

64. Ahn, *Reign of God*, 188 n116, also makes the similar point.

65. On the question of how Luke contrasts Jesus' authority with that of the emperor, see the following chapters.

66. Cassidy, *Jesus, Politics*, 72–76. Somewhat differently, Green argues that "if in this scene Pilate finds no basis for an accusation against Jesus, this is not because Jesus and his message constitute no threat to Rome" (*Luke*, 798), but because he fails to discern such threat.

critiques of the empire, Luke does not give us any evidence that Jesus was an alternative to the emperor's political regime.[67] That is why Pilate declared his innocence three times.

Also, it is noticeable that the Jewish leaders, despite Pilate's declaration (23:4), still tried to associate Jesus' kingship with a political claim by using the verb 'stir up' (ἀνασείω) in 23:5.[68] According to Neagoe, what is different here from the first three charges is that they now focus on Jesus' "teaching" (διδάσκων) and on the "geographical extent of his influence" in order to put him to death.[69] They focused their charges not on truth, but on achieving Jesus' death. Again, their third charge is false on the grounds that Jesus was accused not because of his political messiahship, but because of his teaching (23:5) which had nothing to do with an overthrow of the empire.

Taken together, Luke attempts to highlight that all the charges brought by the Jewish authorities are not true, and that Jesus is innocent of Jewish accusations. In doing so, Luke intrinsically emphasizes the fact that Jesus' authority was not damaged even in the trial scene. Rather, Jewish leaders' traditional authority was regarded as authority with falseness and injustice.

Trial before Herod (Luke 23:6–12)

The scene of Jesus' trial before Herod Antipas occurs only in Luke's Gospel. Whereas he does not appear in Mark after the execution of John the Baptist, he plays one of the major roles in the trial scene of the Lukan narrative. Other Gospel writers do not refer to any kind of allusion to this trial.[70] It seems to me that Luke intends to show something to his audience by inserting this scene between the two trials before Pilate. It is important to discuss Luke's portrait of Herod.

---

67. Neagoe, *Trial*, 73.

68. The use of the Greek term, ἐπίσχυον, in an imperfect form, highlights their continuous action.

69. Neagoe, *Trial*, 74; "The term 'Judaea' may also be understood in its broader Lukan sense of 'Palestine,' 'the land of the Jews' (Luke 1:5; 6:17; 7:17; 23:5), in which case Galilee becomes part of it," at 75 n50.

70. The other reference to it is found only in Acts 4:26–28.

Pilate's Reasons for Sending Jesus over to Herod (Luke 23:7)

First of all, we need to identify why Luke inserts the scene of Pilate's sending Jesus to Herod. T. Mommsen suggests that Luke seems to show the historicity of the proceedings before Herod.[71] For him, the trial was conducted by the authorities of the province to which the accused belonged (*forum domicilii*) in the time of Jesus, but this law was later changed so that the accused were tried in the province in which the crime was committed (*forum delicti*). According to him, that is why Pilate sent Jesus to Herod, who was judicially responsible for the accused. For Mommsen, Pilate in Luke 23:7 acknowledged that Jesus belonged to the "jurisdiction" (ἐξουσία) of Herod.

However, A. N. Sherwin-White, challenging Mommsen's view, asserts that the accused needed to be tried in the province where the crime was committed (*forum delicti*) in the time of Jesus. He further argues that *forum domicilii* was introduced only later.[72] His understanding of trial is more conceivable when looking into Paul's trial in Acts 23:34–24:26. Felix tried Paul for misdeeds in Jerusalem in spite of Luke's description that his home province was Cilicia (Acts 23:34—24:26). Regardless of the question about whether the account is historical or not, Pilate was not legally forced to send Jesus to Herod. It is more important to analyze Luke's report about Pilate's sending Jesus to Herod on a narrative level than on a historical level. For me, the trial before Herod is a literary composition designed to say something about Luke's intention. Then, why does Luke report that Pilate sent Jesus to Herod Antipas within the narrative itself? Scholars have attempted to offer plausible scenarios. Among the most favored explanations are: Pilate wanted to get rid of a complex case;[73] he wanted an independent evaluation from someone legally connected with Jesus[74]; and, after the massacre mentioned in Luke 13:1, Pilate was trying to avoid any further offence to Herod, or even positively to attempt a reconciliation by means of this act of courtesy.[75] Furthermore, somewhat

---

71. Mommsen, *Romisches Strafrecht*, 356–57.

72. Sherwin-White, *Roman Society*, 28–31; also see Hoehner, *Herod Antipas*, 236, and "Why Did Pilate," 88.

73. Hoehner, *Herod Antipas*, 236, and in "Why Did Pilate," 88.

74. See Brown, *Death of the Messiah*, 1:766.

75. See ibid., 1:767; Hoehner, *Herod Antipas*, 236–37; and in 'Why Did Pilate', 88; Sherwin-White, *Roman Society*, 31 n5.

differently, Walaskay suggests that Luke inserted Jesus' trial before Antipas in order to parallel Paul's trial before Agrippa.[76]

However, those views have failed to notice Luke's intrinsic or implicit intention of including the trial before Herod. It seems to me that Luke aims to stress that Herod was, to a great extent, responsible for Jesus' death on a literary level.[77] In this respect, some would argue that Luke attempts to exonerate the Roman authorities by heightening Herod's involvement in Jesus' trial or that the trial before Herod functions as stressing Jewish active involvement in Jesus' death because of Herod's position. Yet, this suggestion does not take seriously Luke's purpose in the account of Herod. The view is partly right: on the one hand, it is correct in arguing that Luke emphasizes Herod's involvement in Jesus' death; on the other hand, it is wrong that Luke exonerates the Roman responsibility for Jesus' crucifixion. Moreover, it is a mistake to argue that Luke uses Herod as a tool for heightening Jewish leaders' responsibility because Herod was not a Jew by birth, but a half Jew. As Hoehner explains:

> It is difficult to see any apologetic purpose in Luke for the inclusion of Jesus' trial by Antipas. With this episode [the trial before Herod], Luke apparently does not attempt to exonerate Rome and blame the Jews. Since Antipas was not a Jew by birth, the Jews did not think of him or the Herodian family as representatives of the Jews.[78]

If Luke had intended simply to emphasize Jewish mistreatment of Jesus and, at the same time, to exonerate Roman responsibility, he would have not inserted the episode of the trial before Herod. If this was his main purpose, he had already achieved his goal in 22:63—23:5. The Jewish leaders were viewed as representatives of the Jews more than Herod was.

Furthermore, we need to consider Jesus' attitude toward Herod in the Lukan narrative. Luke reports that Jesus, when he was sent to Herod's authority, did not cooperate with Herod. He refused not only to perform some sign, but also to give him an answer (23:8–9). As Cassidy rightly asserts, "[Luke's] Jesus did not cooperate with or defer to the authorities

---

76. Walaskay, 'And so We Came', 43.

77. Also, an analysis on a literary level will help us comprehend Luke's portrait of Herod and Pilate's authority, or the former's traditional/ bureaucratic authority and the latter's bureaucratic authority. See below.

78. Hoehner, *Herod Antipas*, 227.

who judged him."⁷⁹ Luke describes that Jesus rejected to cooperate with the holder of false authority. Then why is Herod's traditional/bureaucratic authority considered false? Let us look into Luke 13:31 where Luke's characterization of Herod is described.

Herod as Fox in Luke 13:31

Even though the verse of 13:31 is not part of the trial account, its significance should not be under-estimated. It seems to me that Luke's account of Herod at Luke 13:31 has a double allusion: it serves, first, as presenting Herod's characterization and second, as hinting at Pilate's characterization later in Jesus' trial. This is very clear when analyzing the meaning of 'fox' in Luke 13:31–35 and 'friendship' in 23:12 respectively. In other words, Herod's characterization is related implicitly to that of Pilate in Luke's Gospel, even though not stated directly. Before the trial scene, it is said that Herod imprisoned John the Baptist (Luke 3:19–20). And he was perplexed by Jesus and wanted to see him (9:7–9). Furthermore, in 13:31 even the Pharisees warned Jesus to "get away from here, for Herod wants to kill you."⁸⁰ Bond contends that this verse implies the fate of Jesus who will suffer as John the Baptist did.⁸¹ It can be said that Luke's overall picture of Herod is unfavorable towards Jesus.

More importantly, Herod was referred to as a fox in 13:31. It has been generally recognized that the characterization of a fox in ancient literature employs a very negative meaning. According to Hoehner, those who are called a fox are regarded as "an insignificant person, lacking in true power/*authority* despite the fact that he or she might accomplish things through cunning."⁸² In a different vein, A. A. Plummer, focusing the meaning of fox on craftiness, states:

> Herod's craftiness lay in his trying to get rid of an influential leader and a disquieting power of righteousness by a threat which he had not the courage to execute.⁸³

---

79. Cassidy, *Jesus, Politics*, 73.

80. In this scene, it can be interpreted that Pharisees are portrayed in a positive way.

81. Bond, *Pontius Pilate*, 155.

82. Hoehner, *Herod Antipas*, 343–47 (emphasis mine).

83. Plummer, *Critical and Exegetical Commentary*, 349; Borgman, *Way*, 206, argues that the fox was regarded as not only crafty, but "dishonorable and worthless as well."

Another characterization of fox has been proposed by John A. Darr.[84] His analysis offers a different metaphorical meaning of Luke's reference to Herod as a fox. He denies Hoehner's idea, in arguing that Herod is not insignificant or lacks power, since he executes John the Baptist, an influential figure with charismatic authority among the Jews. In so doing, he asserts that the metaphorical meaning of fox is "destructiveness" on the basis of Herod's two actions: he beheaded John the Baptist and threatened to kill Jesus.[85] In other words, for him Herod is "a destroyer of God's agent, a would-be disputer of the divine economy."[86] However, one of the serious problems with Darr's comprehension of Herod as a fox is his strong rejection of other traits of a fox, such as craftiness and weakness in relation to power or authority. For me, Hoehner implies that Herod's characterization conveys Luke's emphasis on God's superiority (or Jesus' authority) over Herod's power by describing him as an insignificant person in terms of his authority. By portraying Herod as a fox Luke attempts to achieve his aim; that is, he criticizes Herod's false traditional/bureaucratic authority, which played a part in putting Jesus to death. Regardless of the fact that Herod as a fox signifies his destructiveness or lack of his power, it is clear that Luke portrays his authority in a very negative way.

Friendship in Luke 23:12

Along with Herod's characterization as a fox, it is important to clarify the meaningfulness of friendship in Luke 23:12 on a literary level. Luke's account itself does not clearly explain why Pilate and Herod were enemies before. Some would argue that it was due to Pilate's slaughter of the Galileans in 13:1, but this is not really obvious. Goulder claims that they became enemies because of the incident concerning the gilded shields.[87] Whatever it is, the reason for their enmity does not affect my study of their friendship, for my focus is not on their enmity, but on their friendship in the trial scene. It seems to me that Luke wishes to stress the friendship between Pilate and Herod despite their former enmity. They became friends since both were responsible for Jesus' death. As Johnson rightly states, both Herod and Pilate are mentioned "in murderous con-

---

84. Darr, *Herod the Fox*, 180–83.
85. Ibid., 182; also see Luke 13:34.
86. Ibid.; Darr connects this with a doer of evil in Luke 3:19–20.
87. Goulder, *Luke*, 759; see Philo, *Embassy* 229–305.

texts." In other words, Luke brings together two different secular rulers who played their part in Jesus' execution.[88]

As mentioned earlier, Herod under the Roman Empire was not independent from Roman support for his position. In this regard, Herod's cooperation with Pilate was probably explicable. But it seems to me that Luke's reference to this friendship functions as implicitly associating Herod's negative characterization with Pilate's characterization. It does not necessarily mean that Herod's characterization is the same as that of Pilate. In other words, although Pilate's characterization differs, to some extent, from that of Herod as a fox, what we can conclude is that Pilate is regarded, at least, as a very negative figure. More importantly, the reference to 'friend' cements the relationship between the Jewish leaders and Pilate on a narrative level. It means that Herod, as a half-Jew, can be viewed as mediator between two different authorities, such as Jewish authority and Pilate, even though this is not mentioned in Luke's Gospel. John T. Fitzgerald holds that "friend" (φίλος) in the ancient Mediterranean world was "not simply an interpersonal relationship but also a political phenomenon."[89] As seen in the *Introduction*, religion was inseparable from politics in the Roman Empire. Given that the power of Jewish leaders and Herod was under Roman power, their closeness should not be under-rated. Luke stresses their friendship as the basis of their mutuality. In doing so, Luke attempts to combine the Jewish leaders' authority with that of Pilate through Herod's characterization in order to show that Jesus was put to death at the hands of false traditional/bureaucratic authority.[90] As both Herod and the Jewish leaders were responsible for Jesus' death, Luke seems to show that Pilate was also heavily involved in Jesus' death through the insertion of Herod's trial.[91] In order to re-affirm a bond of

---

88. Johnson, *Luke*, 368; see Luke 9:9 and 13:32 for Herod, and 13:1 for Pilate.

89. Fitzgerald, ed., *Greco-Roman Perspective*, 4; also see Mitchell, "Greet the Friends," 225–62; Plutarch's discussion about friendship, such as "How to Tell a Flatter from a Friend" (*Mor.* 48e–74e) and "On Having Many Friends" (*Mor.* 93a–97b).

90. It has been often suggested that Luke's use of Ps 2:1–2 alludes to the bond of Herod and Pilate in order to put Jesus to death (e.g., Cadbury, *Making*, 30). Neagoe also argues that the connection between Psalm 2 and Luke's account of Jesus' trial is explicit in Acts 4:26–27. (*Trial*, 79; "Jesus is God's Χριστός" Acts 4:26; the same term as in Ps 2:2, LXX) But Darr, *Herod the Fox*, 203–207, argues that it is not appropriated for linking Ps 2:1–2 to Luke 23:12. For him, Herod and Pilate were not depicted as gathering against the Lord and his anointed in Luke 23:1–23.

91. Neagoe, *Trial*, 82 claims that the narrative function of the trial before Herod indicates Jesus' political innocence by portraying him as the suffering righteous one

friendship between Pilate and Herod in Luke 23:12, Luke again heightens their cooperation against Jesus' authority in Acts 4:27: ". . . *both Herod and Pontius Pilate*, with the Gentiles and the peoples of Israel, gathered together against your holy servant Jesus [*or against Jesus' authority*], whom you anointed."[92] Thus, it is evident that Luke does portray Herod's traditional/bureaucratic authority very unfavorably through Jesus' trial, and this negative portrait is linked to Pilate's bureaucratic authority later in terms of Jesus' death. The second trial before Pilate indicates that Pilate played a significant role in bringing about Jesus' death.

Second Trial before Pilate (Luke 23:13–25)

Let us first explore whether Pilate was responsible for Jesus' death. Those who argue that the Jewish leaders, not the Roman authorities, were responsible for Jesus' death frequently emphasize that Pilate declared his innocence three times.[93] Their argument is based primarily upon the assumption that Luke uses Pilate's declaration as a marker for heightening the role of the Jews in bringing about Jesus' death. Accordingly, for them Luke exonerates Pilate's culpability in the crucifixion. However, they pay little attention to Luke's implicit intention of Pilate's appearance in two scenes in connection with his declaration of Jesus' innocence. Pilate's involvement in Luke's Gospel should not be weakened.

Let us see why Pilate's announcement of Jesus' innocence cannot be interpreted so that Luke exonerates his culpability. Surprisingly, it becomes clear that Pilate was heavily involved in Jesus' death on the basis of his threefold pronouncement of Jesus' innocence. J. A. Weatherly boldly claims that Pilate "appears all the more culpable for having knowingly turned an innocent man over to execution" by declaring Jesus' innocence

---

(see Luke 23:47; Acts 3:14; 7:52; 22:14).

92. See Stenschke, *Luke's Portrait*, 141–43; he is correct in arguing that both Jews and Gentiles are responsible for Jesus' execution. But he too quickly concludes that all the Gentiles are against Christian mission without a careful consideration of a few positive views of Gentiles. Given the fact that one of the Lukan main purposes is to preach the gospel to the Gentiles, the groups of the Gentiles should be carefully categorized. Cf. Slingerland, "Composition of Acts," 99–133; for him, Luke plays down Jewish responsibility for Jesus' death by emphasizing Roman involvement (103–4).

93. E.g., Cadbury, *Making*; Maddox, *Purpose of Luke-Acts*; Conzelmann, *Theology*; Tyson, *Death of Jesus*; Walaskay, *"And so We Came"*; Esler, *Community and Gospel*.

and then sending him to be crucified.[94] As discussed in the section of his accusations brought by the Jewish leaders, Pilate did not see Jesus as a political rebel. That is why he declared his innocence.

In addition, unlike the view that Luke's omission of the flogging scene of Mark 15:16–20 undermines the involvement of the Roman authorities, for me Luke does not completely omit any sense of scourge. Rather, Luke tends to draw a very different picture of the flogging scene. Pilate's active involvement in Jesus' death becomes much clearer when Pilate's second and third verdicts are examined. By omitting the Markan flogging version, Luke alludes to the scourge in connection with Pilate's order in his second and third verdict in order to stress that he cannot escape from the blame for Jesus' death. According to Stenschke, despite the fact that Jesus was found innocent of any charge, Pilate *still* intended to flog him prior to releasing him (Luke 23:16, 22).[95] Assuming that Luke's main intention is to show the Roman governor's injustice or his failure as a judge rather than the cruelty of the flogging itself, he does not necessarily describe the flogging scenes in detail.

What is more, the significant question is whether Pilate actually ordered Jesus' execution. Luke tells us that Pilate declared death by crucifixion in Luke 23:24–25. Crucifixion was carried out by Roman soldiers under the direction of Pilate.[96] Although Jesus' death was intensely plotted by the chief priests and their allies, it was finally carried out and

---

94. Weatherly, *Jewish Responsibility*, 95; he relates Pilate's pronouncement of innocence to that of Herod. The former is accompanied by crucifixion, and the latter by mock (Luke 23:11); he goes on to argue that such treatment is "hardly commendable handling of an innocent" (95). When taking into account the friendship shown above, this cooperation becomes more evident.

95. Stenschke, *Luke's Portrait*, 121.

96. Ibid., 114–46; and Weatherly, *Jewish Responsibility*, 94–95. Wengst presents a different view in arguing that Luke undermines the negative action of the soldiers in the passion narrative as opposed to the soldiers in Mark. For him, those who carried out Jesus' crucifixion were not the Roman soldiers, but the Jewish soldiers. Wengst, *Pax Romana*, 90, notes: ". . . according to Luke the Roman soldiers only appear at the point when Jesus is already hanging on the cross . . . (Luke 23:36f.)." Also, it is very interesting to note that crucifixion, according to Sanders, was not really a Roman method of execution, but a Jewish form of execution on the basis of Deut 21:22. In doing so, Sanders, *Jews*, 11, argues that Luke intends to stress that Jews, not Romans, put Jesus to death. Yet, his argument is too speculative. We do not have enough evidence that "hanging on a tree" in ancient Palestine was the same form of crucifixion in the Roman Empire.

controlled by the Roman authority.[97] It cannot be denied that Jesus ultimately died under Roman bureaucratic authority.[98] Furthermore, another example which shows Pilate's active involvement in Jesus' death would be Joseph's request for Jesus' body in Luke 23:52. As Weatherly claims, if Pilate has the authority to dispose of Jesus' body, it can "reasonably be assumed that Pilate is the authority under whom Jesus is executed."[99]

Let us now focus on Pilate's judicial procedure in detail. In Luke 23:13–16, the case was returned again to Pilate. He called together the chief priests, the leaders, and the people in v. 14. Luke uses the Greek term ἀνακρίνω ("judge" or "examine") here in v. 14. Bond asserts that the term ἀνακρίνω is "a technical term corresponding to the Latin *cognitio* referring to an examination by a magistrate."[100] With the focus on the word ἀνακρίνω, Luke shows that Jesus' trial before Pilate is expressed by traditional Roman trial proceedings.[101] Two aspects are worth noting. First, in contrast to the meaning of the term ἀνακρίνω, Pilate showed a very brief examination without any proper investigation. It seems that Pilate wanted to avoid dealing with the case or that he did not take the

---

97. Cassidy, *Society and Politics*, 19–20; also see Weatherly, *Jewish Responsibility*, 96, where he argues that the verb "crucify" (σταύρου) in Greek in Luke 23:21 is the second person singular verb, which clearly implies the crowd's expectation that Pilate is the one who will crucify. It is thus clear that Pilate has a share of responsibility for regulating Jesus' death.

98. Bond, *Pontius Pilate*, 158, n84 claims that Pilate's verdict was due to 'the forcefulness of the crowd' on the basis of two Greek terms, such as ἐπίκειμαι ("to be urgent") and κατισχύω ("to overpower") in Luke 23:24. She further argues that Luke seems to stress the crowd's verdict, not the Roman governor's, because Pilate passed sentence: "So Pilate gave his verdict that their demand should be granted" (ἐπέκρινεν in v. 24 has the technical nuance of issuing an official sentence; see also 2 Macc 4:47; 3 Macc 4:2). However, there is a serious problem with her argument. Even if Pilate was, as she argues, forced to give his verdict by the crowd, it does not mean that Luke exonerates Pilate's involvement in Jesus' death. Rather, it is more probable to interpret that the governor lost his control of the crowd. In other words, Luke stresses, at least, that Pilate's bureaucratic authority in connection with his office "governor" failed to be in complete control of the trial.

99. Weatherly, *Jewish Responsibility*, 96; also see Cassidy, "Luke's Audience," 147.

100. Bond, *Pontius Pilate*, 156; the same legal term is used later in Acts 12:19 and 28:18.

101. Neyrey, *Passion*, 77, observes the following judicial procedure: charges are made (23:2), the magistrate conducts his *cognitio* (investigation, 23:3), and pronounces a verdict (23:3). Green, *Luke*, 798, describes it in a slightly different way, as accusation made, charges formulated, opportunity for defense given, and judgment rendered. See also Sherwin-White, *Roman Society*, 24–26.

case seriously. Let us draw attention to Pilate's order right after his pronouncement of Jesus' innocence. In the scene of his first verdict, Pilate sent Jesus off to Herod (23:7) without ordering any proper investigation (23:1–7). As Stenschke, defining him as a quick and careless judge, rightly points out, Pilate does not take Jesus' case seriously.[102] It is hard to say that Pilate acted as a proper judge in this scene. Given that he was sent by the emperor to maintain law and security of part of the empire, Pilate's investigation signifies dereliction of his duty. As he neglected one of his main duties, his bureaucratic authority, as a judge, was accordingly damaged. That is, Luke seems to portray Pilate as the one who failed to use his authority, or, at least, as the one who did not know exactly what the term ἀνακρίνω means. The second aspect is that, when declaring his innocence, Pilate referred to what Herod had done to Jesus. Here, Luke seems to underline that Pilate's verdict is not a far cry from Herod's verdict after becoming friends. It is very likely that the verse of 23:15 functions as re-affirming their friendship; that is, Luke depicts both Pilate and Herod in a negative sense.

Why does Luke portray Pilate as the one who put Jesus to death? What significance does his portrait of Pilate bear? As mentioned above, one of the Roman governors' roles was to maintain peace and law. In this regard, justice was frequently emphasized in the Roman Empire. For example, Virgil, praising Augustus' justice, stresses "peace crowned with justice" to the world (*Aen.* 6.853).[103] In a quite similar vein, Seneca praises the emperor that his absolute power already has issued in 'justice' among other blessings for all his subjects (*Clem.* 1.1.9).[104] Cicero also writes that gods had implanted in the Romans "a love of peace and tranquility which enable justice and good faith more easily to flourish" (*Rep.* 2.31). As P. A. Brunt rightly maintains, one of Cicero's favorite themes is that Roman hegemony "was ordained by the gods, whose favor Rome had deserved by piety and justice."[105] It is clear that justice was one of the main themes in the Roman Empire.

In contrast to Rome's emphasis on the law, Luke seems to show that the reality was different. In order words, Luke strives to indicate that Pilate failed to keep Roman justice through the imperial judicial

---

102. Stenschke, *Luke's Portrait*, 119–20.
103. See also *RG* 34, for Augustus' emphasis on justice.
104. See Galinsky, *Augustan Culture*, 80–90.
105. Brunt, *Roman Imperial Themes*, 288.

procedure. *In spite of* his threefold declaration of Jesus' innocence, Pilate gave a wrong verdict; that is, Luke does not see him as a capable judge with bureaucratic authority. Through Jesus' trial, Luke shows that the Roman judicial system, despite its emphasis on justice, could not protect the innocent, such as Jesus.[106] It could be easily corrupted as seen in trials of Jesus in the Gospel and Paul in Acts. Along with his declaration of Jesus' crucifixion, another example of Pilate's injustice would be his release of Barabbas, who "had been put in prison for insurrection and murder" (Luke 23:25). Tannehill correctly asserts that "a ruler who gives into mob pressure and releases a rebel and murderer to them is hardly a model of justice."[107] Similarly, Ahn points out, "Luke's emphasis is neither on the faithfulness of the Roman official, who carries out the trial in a correct judicial procedure, nor on the fairness of the imperial judicial system."[108]

What is more, another criticism of Pilate's bureaucratic authority can be found in the essence of bureaucratic authority itself. Christopher Adair-Toteff contends that, for Weber, "the holder of bureaucratic authority has been trained to act impartially according to the rules governing his or her office. He or she must be totally impartial; nothing about the person can in any way influence his or her decision."[109] In contrast to Weber's assertion, Pilate's bureaucratic authority was considered partial as indicated, and his decision was influenced by others. Thus, it can be understood that his bureaucratic authority is questioned through Jesus' trial.

Summary

This chapter has dealt with three types of authority based upon Weber's categorization. My use of his three categories makes it easier to see Luke's interest in authority. As we have discussed, Luke heightens Jesus' authority in comparison with John's charismatic authority through the birth narratives. He does so first by comparing Mary and Elizabeth: even before their birth, Luke portrays that John was subordinate to Jesus.

---

106. De Ste. Croix, *Class Struggle*, 330, claims that the injustice of the Roman law would be its double standard, and he further argues that 'there was one law for the rich and another for poor'.

107. Tannehill, *Narrative Unity*, 1:198.

108. Ahn, *Reign of God*, 185.

109. Adair-Toteff, "Max Weber's Charisma," 193; for Weber's extensive treatment of the holder of bureaucratic authority, see *Wirtschaft und Gesellschaft*, esp. 126–31, where rationality is the fundamental character of bureaucratic authority (126 and 129).

Second, he uses the power relationship between Herod and Augustus. Luke, acknowledging that Herod was dependent on Roman power, links John to Herod, and Jesus to Augustus, respectively. With the help of the two different settings, Luke's readers probably recognized that Jesus' charismatic authority was far greater than John's. The reason to present this authority-related parallelism between Jesus and John in the infancy narratives is that Luke prepares his readers for a similar parallelism between Jesus and the emperor in the body of the Gospel, where the issue of authority is implied. That is, it functions as hinting at Luke's implicit comparison between Jesus' authority and the emperor's authority in the following chapters.

With respect to Jesus' death, it is clear that both traditional authority and the bureaucratic authority of Jewish leaders, Herod, and Pilate, were not portrayed in a positive light. Even though Luke does not explicitly show that Jesus' authority is superior to their authority, his account of Jesus' trial plays an important role in devaluing the significance of their authority. The Jewish leaders, as an agent for the trial, challenged Jesus' authority and attempted to accuse him. In this respect, Luke does not say that Jesus' authority given by God was superior to their traditional authority in a direct way. Rather, by depicting their accusation (and accordingly their authority) as false or negative in an indirect way, Luke stresses that they were responsible for Jesus' death. He also implicitly shows that both Herod and Pilate were involved in Jesus' death. By inserting Herod's trial between Pilate's two trial scenes, Luke focuses on their friendship which finally put Jesus to death. In Luke's view, their authority first denied Jesus as a holder of true authority, and second they did not know that they were abusing their authority. Luke underscores that Pilate's authority leads to Jesus' death by hinting that his death was partly due to the injustice of the Roman judicial procedure. In other words, Luke, given that Pilate was regarded as a representative of the emperor, implicitly criticizes both Pilate's injustice and the imperfection of the Roman law. He also indirectly questions the emperor's claim to justice. In Jesus' trial, the one whose authority is devalued is not Jesus, but the holders of traditional authority and bureaucratic authority, namely, Jewish leaders, Herod, and Pilate who were all under the emperor's authority.

2

Census, Tribute, and Tax Collectors

IN CHAPTER 1, WE discussed two topics on the basis of Weber's categorization of authority: first, Luke's description of Jesus' superiority over John (charismatic authority), and, second, his critical attitude towards the empire (traditional/bureaucratic authority) through the account of Jesus' trial. Luke's negative portrayal of the empire is not isolated from his depiction of the emperor's authority. This chapter deals mainly with Luke's deep interest in Jesus' authority in comparison with that of the emperor, while the previous chapter discusses his general view on the empire. With the focus on Roman taxation, in particular, it analyses in what ways tax-related issues in Luke 2:1:2, 20:19–26, and 23:3 are linked to the empire's authority.

The importance of the tax-related issues in Luke's Gospel should not be under-evaluated because his accounts are expressed more in detail than other evangelists' accounts are. It is interesting to note that three accounts, Luke 2:1:2, 20:19–26, and 23:3, have some similarities. First, all these accounts are related directly/indirectly to paying taxes to the emperor. Second, the Roman governor, delegated by the emperor, is mentioned in each account. Quirinius and 'the jurisdiction and authority of governor' (although the name has not been referred to) are mentioned in Luke 2:2 and 20:20, respectively. As for Jesus' trial, the Roman governor, Pilate (23:3), is mentioned as a judge in relation partly to tax. Most importantly, the emperors are referred to in all three accounts: Augustus in Luke 2:1, and Tiberius in two other cases, even though his name is not mentioned. It seems to me that these similarities can provide us with a clue to the relationship between taxation and the Roman power, particularly, the emperor's authority. With the recognition of this relationship, I will attempt to answer the question as to how Luke understands Augustus' (or emperors' in general) authority. That is, his portrayal of the emperor's authority will aid us to analyze why he places so much emphasis on tax-related accounts.

In this chapter, several questions will be answered: Were tax collectors viewed unfavorably? If so, what were the reasons? Why does Luke include more accounts about tax-related issues than other evangelists do? What is he trying to tell his audience? In what ways does he utilize the stories of the tax collectors? What is the function of Jesus' table fellowship with the tax collectors in this narrative? What significance does the census account bear in the Roman Empire? How can we make a strong link between tax collectors and the emperor in terms of Jesus' authority? With the focus on such questions, this chapter intends to explore how Luke emphasizes Jesus' superiority over the emperor's authority through the tax-related issues. My methodology is rather different from other scholars who simply focus on the emperor's authority or power. To put it differently, in order more concretely to compare and contrast Jesus' authority and that of the emperor, I will split the emperor's power into two realms: *imperium* and *auctoritas*.[1] On the basis of such division, I will analyze in what ways the emperor's claim to *auctoritas* is questioned in Luke. Moreover, such analysis will be helpful in turning to the next topic about Luke's view on the emperor's titles: benefactor (Chapter 3) and savior (Chapter 4).

Census and Tribute

Prior to evaluating the significance of tribute in Luke 20:20–26 in relation to the census in Luke 2:1–2, it is necessary to briefly analyze the main purpose of the census in the Roman Empire. It is noteworthy that the purpose of the census under the empire was not the same as that of the Republican census in Italy. While the Republican census was concerned more with recruiting for the legions as well as voting rights, the Roman census under the empire, as Capponi suggests, was associated more with keeping "a record of people liable to compulsory services such as the *corvee* works on the canals, and to extract other capitation taxes."[2]

---

1. Even though he writes his books in Greek, not in Latin, it is very probable that Luke has some knowledge of Latin words used for the Roman imperial cults or propaganda.

2. Capponi, *Augustan Egypt*, 84; also see Bagnall and Frier, *Demography of Roman Egypt*; on the Italian census figures under Augustus, see Brunt, *Italian Manpower*, 113–20; Rousseau, and Arav, *Jesus and His World*.

Unlike the Republican census, in general, Brook W. R. Pearson claims that the Roman census had a dual purpose, taxation and social control.[3] As Augustus himself implies, census is associated directly with counting the population.[4] He began the practice of a regular and periodic count of the population and a valuation of property for the assessment of tax liabilities.[5] Taxation was therefore based primarily upon census.

Collecting taxes was very important in the Roman Empire, since the emperor's wealth, which was one of the main sources of his power, was largely accumulated by tax.[6] Taxes were the main source of imperial income, along with war and the produce of imperial gold and silver mines and leasing the public domain.[7] This kind of money became a main source for the emperor's power, which was needed to pay the army.[8] In other words, taxation was extremely important for the emperor, and tax-power enabled him, in some sense, to ensure his power/authority. It is not an exaggeration to say that census was an exercise of the Roman power, and that taxation was rooted in census.

Luke's census account in Luke 2:1–2 is related directly to the dispute about tribute to Caesar at Luke 20:20–26, since the tribute including other taxes is not separable from the census. As briefly mentioned, the amount of tax was calculated or assessed on the basis of the census. Luke, who probably knows the significance of the relationship between census and tribute, strives to place more emphasis on tax-related issues in his writing. His tribute account at 20:20–26 is not the same as that of Mark or Matthew. Even though all three Gospels tell that Jesus' opponents wish to trap him, only Luke's account displays their motive in detail.[9] Among the

---

3. Pearson, "Lukan Censuses," 276, claims that census was a very useful tool for controlling Rome's subjects in various ways.

4. See *RG* 8.2–4; in Josephus, *War* 2.385, King Agrippa II of Judaea estimated the population of Egypt (excluding Alexandria) to 7.5 million people from the total amount of poll tax collected.

5. On the discussion of various taxes in the Roman Empire, see below.

6. See Tacitus, *Ann.* 4.6.

7. See Pliny, *NH* 12.111–23.

8. Rousseau and Arav, *Jesus and His World*, 277, assert that "the financial procurators, prefects of Egypt and Judaea, and procurators assigned to the legate of Syria, made decisions in matters of taxation, including the inheritance tax. They established the structure of the tax base and were receivers and payers. One of their most important duties was to assure the timely payment of the troops' salaries."

9. The people who were sent by Jesus' opponents are all different in the three Gospels: some Pharisees and some Herodians in Mark, the disciples of the Pharisees and

marked differences, Luke explicitly tells us that Jesus' opponents wished to hand him over to "the jurisdiction and authority of the governor" (τῇ ἀρχῇ καὶ τῇ ἐξουσίᾳ τοῦ ἡγεμόνος) in his tribute account, while neither Mark nor Matthew refers to them.[10] In my opinion, Luke seems to highlight that this dispute over the tribute is the issue about authority between Jesus and the emperor, because the census itself was decreed by the latter's authority (2:1).[11] Accordingly, the tribute to Caesar (20:20–26) is linked directly to his power, even though in this scene Caesar is Tiberius, not Augustus.[12]

In Luke 20:22 Jesus' interrogators asked: "Is it lawful for us to pay taxes to the emperor, or not?" (ἔξεστιν ἡμᾶς Καίσαρι φόρον δοῦναι ἢ οὔ;).[13] Their question can be interpreted in a Jewish society as follows: whether it is lawful either in terms of the law of Israel's God or in terms of the law of the Roman empire. In either way, it seems that Jesus' authority was in danger. If his answer is given in terms of the law of Israel's God, then he will be handed over to the Roman authority. Or, if he answers in terms of the law of the empire, he will be blamed by the Jewish people. It is often argued that the former is a matter of piety, the latter politics. Despite their elusive plot, it is interesting to note that Luke's Jesus, acknowledging that his opponents were striving to cause him trouble with the emperor's authority, asked them to show him a denarius with a simple question as a way of avoiding such a dilemma.[14] Before the discussion of Jesus' reaction to their question, let us first analyze two things: first, identification of a

---

the Herodians, and the spies (ἐγκάθετοι) in Luke. On the discussion of the meaning of ἐγκάθετος, see Derrett, "Luke's Perspective," 38–48; Plutarch, *Pyrrh.* 11.4; Josephus, *War* 6.286.

10. According to Derrett, "Luke' Perspective," 40, the expression "handing over" (παραδίδωμι) is a technical one; for its use, see Josephus, *War* 6.301–305.

11. For the relationship between authority and decree, see below.

12. What is interesting is that Jesus' opponents understood the tribute issue only in terms of the emperor's *imperium* with the reference of Roman governor, when attempting to put him in danger. However, Luke has Jesus understand this dispute in a different way in which he interpreted this issue in terms of the emperor's moral *acutoritas*. See below.

13. Luke uses φόρος, whereas both Matthew and Mark use the Greek term, κῆνσον, a loanword from Latin census.

14. In Matt 22:18, Jesus was aware of their malice (τὴν πονηρίαν); in Mark 12:15, Jesus was aware of their hypocrisy (τὴν ὑπόκρισιν); in Luke 20:23, Jesus perceived their craftiness (τὴν πανουργίαν).

denarius in relation to the emperor's authority and, second, tribute to the emperor as idolatrous actions among the Jews.

Identification of Denarius and Authority of Coin-Mint

It is important to answer the question as to why the tribute to the emperor could be viewed as idolatrous. In order to answer this question, two aspects should be noted first: the identification of the denarius in the dispute over tribute, and the relation between coinage and one's authority. The analysis of these aspects will help understand Luke's intention that he makes comparisons between Jesus' authority and the emperor's authority through his tax-related accounts.

As a rule, the Roman tribute was to be paid in Roman coins. There is a rescript of Germanicus Caesar to Statilius[15], "directing that all state taxes are to be collected in asses, i.e., in Roman coinage (the *aes* being then one-sixteenth of a denarius in value)."[16] This evidence says that Roman coinage was used when the tax was paid. Likewise, the denarius was mainly used as the coin of the tribute. This is evidenced on a Greek inscription, for instance, *OGIS* 629 (lines 153–6): various dues were to be paid in the Roman coin, *denarii* (εἰς δηνάριον).

With respect to the identification of the coin in Lk 20:24, it is very probable that the *denarius* was a *denarius* of Tiberius himself. Harold Mattingly illustrates a list of the imperial mints of Tiberius, arguing that all his *denarii* are attributed to the mint of Lugdunum in Gaul.[17] According to his categorization, there are only two series: first, a series dated to AD 15/16 (TR POT XVII) which was not continued[18]; and second, a series of the standard "identification,"[19] which bear no dates, but the titles of the emperor are continued on the reverse with PONTIF MAXIM; Tiberius became *Pontifex Maximus* on 10 March AD 15.[20] In a quite similar vein, M. Grant notes:

---

15. Perhaps he was a financial procurator in Syria.
16. Bruce, "Render to Caesar," 252.
17. Mattingly, *Coins*, 120ff.
18. Ibid., 121, ##7–11.
19. Ibid., 125ff, ## 34–38, 42–45, 48–60.
20. See EJ, 47; those coins were issued in quite extraordinary numbers at intervals throughout the rest of Tiberius' reign. Also see Sutherland, *Roman Imperial Coinage*, 84.

> [This standard "identification"] type is of special significance because, when the *princeps* [Augustus] died soon afterwards, his successor Tiberius -changing only the obverse- continued to use the same reverse type, and scarcely any other, throughout the twenty-three years of his reign . . . this type was issued in many millions of examples (including, perhaps, the "Tribute Penny" of the New Testament) over a period of nearly a quarter of a century. This duration is more characteristic of our modern coinage than of the incessantly changing coin-types of the Roman Empire . . .[21]

Can we say that such series of Roman imperial *denarii* were the denarius shown to Jesus? And, is it consistent with the monetary situation in Roman "Palestine" in the period of the ministry of Jesus? It is very likely that the series of the imperial *denarii* were identical with, or, at least, very similar to the denarius shown to Jesus.[22] According to, J. Spencer Kennard, only four specimens of the *denarius* of the standard "identification" which were known to us have been found in Palestine.[23] He agrees that a *denarius* was indeed shown to Jesus, and that it was likely to have been a specimen of the standard "identification." But he denies that it was the money of the tribute, saying that "The denarius represented the coinage of the West; it was not the coin of tribute."[24] He sees the denarius as a rare novelty in the context of the Gospels. He goes on to assert that the tribute would have been paid in other silver currency, not minted far away at Lugdunum in Gaul. However, Kennard's view should be criticized for several reasons. As Hart claims, Kennard's argument is "very questionable, since there has been no systematic recording of the detail and locality of finds until quite recent decades."[25] Also, the Greek texts in Luke, as it stands, specifically refer to a denarius; this smallest silver coin was widely circulated because it was a day's wage for an agricultural worker.[26] That

---

21. Grant, *Roman Imperial Money*, 133–34.
22. See Hart, "Coin of 'Render to Caesar,'" 244.
23. Kennard, *Render to God*, 50.
24. Ibid., 51.
25. Hart, "Coin of 'Render to Caesar,'" 244; he goes on to claim: "It remains highly probable that the coin shown to Jesus was one of the huge second series of *denarii* of Tiberius according to the standard 'identification'. To determine between this and his earlier series, or some earlier *denarius* of Caesar Augustus himself, also bearing the εἰκών and ἐπιγραφή of Caesar, is not now in our power, nor is it probable that it ever will be" (248).
26. Rousseau and Arav, *Jesus and His World*, 59; also see *OGIS* 629 (lines 153–56);

is, the coins were readily available. The question in Luke 20:22, "ἔξεστιν ἡμᾶς Καίσαρι φόρον δοῦναι ἢ οὔ;" (Is it lawful for us to pay taxes to the emperor, or not?), logically affirms that the tribute was paid in denarius. A profile of Tiberius on the obverse is coherent with Jesus teaching of "render to Caesar." Thus, it is very likely that the imperial *denarii* of the standard "identification" were probably used as tribute money.

Concerning the relation between coinage and authority, Jesus' question in Luke 20:24, "τίνος ἔχει εἰκόνα καὶ ἐπιγραφήν;" (Whose head and whose title does it bear?), which comes after his opponents' question, can be interpreted as a question about authority. When the coin is called for, Jesus' question focuses on both εἰκών and ἐπιγραφή on the coin. In this respect, Hart argues that both portrait and subscription testify the fact that the coin is Caesar's money.[27] Hart is right in stating that the money belongs to the emperor, but he does not explore whether it symbolizes his authority. In other words, the coin itself with εἰκών and ἐπιγραφή signifies the emperor's authority in the Roman Empire. Andrew Wallace-Hadrill's article presents a strong bond between image (εἰκών) and authority in Roman imperial coinage.[28] As he correctly suggests, the head of the emperor on the imperial coins was viewed as a symbol of authority.

Moreover, coin-minting itself frequently implies a ruler's authority in the ancient world. There are various examples of direct links between coin-minting and one's authority. All too often, the rulers are shown on the coins in order to express their authority/power. The Herodian kings minted coins, although their coins were somewhat different from Caesar's coins in terms of designs. For example, the Herodian dynasty did not use Hebrew letters on coins (in contrast with the Hasmonean coins) and favored neutral, non-provocative symbols, such as cornucopias, pomegranates, palms, the prow of a ship and a helmet. In the third year of his appointment to kingship by the Roman Senate, Herod the Great minted coins representing utensils from the temple, probably to indicate that he attempted to avoid the people's religious rage.[29] Antipas also established a mint. His coins represent the emperor Tiberius on the obverse and on the reverse a palm or a reed, symbols of Tiberius. In addition, some portraits of the Jewish rulers, such as Herod Philip II (Luke 3:1), Agrippa

---

this does not mean that agricultural workers were paid in *denarii*; rather, it means that their daily wage was almost equivalent to one denarius.

27. Ibid., 242.
28. Wallace-Hadrill, "Image and Authority," 66–87; also see below.
29. Ibid., 55–56.

I (Acts 12:1–3; 12:21–23) and Herod Agrippa II (Acts 25:13; 26:2, 28), are viewed on ancient coins. A good example is the small bronze coin of Herod Agrippa I (AD 37–44) which has on its obverse a bust portrait of the king surrounded by the inscription ΒΑΣΙΛΕΥΣ ΜΕΓΑΣ ΑΓΡΙΠΠΑΣ ΦΙΛΟΚΑΙΣΑΡ. The reverse of the coin shows an image of *Fortuna* standing to the left and holding a cornucopia in her left hand and balancing a rudder with an extended right hand.[30] Similarly, Herod Agrippa II (AD 56–95) minted a small bronze coin in AD 66 which has a bust of the king on the obverse surrounded by the inscription ΒΑΣΙΛΕΩΣ ΑΓΡΙΠΠΟΥ.[31]

Along with the Herodian kings, the Roman prefects on behalf of the emperor minted coins.[32] They followed Herod's example by avoiding the use of symbols that could have offended the Jewish population. Those who minted coins, Coponius (AD 6–9), Valerius Gratus (15–26), and Pontius Pilate (26–36) did not represent the head of the emperor as was customary in the rest of the empire, but instead used symbols of authority or images representing the country.[33] Regardless of the differences of style of the coins, they all represent, to a certain degree, rulers' authority.

More importantly, the emperors often issued the coins during their reign to highlight their authority by linking it to their control of minting. Caesar, even though he is not the emperor, controlled the central mint when he achieved ultimate supremacy in Rome. He also received the right of portraiture and exercised the right of imperial coinage.[34] After Augustus onwards, the emperors, or sometimes imperial officials on their behalf, also controlled the coin types more or less directly.[35] For instance, the coin types of the gold and silver of Lugdunum were a mint operated exclusively through Tiberius' authority.[36] Therefore, it is clear

---

30. See those coins in Kreitzer, *Striking New Images*, 21.

31. See the coins in ibid., 22.

32. Rousseau and Arav, *Jesus and His World*, 62.

33. Wallace-Hadrill, "Image and Authority," 58; Bond, *Pontius Pilate*, 203, notes: "Archaeological evidence shows that Pilate, unlike other governors of Judaea, minted coins containing both Jewish and Roman designs. Although the pagan designs may not have been particularly offensive, the coins do seem to reflect a tendency to want to bring Judaea into line with other Roman provinces." For the discussion of the custom of the prefects, such as minting coins, see Rousseau and Arav, *Jesus and His World*, 60–65.

34. Sutherland, *Coinage*, 1–13.

35. Ibid., 93; Miles, "Communicating Culture," 29–62, argues that coins were an important medium which represented the emperor's power (esp. 42).

36. A similar point is also made in Rousseau and Arav, *Jesus and His World*, 56,

that imperial coinage represents, to a large extent, the emperor's supreme authority in his territory.[37] As symbols on the coins in the Roman Empire are related closely to his authority, coin-minting itself also represents the emperor's supreme authority.

Revolt in Relation to Religious Reasons

Let us go back to the question as to why paying taxes to the emperor was regarded as idolatrous among Jews. Many of Jesus' Jewish contemporaries tended to regard any act of paying taxes as an act of submission to the emperor. They also viewed paying taxes to the emperor as treason to God. According to Bruce, one of the main reasons is that, after a new decree in AD 6, for some Jews the payment of tribute to the Romans was "incompatible with Israel's theocratic ideals."[38] The revolt of Judas of Gamala in Gaulanitis or Judas the Galilean would be a good example.[39] Josephus tells us that he was the founder of the "fourth philosophy" among the Jews (*Ant.* 18.9.23).[40] According to Judas, loyal Jews should not pay taxes to the emperor. He insisted that it would be sinful to pay tribute to a Gentile ruler. In this respect, many Judeans regarded image-bearing coins as so blasphemous that one should not even look on them, much less possess them. For them, paying taxes could be the breach of the Second Commandment: as it is recorded in Lev 19:4, "do not turn (your face) to idols."

Similarly, Hippolytus tells that imperial coins were viewed as idolatrous objects to strict sectarians.[41] He tells of some Essenes whose practice of self-discipline went beyond the normal rules of their order in that they would not even touch such a coin, since they held it unlawful not

---

arguing that Augustus and Tiberius had a monopoly on issuing gold coins, which were minted in Rome and in some provinces. On the discussion of the *aes* of the mint of Rome, see Sutherland, *Coinage*, 93 and 190; Grant, *From Imperium to Auctoritas*, 116f.

37. In 1 Macc 15:6, the right to issue one's own coinage was viewed as a symbol of independence.

38. Bruce, "Render to Caesar," 255.

39. Gamala in Gaulanitis in *Ant.* 18.4, and Judas the Galilean in *War* 2.118, 433; cf. 2.433 and *Ant.* 18.23; 20.102 (Acts 5:37).

40. Josephus, *War* 2.118, represents the Jewish religious parties as "philosophies," for the same reason he refers to Judas as a "sophist."

41. Hippolytus, *Refutatio omnuim Haeresium*, 9.21.

only to make, but even to carry or look at images of any kind.[42] Thus, they refused the payment of tribute to the emperor, for such an activity was considered contrary to the law of their God. They rejected the idea of the tribute to the emperor due to εἰκών and ἐπιγραφή, which symbolize his authority, on the coins as discussed above. In this regard, paying taxes to the emperor, for them, was perceived as their admittance of his power and authority.

Jesus' Response

Luke reports that Jesus' reaction to the imperial money is quite different from his contemporaries' response, as Luke 20:25 shows: "Then give to the emperor the things that are the emperor's, and to God the things that are God's." Luke's Jesus does not see that Judeans' use of Caesar's coins necessarily implies their recognition of the emperor's sovereignty, which was considered greater than that of God.[43] In other words, he does not interpret paying taxes to the emperor as idolatrous activities. It is therefore wrong to argue that he is in opposition to paying the tribute to Caesar.[44] Jesus' answer cannot be understood as objection to the tribute itself. Luke hints at such a theme in his earlier account. When the census was conducted in Luke 2:1–4, he reports that Joseph and Mary returned to his own hometown, Bethlehem, in order to be registered. Here, Luke seems to tell us that Jesus had nothing to do with refusal to pay taxes even in his birth account.

Furthermore, the fact that Luke's Jesus does not object to the tribute to the emperor is re-affirmed in his trial scene; that is, the dispute in Luke 20 is related closely to the charge against Jesus brought by Jewish leaders (Luke 23:2). As mentioned in the previous chapter, Luke heightens that Jesus did not forbid people to pay taxes to the emperor, first, by showing

42. Hippolytus, *Refutatio omnuim Haeresium*, 9.21.

43. According to Derrett, *Law in the New Testament*, 321, Jews in Judaea and elsewhere used Tyrian coinage at this time to pay their temple dues, but this would not be taken to mean that they acknowledged Tyrian sovereignty. Derrett pays little attention, however, to the difference between Tyrian coins and Roman tribute coins in terms of the designs on them. As Bruce, "Render to Caesar," 259, mentions, the Tyrian coins bore no human ruler's name or image, and in any case the use of Tyrian coins for the payment of the temple tax was not a political issue.

44. But this should not be confused with the idea that rendering to Caesar, for Jesus, means unquestioning obedience to imperial authorities, as Derrett rightly argues, "Luke's Perspective," 38–48.

Pilate's declaration of Jesus' innocence, and, second, by showing his accusers' falseness.

In addition, the Greek term ἀποδίδωμι ('render' or 'give back') in Luke 20:25 supports the idea that Jesus did not object to the tribute. This word is used when Jesus is giving back the scroll in the Nazareth synagogue to its lawful attendant (Luke 4:20; ἀποδούς). As Bruce rightly asserts, this word indicates that something will be given back to its owner, saying:

> It is specially used of paying various kinds of dues -of returning a deposit to its owner (Lev. 6:4, LXX), of refunding an advance, as in the parable of the good Samaritan (Luke 10:35), of restoring goods wrongfully taken, as in the Zacchaeus incident (Luke 19:8), of repaying debts to a creditor, as in the parables of the unforgiving servant (Matt 18:34) and the two debtors (Luke 7:42), of paying a fine or damages, as in Matt 5:26 par. Luke 12:59, or (as here) of paying taxes (cf. Rome. 13:7). In these instances it is implied that the person to whom payment or repayment is made is the rightful owner or recipient of whatever is paid or repaid; the action amounts to giving back to someone property to which he is entitled. Caesar, it is implied, is entitled to demand tribute; to pay him tribute is to give back him what is in any case his.[45]

---

45. Bruce, "Render to Caesar," 258. For a detailed discussion of the meaning of Jesus' saying at 20:25, see Brandon, *Jesus and the Zealots*, 345-47, maintaining that Jesus' answer could be interpreted as an interdiction for paying the tribute on the reasoning that, because everything belonged to God, nothing belonged to Caesar, who should not receive anything. Conversely, Grant, *Economic Background,* 100 and 102, sees "what belongs to God" as the temple tax, asserting that Jesus meant, "You must pay your tribute to Caesar, and you must also pay your annual half-shekel to God." However, "the things that are God's" should not be limited only to an annual half-shekel. It should be interpreted in a broad sense. As Bruce, "Render to Caesar," 261, rightly asserts, it "has much broader meaning, such as the dedication of one's whole life: the seeking of his kingdom and righteousness. Obedience to God's will is not compromised by letting Caesar have the money which bears his name." In a different vein, Derrett, *Law in the New Testament*, 335ff., claims that Jesus meant that by giving Caesar what was Caesar's they would be giving God what was God's, saying: "Obey the commands of the king [emperor] and obey (thereby) the commandments of God", or "Obey the commands of Caesar provided that the commandments of God are not broken in your doing so." His argument is rooted in Eccl 8:2, "Keep the king's command." Also he holds that "the things of Caesar" implies the rights of Caesar, just as the "things of God" means the rights of God ("Luke' Perspective," 42). In addition, Wright, *Jesus and the Victory of God*, points out that on the basis of 1 Macc 2:66-68 ("Pay back the Gentiles in full, and obey the commands of the law"), where Mattathias instructed his sons to give back to the pagans an equal repayment, the saying is unambiguously revolutionary. For him, it has "a double thrust: your duty towards the pagans is to

Moreover, what a king does is defined in the passage in 1 Sam 8:10–17 (see especially LXX version); that is, he imposes taxes and impresses labor.[46] Thus, Luke's three accounts (census in the birth narrative, dispute over the tribute, and Jesus' trial), point out, first, that they are all interrelated in terms of signifying the emperor's authority, and, second, that Jesus was not in opposition to the tribute to the emperor.

As seen above, Luke's Jesus does not advocate rebellion against the payment of the tribute to Caesar. Then, what does Luke intend to show through the tax-related accounts? For me, Luke seems to challenge the Roman authority that farmed out the excessive taxes from the people, while not rejecting the tribute to the emperor. To put it another way, Luke portrays that Jesus was on the side of the poor who were exploited by the Roman authority, along with the tax collectors. Luke is concerned more with the burden of taxes (both direct and indirect) in relation to morality, rather than with paying taxes itself. In this respect, Bruce, who attempts to analyze the burden of taxation, emphasizes that it was "not because of the sheer weight of taxation that the question of tribute to Caesar was such a burning one in Jesus' day."[47] He goes on to assert that the Herodian tribute had already been payable over and above the religious dues, and that it may have been as high as the Roman tribute which replaced it. Bruce, however, fails to understand the actual burden that resulted from various taxes. Luke not only avoids the dilemma but turns it to emphasize his critical stance against the immorality of the emperor's authority.

Various Taxes

We need to look into the seriousness of tax burden in the first century from the perspective of the oppressed, not from the rulers.[48] At the be-

---

fight them, and your duty to our God is to keep his commandments"; the former was subsumed, ultimately, within the latter. Furthermore, according to Rousseau and Arav, *Jesus and His World*, 278, it could be understood as "an attitude of indifference to the domain of a foreign power in that God allowed it to be."

46. Derrett, "Luke's Perspective," 44.
47. Bruce, "Render to Caesar," 254.
48. The emperors, of course, did not say that they collected taxes from their subjects purely for their own amusement. According to Derrett, "Luke's Perspective," 42, the rulers or the emperors, in general, claimed that they collected taxes in order to provide for security, the buildings of public work, and the like "even under the extremely disagreeable and inefficient systems of tax-collection."

ginning of the first century AD, the people of Judaea, according to Josephus, complained to the emperor about the excessive taxes imposed on them by Herod the Great and Archelaus; they even requested that their country be annexed to the province of Syria under Roman rule.[49] In this respect, the economic burden that resulted from various taxes should not be under-estimated in the discussion of the tax-related issues in Luke's Gospel.

The Roman Empire exacted a number of taxes under the name of direct and indirect taxations. As a rule, two kinds of direct taxes were levied on the people: first, a tax on landed property (*tributum agri* or *tributum soli*), calculated on the estimated annual yield in crops and cattle, and, second, a head tax (*tributum capitis*).[50] As mentioned, the poll tax was determined by census (Luke 2:1-2; Acts 5:37). Under Herod the Great (37–4 BC) direct taxes were collected by royal officials, attached to the court. When Judaea came under the Roman prefects[51] in 6 AD, the direct taxes, the "head" or poll tax and the land tax were collected by officials in direct employ of the Romans.[52] Rousseau and Arav claim that, if the same rules as the ones existing in Syria applied, all men 14 to 65 and women 12 to 65 years of age were subject to the *tributum capitis*.[53] Its amount was probably one denarius.[54]

---

49. Josephus, *Ant.* 17.11.2; *War* 2.6.2; also see the revolt of AD 6; according to Rousseau and Arav, *Jesus and His World*, 276, Herod in Judaea was in charge of collecting the tribute. At his death, his sons were authorized to collect a tribute from their peoples. For instance, Archelaus collected 600 talents (400 talents according to *War* 2.6.3), Antipas 200, and Philip 100 (*Ant.* 17.11.4), respectively. They, *Jesus and His World*, 277, further note: "Although direct information is lacking, it is generally assumed that most of the Roman tax system applied directly to the sub-province of Judaea, and that Antipas and Philip instituted identical systems in their territories."

50. *Digest* L. 15.4.2; 8.7. According to both Oakman and Freyne, the *tributum soli* laid upon Palestine by Pompey, Herod (Josephus, *Ant.* 14.202-3), and Tiberius (Tacitus, *Ann.* 2.42) was heavier than that prevailing elsewhere in the provinces (Oakman, *Jesus and Economic Questions*, 68-9; Freyne, *Galilee from Alexander*, 188-92; cf. Jones, *Roman Economy*, 164-65). On the influence of over-taxation on landowners, and the resulting depopulation and secession of property, see Jones, *Roman Economy*, 82-88 and Oakman, *Jesus and Economic Questions*, 66-72.

51. They were called procurators after AD 44.

52. In Galilee, similar officials were under the supervision of Herod Antipas (4 BC–AD 39). See *ABD*, 337.

53. Rousseau and Arav, *Jesus and His World*, 276.

54. Heichelheim, "Roman Syria," 237; also see below.

Second, in addition to direct taxes, the Roman tax system included indirect taxes. Many kinds of indirect taxation were superimposed on the direct taxation in the form of tribute.[55] Indirect taxes comprised "the *portorium*, a tax *ad valorem*, 'based on value,' on the transport of goods, including slaves and animals, the *vicesima hereditatium*, an 'inheritance tax,' created by Augustus in 6 AD with other taxes on transfer of real property, and the *centensima rerum venalium*, a 'sales tax' on all items bought and sold (Josephus, *Ant.* 17.8.4), instituted by Augustus."[56] Also, there already had been a tax of 4 percent on the sale of slaves since 7 AD Moreover, a business license fee appeared under the name of *aurum negotiatorium*. It was levied on merchants, artisans, and members of professional or craft guilds.

In the case of Judaea, along with the taxes above, the people should have paid more kinds of taxes or dues. These were distinct from temple and priestly taxes. In other words, in addition to the Roman tribute and other secular dues, the Jews of Judaea were obliged by religious law to pay for the maintenance of the Jerusalem temple and priests, Levites and others.[57] For example, a half-shekel tax, which at first had been only a third of a shekel according to Neh 10:32–33, was exacted by religious leaders for the maintenance of the temple. Josephus (*Ant.* 18.9.1) describes that it was collected each year from every Jew twenty years of age and older in the land of Israel and abroad. Furthermore, the Jews had the additional burden of the tithe on all crops to be paid to the priests and Levites.[58]

Rousseau and Arav's analysis of taxation would be helpful for a better understanding of the situation of the oppressed in Judaea.

---

55. See Rousseau and Arav, *Jesus and His World*, 276–77.

56. Ibid., 276.

57. Perkins, "Taxes in the New Testament," 185–86. Many forms of taxation developed in Israel during the monarchy, such as contribution of services, in addition to those already provided by conquered people (2 Sam 20:24; 1 Kgs 5:13; 9:20; 12:4, 18; 2 Chr 2:2, 17–18; 8:7–10), contribution of food (1 Kgs 4:7), tolls collected from traders and caravans (1 Kgs 10:14–29; 2 Chr 9:13–28), and the first property tax mentioned in the Bible is that assessed by King Jehoiakim of Judah on land owners in order to pay tribute to Pharaoh Neco (2 Kgs 23:35).

58. See Rousseau and Arav, *Jesus and His World*, 277; Bruce, 'Render to Caesar', 254; Num 18:21ff.

Census, Tribute, and Tax Collectors

Taxation by the Romans and Tetrarchs

1. *Tributum soli* on crops. Yearly average, excluding the sabbatical year:
   (25% + 5 x 33%)/6 = 31.7%
   Estimated at 60% of all crops and income = 19%

2. *Tributum capitis*, for a family of six: 6 *denarii* of income for 250 days (one worker assumed) = 1%

3. Sales, inheritance taxes. Total impact = 5%

4. *Portorium*. Total impact = 4%

5. Gifts to official = 3%
   Total civic taxes = 32%

Traditional Jewish Taxes

1. Tithes on all crops. Total impact = 8%

2. Half-shekel (2 *dinarii*) tax on males = 1%

3. Sacrifices. Total impact = 3%
   Total Jewish Taxes = 12%

Forced exactions

1. Officials' persecution, banditry = 5 %
   Total burden = 49%[59]

From Rousseau and Arav's analysis, it is very likely that first-century Jews suffered from a serious economic burden caused by paying various taxes to the emperor, to local authorities, and to religious leaders.

Palestine at the time of Jesus gave certain advantages of the Roman Empire to some of the Jews. In this regard, some scholars claim that being a part of the Roman Empire secured certain benefits like possible citizenship, military protection, personal status, trade, transport systems and access to roads, and overall political stability.[60] This, however, should not be over-evaluated. For example, as Rousseau and Arav's analysis of taxation indicates, the Jewish people had to pay various taxes to the emperor and to religious leaders. The double burden of taxation (direct and

---

59. Rousseau and Arav, *Jesus and His World*, 278. According to Bruce, "Render to Caesar," 254, the total taxation could have approached something like 40 per cent of the provincial income.

60. E.g., in particular, the proponents of an apologia *pro imperio*.

indirect taxation) caused considerable hardship and often precipitated both passive and violent resistance.[61] As Luke Timothy Johnson notes, "the empire grew by conquest … and two significant aspects of life within it were shaped by that fact."[62] The first aspect, according to him, was the growing social unrest caused by dissidents of Rome and the congregation of displaced persons in urban centers which drew the attention of the military to quell disturbances.[63] The second significant aspect was "the constant pressure of taxation of the provinces" in order to feed people and to support the machinations and spread of the Roman Empire; taxes which, Johnson argues, were especially severe for subjected persons, thereby furthering their oppression and subjection.[64] Given that the tax-burden among the first-century Jews was serious, it is necessary to draw particular attention to Luke's special interest in tax collectors in association with the economic burden. He, probably aware of the seriousness of burden, seemed to focus on tax collectors' immorality by means of critique of the emperor's authority. Again, this does not mean that he was in opposition to tax collecting itself. We need to explore how the tax collectors in Luke's Gospel are portrayed prior to the discussion of Luke's comparison between Jesus and the emperor.

Tax Collectors

Among biblical writings, the Greek term "tax collector" (τελώνης) occurs only in the Gospels. It does not appear in the Septuagint or any other Greek Old Testament versions including the Apocrypha, even though tax collectors were existent in all the provinces of the empire.[65] It is necessary to consider a general picture of tax collectors in the empire since Luke's Palestinian context is not isolated from the wider context, that is, the influence of the Roman Empire. In this regard, the role of tax collectors or other people's attitudes toward them in the empire should be taken into account. The tax system in the Roman Empire cannot be explained without considering the tax collectors (τελώνης), who played

---

61. See Freyne, *Galilee from Alexander*, 281–87.
62. Johnson, *Writings of the New Testament*, 26.
63. Johnson, *Writings of New Testament*, 26.
64. Johnson, *Writings of New Testament*, 26.
65. Another form of the term, 'chief tax collector' (ἀρχιτελώνης), is referred to only in Luke 19:2.

a vital role in farming out taxes from their people. What is noticeable is that the collecting of taxes was farmed out to the highest bidder, creating the "tax farmer" whereby "Rome received its money in advance, and the tax collector made his living from commissions on tolls and customs."[66] As seen in its origin, the Greek word τελώνης is derived from *telos*, "tax," and *oneomai*, "I buy." Thus, τελώνης designates a person who purchases *from the empire* the rights to official taxes and dues, and who collects these from the people who owe them. In this respect, it should be highlighted that their authority of farming out taxes was given ultimately by the emperor.[67]

Let us see how tax collectors were viewed among first century people in the empire. With the help of the analysis of a person's or a group's characterization, we can better understand Luke's intention in his stories about tax collectors in connection with the emperor's authority. A. S. Hoffman suggests, "Every time you give a definite trait to a character you add a potential, dynamic, dramatic force to help build your plot."[68] Similarly, Robert Alter, emphasizing the function of characterization in literature, points out that act or gesture is not incidental, and, accordingly, that the sequence of events is not accidental.[69]

In the Gospels, it is common to associate a person's characterization with another, which is not accidental. In many cases, tax collectors are often coupled with other people or groups, such as prostitutes (Matt 21:31b–32), sinners (Matt 11:18–19a/ Luke 7:33–34; Matt 9:10–13/ Mark 2:14–17/ Luke 5:29–32; Luke 15:1–2; 18:9–14; 19:1–10), gentiles (Matt 5:46–47; 18:15–17) and the like. As prostitutes and sinners were all regarded as outcasts in a Jewish society, tax collectors, coupled with them, were portrayed in a negative light in all the Gospels. In Luke 18:11, the Pharisee prays, "God, I thank you that I am not like other people: thieves, rogues, adulterers, or even like this tax-collector." In general, this shows Jewish people's negative attitude toward those outcasts. Tax collectors were not an exception.

Why were tax collectors interpreted as such in Luke? First, it is because of their active involvement in the Roman Empire. Such an involvement was interpreted that they, while being against their own people, sold

---

66. Schmidt, "Taxes," 805.

67. Tax collectors were like sub-contractors, who agreed to pay the chief tax collector a given sum.

68. Hoffman, *Writing of Fiction*, 130.

69. Alter, *Art of Biblical Narrative*, 88–113.

their services to the foreign conquerors. As indicated above, this reason is sometimes related to nationalistic movement in the Jewish society. They were understood as employees of the Roman imperial oppressors or as a means of the emperor's power. Second, from the perspective of social science, they were viewed as impure. They entered the homes of unclean people, touched unclean objects, and handled unclean money. The third reason, which I wish to highlight, is due to their exploitation and corruption as well as immorality.

Along with various taxes, another serious problem in the Roman Empire was that taxation was abused by tax collectors and financial authorities.[70] A classic example in the Lukan Gospel would be John the Baptist's preaching. When tax collectors came to him to be baptized, he said to them, "Collect no more than the amount prescribed for you" (Luke 3:12–13).[71] In this account the tax collectors whose role was given by the Roman Empire were viewed as crafty, dishonest, and unjust in their official duties.

Pearson claims that the office "village scribes," responsible for the collection of statistics regarding property and its taxation in Egypt, was the target of people's complaint.[72] For instance, *POxy.* 488 on papyrus shows a complaint against a dishonest village scribe who, by reporting that certain people had much more property than they actually had, forced them to pay more taxes.[73] Their dishonesty and exploitation were notorious among the tax payers. Similarly, MacMullen summarizes a wealth of evidence for first-century Roman Egypt, drawing a general picture of the "predatory arrogance of long latent in the *pax Romana*" in connection with tax collectors' extortion.[74] He quotes a petition from the village of Euhemerus to their Roman "master and patron," indicating that they were willing to sacrifice some of their young men in order to meet an unsustainable tax burden.[75] More seriously, defrauding people went hand

---

70. *Ant.* 18.6.5; *War* 2.14.1; Philo, *Legatio ad Caius*, 199.

71. According to Okorie, "Characterization," 28, the term πράσσετε (collect) is "used in the present imperative tense which forbids the continuation of an act."

72. Pearson, "Lucan Censuses," 271; he further (271) asserts: "at least in Egypt, the office of village scribe was intricately tied to the census. It is difficult to believe that this office was drastically different in Herod's kingdom."

73. Also, see *POxy.* 254, 255 and 288.

74. MacMullen, *Roman Social Relations*, 36.

75. MacMullen, *Roman Social Relations*, 44–45, citing *Papyri russischer und georgischer Sammlungen*, vol. 3, no.8. He also summarizes some seventy such pleas for

in hand with being a tax collector.[76] Philo of Alexandria called on "rulers of cities" to "cease from racking them with taxes and tolls as heavy as they are constant." He objected not only to the injustice of the taxes, but also to the violence by which they were collected. The Romans had intentionally appointed as tax-collectors "the most ruthless of men, brimful of inhumanity, and put into their hands resources for over-reaching."[77]

As a result of their abuse, tax collectors became infamous for dishonesty, exploitation, mistreatment, overcharging, and their aggressive methods of enrichment. Tax collecting became a lucrative and politically important occupation[78] by using their office with some authority, and even Roman writers describe that tax collectors often exploited the provinces.[79] As an astonishing number of materials indicate, the tax collectors stood at the centre of exploitation in the empire. MacMullen, regarding the exploitation of tax collectors as a "common pattern of desperation," aptly states that their corruption was one of the serious problems.[80] In a similar vein, Schmidt stresses that additional amounts, often in large sums, were added to pay the commissions of tax collectors which created a form of "institutionalized robbery."[81] They lived on what they could collect in addition to what was required as noted in Luke 3:12–13. Also, Corbin-Reuschling summarizes: "It is no wonder that tax collectors were universally reviled, were viewed as the worst of all sinners, and were often characterized as unclean by religious leaders as well as those who

---

justice.

76. Harrison, "Case of Pharisee," 103.

77. Philo, *Spec. Leg.* 2.92–94; 3.158–62; for a detailed discussion of tax collector's use of violence, see MacMullen, *Roman Social Relations*, 11, emphasizing "the recurrence of physical outrage, the beatings, mauling, and murders. They accompany a robbery (thefts being frequent) or play a part in intimidation. The plaintiff may allege an attempt to drive him clean out of the village; his enemies want his land, or access to water, which was scarce."

78. Finley, *Ancient Economy*, 60.

79. Although the system was drastically curtailed, first by Julius Caesar and later, by Augustus (see Garnsey and Saller, *Roman Empire,* 87), their exploitation was still all too rife. Also, see Pliny, *Letters* 10.23.24.

80. MacMullen, *Roman Social Relations*, 47. Actually, Roman power created such conditions. In particular, the emperor's failed moral *auctoritas* let tax collectors' exploitation happen. See below.

81. Schmidt, "Taxes," 806.

associated with them, such as Jesus."[82] Thus, tax collectors had an image of a much-hated group.

As with this image or characterization of tax collectors, relatively frequent repetitions of the term "tax collector" are important for understanding Luke's special interest in taxation of the Roman Empire. As Okorie points out, "Characterization in the Bible is often inferred rather than directly stated . . . Though characterization can be revealed through what a character says or does - it is also shown through techniques of repetition or redundancy."[83] In this respect, it is necessary to count how often Luke refers to tax collector(s) in his Gospel in comparison with other evangelists. Luke uses the term "tax collector(s)" (or the terms related to tax) more often than other evangelists do. The word τελώνης occurs ten times in Luke (Luke 3:12; 5:27, 29, 30; 7:29, 34; 15:1; 18:10, 11, 13), while eight times in Matthew and three times in Mark. Statistically speaking, this indicates that Luke has more interest in tax collectors than Mark does. This is not the only reason that I focus on Luke's interest in them. Along with his relatively frequent use of the term, his interest in "tax collectors" is also existent in tax-related accounts, such as census and tribute, although the term is not mentioned.[84]

In my opinion, Luke, acknowledging that tax was related directly/indirectly to the emperor's authority, attempts to link the corruption of tax collectors to the failure of the emperor's authority. Also, he contrasts this with Jesus' reaction to tax collectors in order to highlight his authority. Prior to the discussion of how Luke contrasts Jesus' authority with the emperor's, it is necessary to differentiate the emperor's *imperium* from his *auctoritas*.

Emperor's Imperium and Auctoritas

In general, the emperor's power can be divided into two elements. In this regard, I wish to make a distinction between the emperor's *imperium* and his *auctoritas* in terms of census and tribute of the Roman Empire. Let us first define the meaning of *imperium* and *auctoritas* individually in order to understand in what ways Luke criticizes the emperor's morality

---

82. Corbin-Reuschling, "Zacchaeus's Conversion," 72; Neale, *None but the Sinners*.

83. Okorie, "Characterization," 27; on the characterization of sinners, and thus, by extension, see Neal, *None but the Sinners*.

84. See above.

through tax-related accounts. My assumption is that Luke's understanding of tax is based partly on his recognition of differences between the emperor's *imperium* and *auctoritas*.

Imperium

It is difficult to define the meaning of *imperium* because it has "undergone a shift, or more precisely an extension, of meaning" throughout Roman history.[85] Even though it is not easy to identify its original nuances, it has been generally accepted that the term 'empire' derives from *imperium*; that is, at least from the second half of the first century AD *imperium Romanum* is used as we would use "Roman Empire."[86] Also, its cognate *imperator*, who exercises *imperium*, comes to mean "emperor."[87]

It is almost impossible to grasp Augustus' power without considering the significance of his *imperium*. For example, the first "Augustan Settlement" of 27 BC allowed him to hold the consulship each year and extended his proconsular *imperium* over the provinces of Gaul, Spain, and Syria for a ten-year period. In the second settlement of 23 BC, according to Dio Cassius, Augustus' powers were re-defined: his proconsular *imperium* became broader (*imperium maius*), putting him in control of all military provinces; he could intervene legally in all of them; and his proconsular *imperium* did not lapse even when he entered Rome's *pomerium*.[88] That is, Augustus' *imperium* became superior to that of the other magistrates and pro-magistrates. As Dio (53. 32.5) stresses, superiority of Augustus' power was based on his *imperium*, which signified his power.

A question can be raised here. In what is Augustus' *imperium* rooted? Rehak argues that *imperium* was based partly on coercive power and partly on administrative power although they were often interrelated, stating:

---

85. Richardson,"*Imperium Romanum*, 1.

86. Plilny, *NH* 6.26.120: "*durant, ut fuere, Thebata et, ductu Pompei Magni terminus Romani imperi, Orutos, a Zeugmate L. CC.*"; also see Lintott, 'What Was," 54f.

87. Grant, *From Imperium to Auctoritas*, 412f.

88. Dio, 53.32.5; at this time Augustus gave up the annual consulship and was granted tribunician power in its place. Rehak, *Imperium and Cosmos*, 4, contrasting Augustus' *imperium* with others' *imperium*, asserts that their *imperium* was geographically finite unlike Augustus' *imperium*, saying that their "military *imperium* could not be wielded within the *pomerium*, nor could a city magistrate's *imperium* be exercised outside it without retaking the auspices upon re-entering."

> The Romans recognized two types of *imperium*: the exercise of military power (*imperium militare*), by a field commander whose troops might acclaim him imperator on the battlefield, and the executive power of magistrates (*imperium domi*), awarded to consuls and praetors.[89]

On one level, it is noticeable that the military power of *imperium* was to be viewed primarily in relation to the security of the frontiers and the provinces against the enemies of the empire. The emperor's world domination was based upon his military *imperium*: either the Romans were preoccupied with military glory, or the Romans sometimes used the threat of force rather than force itself. The coin types of the Julio-Claudian period clearly reflect that the emperor's exercise of *imperium* was used for military glory or achievement.[90] It is therefore impossible to assume that *imperium* could be achieved without military force. In other words, the emperor's *imperium*, a sign of his coercive power, had a major role in achieving sovereignty over his enemies.[91] As shown on Octavian's *denarii* of the year 28 BC, without the *imperium* Octavian could neither have received his salutation in 31, nor have triumphed for Actium and Egypt.[92]

On another level, the role of *imperium* is, as Rehak suggests, associated partly with civil or administrative power. A classic example is the emperor's conduct of census. In other words, census was conducted by the exercise of the emperor's administrative *imperium*. Augustus used his *imperium* (not *auctoritas*) when conducting a lustrum after a census. Augustus himself says:

> I revised the roll of the Senate three times. In my sixth consulship with Marcus Agrippa as colleague, I carried out a census of the people, and I performed a *lustrum* after a lapse of forty-two years; at that *lustrum* 4,063,000 Roman citizens were registered. Then a second time I performed a *lustrum* with consular *imperium* and without a colleague, in the consulship of Gaius Censorinus and Gaius Asinius; at that lustrum 4,233,000 citizens were registered. Thirdly I performed a *lustrum* with consular

---

89. Rehak, *Imperium and Cosmos*, 4.

90. For such coins, see Sutherland, *Coinage*, 177; Augustus' military *imperium* in connection with his title "savior" is to be dealt with in detail in Ch. 4.

91. As Grant, *From Imperium*, 415, rightly asserts, *imperator*, the holder of *imperium*, is "a title of competence," and "competence is the *imperium maius*."

92. See the coins in Mattingly, *British Museum Catalogues*, xciii; Grant, *From Imperium*, 419.

imperium, with Tiberius Caesar, my son, as colleague, in the consulship of Sextus Pompeius and Sextus Appuleius; at that lustrum 4,937,000 citizens were registered.[93]

It can be said that the executive *imperium* gave Augustus the legal capacity to undertake the census. Even though it is not easy to draw a clear distinction between *imperium* and *auctoritas*, the decree of census and that of *lustrum* are rooted more in his civic *imperium* than in his *auctoritas*.[94]

Auctoritas

Let us consider another aspect of the emperor's power, *auctoritas*.[95] Tacitus refers to the emperor's *auctoritas* as "*Omnes iussa principis aspectare.*"[96] Sutherland asserts that his *auctoritas* was based upon his supreme authority, viewed as the universal instrument of civil administration.[97] Describing the emperor's *auctoritas*, Werner Eck states:

> The sum of his power derived first of all from various powers of office delegated to him by the Senate and people, secondly from his immense private fortune, and thirdly from numerous patron-client relationships he established with individuals and groups throughout the empire. All of them taken together formed the basis of his *auctoritas*, which he himself emphasized as the foundation of his political actions.[98]

As Eck states, the way of acquisition of *auctoritas* is not the same as that of *imperium*. Similarly, Sutherland puts it: "*auctoritas* or the willing and admiring respect of the governed, must be earned, and earned in other

---

93. *RG* 8, 2–4, trans. Brunt and Moore; also see EJ, 35.

94. However, this does not necessarily mean that the census was based solely upon his *imperium*, since his various power sources were all correlated. His *imperium* is concerned more with *lustrum* (part of census) and decree, while his moral *auctoritas* is associated more with the role of censor. For the discussion of the emperor's role as a censor in connection with his *auctoritas*, see below.

95. The emphasis on *auctoritas* is shown on some inscriptions; e.g. *CIL* 10.5393: *ex auctoritate Ti. Caesaris Augusti et permissu eius*. Augustus' *auctoritas* is also emphasized in the description of events 28–27 BC: *sentene post id tempus auctoritate omnibus praestiti* (*PIR*2 1.961.187).

96. Tacitus *Ann.* 1.4.

97. Sutherland, *Coinage*, 41; he further argues that this insistence was to be seen most plainly on the *aes* coinage rather than on those of gold and silver.

98. Eck, *Age of Augustus*, 113.

ways. It was the fruit of wise statesmanship in the civil sphere."⁹⁹ In a similar manner, Grant describes Augustus' *auctoritas* as an important source of his power, saying:

> Every office, every power, and every success -the constituents of *dignitas*- enhanced the inherited *auctoritas* of Augustus until it became his unique and personal attribute or characteristic, enabling him to act without *potestas* or *imperium* . . . Such was the force of his record and character that his hints and words of advice, unlike those of anyone else, only needed to be offered to be accepted . . . The word *auctoritas*, when referred to Augustus, comprises all the elements in his power which were apart from *potestas* or *imperium* . . . Among its outward manifestations are the exceptional titles of *princeps, dux-ductor, conditor*-κτιστης, ἡγεμων, Augustus, *pater patriae* and *Imperator*, which can, in the briefest possible generalization, be said to crystallize the civilian, national, reconstructive, Hellenistic, religious, Romulean (or cliental) and victorious aspects of his rule respectively.¹⁰⁰

It is evident that Augustus' power by *auctoritas*, based mainly upon his own personality, advice, and influence, should be differentiated from that by military *imperium*, rooted primarily in coercive power. For instance, Octavian built up his *auctoritas* on the grounds that he was an adopted son and heir of Caesar, and, accordingly, that his distinctive status, as *divi filius*, was conferred on him in 36 BC.¹⁰¹

Then, why is the emperor's *auctoritas* so important in the discussion of Luke's tax-relating accounts? What is the relationship between Luke's concern for morality and Augustus' census in Luke's writing? These questions can be answered, first, by considering the emperor's emphasis on moral *auctoritas*, and second, by analyzing his role as a censor. Unlike his *imperium*, the emperor focused his *auctoritas* on moral issues. His moral *auctoritas* was frequently employed as a power resource to construct and define the rules of his sovereignty.

A number of sources state that Augustus attempted to emphasize and enhance his moral *auctoritas*.¹⁰² According to *Res Gestae*, he was

99. Sutherland, *Coinage*, 177.

100. Grant, *From Imperium*, 443 and 444.

101. See also, ILS 72=CLS IX, 2628: "*quem senatus populusque in deorum numerum rettulit.*"

102. Augustus is not the only figure who emphasizes the importance of morality. Plutarch also stresses (*Cato Minor* 24.1; 37.5) and encourages others to develop their own moral character by imitating their virtues and avoiding their vices (*Pericles*

aiming to create the new order and the new constitutionalism in order to highlight his *auctoritas*. In doing so, he received the marks of honour and gratitude through such things. After 23 BC, his *auctoritas*, as supreme authority, became ubiquitous and undeniable, proclaiming openly that he exceeded all of his contemporaries in influence (*auctoritas*), but that he possessed no more official power (*potestas*) than the magistrates who were his colleagues.[103] At the same time, the source of the Augustan power derived, to a large extent, from his restoration of the traditional principles, since he was very interested in restoration of stability and peace.[104] As Wells puts it, Augustus was "concerned to placate conservative sentiment by appeals to precedent and by maintaining and restoring traditional values, ceremonies, and procedures."[105] That is, Augustus brought peace to his world by restoring legitimate government based on conservative law and the restoration of public virtues.[106] In doing so, his moral *auctoritas* was enhanced and stressed.

It is not difficult to find that Augustus tended to place much emphasis on the restoration of morality. The Augustan poet Horace celebrated the restoration of morality in the Age of Augustus in his *Carmina* (3.6):

> O most immoral age! First you tainted marriage, the house, and the family. Now from the same source flows pollution over fatherland and people![107]

Augustus sought to restore Rome's lost ancestral virtue through legislation regarding bribery, adultery, chastity, and extravagance. Although the Roman laws could not completely change what was happening in the empire, at least they demonstrated recognition and pervasiveness of

---

1; *Aemilius Paullus* 1). Concerning Plutarch's primary focus on morals, see Russell, *Plutarch*, 103–4. Similarly, Xenophon's picture of Agesilaus is an example for others to follow to become better people (*Agesilaus* 10.2). Such ethical exemplary motives are also expressed by Isocrates (*Evagoras* 73–81) and Lucian (*Demonax* 2).

103. RG, 34.3; see Brunt and Moor, *Res Gestae*, 5.

104. On the eastern coinage which signifies such principles, see Sutherland, *Coinage*, 31; also see Velleius Paterculus, 2.89; Fabius' Decree in *Introduction*.

105. Wells, *Roman Empire*, 100.

106. Jewett, *Romans*, 46–47; also see Knust, "Paul and Politics," 155–73, where he argues that a ruler's virtue legitimates his rule.

107. Also see his *Odes* 4.15.

immorality and a desire for change.[108] Augustan poets, such as Virgil[109] and Horace, frequently praised him as a defender of Rome, a guardian of moral justice, and an individual who bore the force of responsibility in maintaining the imperial security. Likewise, Augustus' successors were also interested deeply in morality. For instance, Tacitus records that Tiberius made efforts to limit corruption (*Ann.* 5.6). Similarly, Suetonius quotes Tiberius as saying "a good shepherd does not flay his flock" (*Tib.* 32).[110] Thus, it can be said that the emperors as the holders of supreme *auctoritas* were responsible for morality in the empire.

Besides, the fact that Augustus' concern for morality is associated more with his *auctoritas* than with his *imperium* is found in his titles, which serve as heightening his moral responsibility; the honorific tittles *pater patriae* and *princeps* to name but a few. Grant emphasizes that those titles were based mainly upon the emperor's *auctoritas*,[111] which played an important role in signifying the restoration of morality. For instance, Augustus' emphasis on ancestral virtues is expressed in his title *pater patriae*. In 2 BC he accepted the title *pater patriae* that had been offered to him many times before.[112] It seems that Augustus' *auctoritas*, based upon *pater patriae*, placed a growing emphasis on the morality in order to secure his empire,[113] since the identification and veneration of ancestors served as a way of building up his *auctoritas*. The title *pater patriae* in association with the ancestors functioned as building up Augustus' *auctoritas* in the empire.[114] That is, the title *pater patriae*, along with *princeps*, whose basis was the *auctoritas*, had great moral responsibilities.[115]

---

108. Suetonius, *Aug.* 31, also reports: "And so [Augustus] restored the public works of each of them . . ." See also Zanker, *Power of Images*; Knust, 'Paul and Politics', 160.

109. Virgil, *Ecl.* 4.11.48.

110. Cf. Matt 9:10–11; 11:19; 18:17; 21:3; Mark 2:15–16; Luke 5:30.

111. Grant, *From Imperium*, 444.

112. Rehak, *Imperium and Cosmos*, 138; the title was already in use in Spain by 6 BC.

113. On the Augustan coinage, see Sutherland, *Coinage*, 27.

114. In this regard, Rehak, *Imperium and Cosmos*, 144, attempts to link architecture to Augustus' power, arguing that "ancestral" buildings may serve as proto-types or archetypes for imitation. He goes on to claim (144): "By creating a monumental dynastic tomb for himself, his relatives, and associates, Augustus effectively declared himself a new ancestor while he was still alive, deliberately bypassing in the process his natural father, Octavius, and his adoptive father, Julius Caesar."

115. See Grant, *From Imperium*, 444; cf. 452 n5.

Census, Tribute, and Tax Collectors 79

It cannot be denied that the emperor's particular interest in morality was expressed by means of his *auctoritas* on which several titles were based.

When the significance of census is taken into account, the emperor's moral *auctoritas* becomes more evident. Even though the decree of census itself was conducted primarily on the basis of the emperor's administrative *imperium*, his role of censor was linked directly to his moral *auctoritas*. Let us analyze first whether Augustus was a censor. In terms of his censorship, it is said that Augustus did not accept the censorship for life, appointing instead two men as censors.[116] For instance, Augustus himself records: he refused the post of "supervisor of laws and morals without a colleague and with supreme power" given by the Senate and the people, because it was inconsistent with ancestral custom (*mos maiorum*); instead, "the measures that the Senate then desired me to take I carried out in virtue of my tribunician power."[117] However, unlike his record, Augustus' attempt to restore morality is clearly found in his role as a censor. His record is inconsistent with Dio (54.10) and Suetonius. First, Dio describes that Augustus in the winter of 22/21 BC accepted a five-year appointment as supervisor of morals (*praefectus moribus*) and censor, along with consular authority for life (54.10). In other words, Augustus exercised censorial power, and that this power was considered in connexion with the Augustan censuses.[118] Dio also records that Augustus had another five-year term as supervisor of morality in 12 BC (54.10), stating:

> Augustus was chosen supervisor and corrector of morals for another five years; for he received this office also for limited periods, as he did the monarchy. He ordered the senators to burn incense in their assembly hall whenever the held a session . . . they should show reverence to the gods.

In a similar way, Suetonius, arguing that Augustus emphasized his morality in association with census, records:

> [Augustus] accepted of the tribunitian power for life, but more than once chose a colleague in that office for two lustra successively. He also had the supervision of morality and observance

---

116. For the explanation of two censors, see *The Oxford Dictionary of Classical World*, J. W. Roberts (John Willoby) (3rd edn.; Oxford: Oxford University Press, 2005), p.139; *The New Interpreter's Bible*, vol. 9 (Luke-John), ed. by Leander E. Keck (Abingdon Press, 2003), p.7.

117. *RG* 6.1; also see *RG* 19, 18 and 11.

118. Dio, 50.30.1.

of the laws, for life, but without the tile of censor (*recepit et morum legumque regimen aeque perpetuum, quo iure, quamquam sine censurae honore*); yet he thrice took a census of the people, the first and third time with a colleague, but the second by himself.[119]

Suetonius' record clearly indicates that Augustus was "a supervisor of morality" through his census. Although he did not bear the office of censor, he carried out the actual role of censor, which was control of morals. What is noticeable is that Augustus, with or without censorship, was viewed as the supervisor of morals in the process of census.[120]

Moreover, it seems that Quirinius as a legate in the province of Syria was in charge of conducting the census according to Luke 2:2. In the provinces, cities were normally liable for collecting tax and remitting it to Roman officials. However, what should be stressed here is that Quirinius was delegated by Augustus with his full authority. In other words, even though Quirinius was responsible for the census, his authority was fully given by Augustus' authority. This fact is affirmed in Luke 2:1, saying that "a decree (*about the census*) went out from Emperor Augustus." Luke uses the term δόγμα here in 2:1.[121] This term is also found in other ancient writings, such as Josephus, *War* 1.393 and P. Fayum 20, 22, with the sense of imperial edict.[122] Yamazaki-Ransom argues that the term "is used of an imperial decree," implying a formal action of the empire[123] and representing the emperor's authority/power in the empire; that is, the decree was declared ultimately by the emperor although Quirinius was in charge of the census. Again, although there are no references to Augustus' role as a censor in Luke's writing, it hints, at least, that the actual and ultimate censor was Augustus.

With a particular focus on the emperor's moral *auctoritas*, let us take a look at the identity and status of tax collectors from the perspective

---

119. Suetonius, *Aug.* 27; cf. Cicero, *de Leg.* 3. 3, 7; Livy, 4.8, 24.18, 40.46, 41.27, 42.3.

120. Augustus carried out various measures himself which more properly belonged to the censors. Along with his concern for morality, Augustus' role of censor was responsible for the grain supply, "delegating responsibility to annual commissioners of praetorian rank" (Wells, *Roman Empire*, 54), because of Rome's dependence on imported supplies.

121. See also Acts 17:7.

122. Porter, "Reasons for Lukan Census," 180.

123. Yamazaki-Ransom, *Roman Empire*, 73; also see Marshall, *Luke*, 98; Brown, *Birth of the Messiah*, 394; Bock, *Luke*, 1:202.

of the moral evaluation. As discussed, while he was not in opposition to paying taxes, Luke is very critical of tax collectors' immorality relating to tax-farming. In this respect, he attempts to devalue Augustus' moral *auctoritas* by referring to tax collectors' immorality. That is, with the help of a negative portrait of tax collectors, Luke strives to link this negative characterization to the emperor who was in charge of their immorality. Given that the tax system was abused and exploited by tax collectors, Augustus and his successors could not avoid responsibility for their immorality, because the emperor as the actual censor was the one who was ultimately responsible for morality. It seems very likely that Luke implicitly blames Augustus' moral *auctoritas* for the lack of tax collectors' morality. In doing so, Luke shows the imperfection of the emperor's moral *auctoritas*, for his power failed to maintain the morality under the Roman tax system. On the contrary, Luke's Jesus summoned the tax collectors in order to make it possible for them to repent and reform; that is, his association with tax collectors serves as both his correction of their immorality and Luke's critique of the emperor's moral *auctoritas*. Luke's accounts of Levi and Zacchaeus would be good examples, for they clearly indicate that Luke's Jesus was successful in correcting tax collectors' immorality as opposed to the emperor's unsuccessful attempt.

Levi (Luke 5:27–32)

Let us look at the issue of tax collector's corruption and immorality implied in Luke's Gospel. We shall analyze two stories about a tax collector (Levi) and a chief tax collector (Zacchaeus) in order to associate their corruption with the emperor's failure to exercise his moral *auctoritas*. Luke's Jesus encounters the first tax collector named Levi (5:27–32).[124] In this account, two significant aspects are to be noted. The first aspect is whether Levi, as a tax collector, was relatively rich. It is noticeable that only Luke clearly identifies Levi's occupation as a tax collector. He di-

---

124. Walker, "Jesus and Tax Collectors," 232, claims that "the call story and the meal story were originally separate traditions, since only Luke connects the two in anything other than a quite abrupt and awkward manner." Bultmann, *History of the Synoptic Tradition*, 18, 47–49, 66, also argues that Jesus' eating with tax collectors and sinners is a creation of the early church. Concerning Levi's identity, in Mark and Luke, he is called Levi, while he is called Matthew in Matthew. And Mark alone tells us that he was "the son of Alpheus"- the same probably, with the father of James the less (Mark 2:14). On a detailed discussion of Levi's identity, see Brown, *Four Gospels*, 56.

rectly tells us that Jesus saw "*a tax collector* named Levi, sitting at the tax booth" (Luke 5:27), while Mark and Matthew do not refer to Levi's occupation in such a direct way. Rather, both Mark and Matthew just say that Jesus saw Levi, "sitting at the tax booth" (Mark 2:14; Matt 9:9). It is correct to assume that Mark's or Matthew's readers probably guessed Levi's occupation without a direct reference to a tax collector. A critical question is why Luke alone explicitly identifies Levi as a tax collector. In brief, my answer is that Luke, unlike the two evangelists, aims to link such an occupation to corruption and exploitation in more detail. In this regard, he wishes to clarify the relationship between Levi's occupation (tax collector) and his wealth.

As mentioned above, tax collectors exploited others by using their authority given by the Roman power. In this process, they accumulated their wealth. In Luke's Gospel, there are several clues to the fact that Levi was relatively rich. Luke says that "Levi gave a great banquet for Jesus in his house" (Luke 5:29: ἐποίησεν δοχὴν μεγάλην Λευὶς αὐτῷ ἐν τῇ οἰκίᾳ αὐτοῦ). Luke alone refers to the term "δοχὴν μεγάλην," which is a sign of Levi's economic status. This phrase of δοχὴν μεγάλην is not found elsewhere in the New Testament, but its use is found in LXX. For instance, it is reported that "Abraham made a great feast (δοχὴν μεγάλην) on the day Isaac was weaned" (Gen 21:8). Also, in 1 Esdras 3:1, it is written that "King Darius gave a great banquet (δοχὴν μεγάλην) for all that were under him, all that were born in his house, and all the nobles of Media and Persia." Similarly, Belshazzar the king held a great feast (δοχὴν μεγάλην) for a thousand of his nobles in Dan 5:1. Here, those who gave a great feast were Abraham and two kings, who were conceivably richer than the normal people around them. Thus, Luke uses the term in order to imply that Levi, who offers δοχὴν μεγάλην, was, at least, relatively wealthy. Also, when Levi gave a great feast (δοχὴν μεγάλην), Jesus was not the only participant. There were many tax collectors and others (v. 29; ἦν ὄχλος πολὺς τελωνῶν καὶ ἄλλων οἳ ἦσαν). This implies, first, that Levi was rich enough to host such a great feast, and, second, that Luke depicts him as having some means because he was capable of throwing a banquet for Jesus and many people.[125]

---

125. But this does not mean that he was as rich as Zacchaeus. As Hays, *Luke's Wealth Ethics*, 83 n49, rightly points out, "we ought not assume he possesses the same type of riches that the Rich Ruler (Luke 18:18–23) or Zacchaeus do (19:1–10), since he is not a 'chief tax collector' (Luke 19:2) who has sufficient money to purchase the right to collect taxes, but likely a subsidiary to the tax farmer, employed to sit in the toll

Moreover, another indication of Levi's wealth can be found in v. 29. Luke records that it was in Levi's own house ("ἐν τῇ οἰκίᾳ αὐτοῦ"; 5:29; Mark 2:15), while Matthew says, "He sat at dinner *in the house*"(Matt 9:10, "ἐν τῇ οἰκίᾳ"). In Matthew we are not sure whether the house belonged to Levi. But Luke reports that the house, which was probably spacious enough to invite many people, was possessed by Levi himself in v. 29.[126] Luke's account is more specific than Matthew's account in terms of the relationship between Levi's occupation as a tax collector and his economic status. Taken together, it seems to me that Luke is concerned more with linking Levi's occupation to his economic status than the other two evangelists are.

The second point I wish to make is whether Luke's Jesus sees tax collectors' corruption as sin. When the Pharisees and scribes complained about Jesus' fellowship with a large company of tax collectors and others (5:29), it is indicated how tax collectors were portrayed in their society. Tax collectors were coupled with sinners in their question (5:30). As shown, tax collectors in the empire were described in a negative light, often with reference to other groups. Likewise, the Pharisees and scribes saw them as sinners.[127]

Here, a critical question arises because they were described as sinners by the Pharisees and scribes. Did Luke's Jesus also see them as sinners? This question can be answered on the basis of Jesus' answer in vv. 31–32. While it is obvious that Jesus' opponents such as Pharisees and scribes viewed tax collectors as sinners, Jesus' attitude toward them could be considered somewhat ambivalent primarily because Jesus had a table fellowship with the tax collectors.

It is necessary to analyze what Jesus' answer means because this analysis helps us to see his attitude toward them. Jesus answered, "Those

---

booth and collect the *portatorium*." Cf. Petracca and Klauck have suggested that the banquet should be understood as a "parting meal," which implies that Levi will subsequently divest himself of his possessions; Petracca, *Gott order das Geld*, 100; Klauck, "Die Armut der Junger," 175.

126. Theissen, *Social Setting*, 85–87, analyzing a house-owner's economic status at 1 Cor. 1:16, distinguishes οἶκος from οἰκία, arguing that οἶκος is a larger house than οἰκία. For him, reference to an οἶκος was used for house more than just parents and children. See Horrell's critique of Theissen's view, "Domestic Space," 359, and his *Social Ethos*, 96.

127. The epithet 'tax collectors and sinners' appears together also in Luke 7:34 and 15:1, while separately in 18:11, 13 and 19:2, 10. In Matthew, only the Pharisees are Jesus' critics. The group of scribes does not appear in this scene.

who are well have no need of a physician, but those who are sick; I have come to call not the righteous but sinners to repentance" (Luke 5:31–32). In this respect, Walker argues that Luke did not see tax collectors in a negative tone because of his description of Jesus' fellowship with them.[128] This is in accordance with Okorie who stresses that the tax collectors were expressed 'in a sympathetic light' on the basis of Jesus' eating dinner with them.[129] In Luke, Jesus' table fellowship with tax collectors can be interpreted as consistent with the accounts of Jesus' concern for other marginal people such as Samaritans (Luke 10:29–37; 17:16), widows (Mark 12:40–44; Luke 20:47—21:4; Luke 7:11–17) and the poor (Luke 6:20–23). It is true that Jesus' table fellowship with the tax collectors signifies his open acceptance of outcasts.[130]

However, Jesus' inclusive attitude in Luke does not necessarily mean that he sees the tax collectors in a positive light. In my opinion, both Walker and Okorie, although acknowledging some aspects of their dishonesty, tend to focus primarily on Jesus' acceptance without a careful examination of the economic status relating to their occupation. For me, Luke seems to highlight that Jesus' answer is more critical of tax collectors' exploitation, as a means of accumulating their wealth, than Okorie suggested. Moreover, as the structure (Luke 5:31–32) itself tells us, the words of Jesus' answer take binary composition: well/sick, righteous/sinners, not come/come.[131] From this binary composition, it is evident that the tax collectors are portrayed as sinners who are sick and who need a physician (Jesus). Clearly, Luke does not emphasize that Jesus tolerated tax collectors' immoral activities.

128. Walker, "Jesus and Tax Collectors," 232.

129. Okorie, "Characterization of Tax Collectors," 29.

130. Garrison's monograph, *Graeco-Roman Context*, 41–47 and 87–88, compares Jesus' table fellowship in Luke with Greco-Roman symposia but also contrasts his open acceptance of people with the more usual concern for the right guests. Also see Borg, *Conflict, Holiness*, 82 and 93–94, who concludes that Jesus used table fellowship with such a wide range of people "as a weapon . . . an acted parable of acceptance . . . an acted parable of what Israel should be, embodying a different understanding of Israel's nature and purpose." For more instances of Jesus' open acceptance of social outcasts, see Luke 4:14–19; 5:12–16; 7:36–50; 10:25–37; 13:10–17; 14:15–24; 16:19–31; 21:1–4; 24:1–12.

131. Okorie, "Characterization of Tax Collectors," 27, suggests, "Characterization often dwells on contrasting traits represented by two or more people, resulting in binary opposition. Such contrasts are seen in the Pharisee and the sinful woman (Luke 7:36–50), the rich man and Lazarus (Luke 16:19–31), and the Pharisee and the tax collector (18:9–14)."

What Luke emphasizes is that Jesus, in spite of their negative characterization or their exploitation, was willing to eat with the tax collectors to correct their wrongs and to save them.[132] To put it another way, Luke does not focus on Jesus' meal with the tax collectors, but on the fact that they could be saved by repenting of their sins while eating with Jesus.[133] In the final part of Levi's story, Levi gave up his post as collector of tolls in order to become a disciple through his encounter with Jesus. In this respect, it is very noticeable that only Luke, among the Synoptic writers, emphasizes the need of "repentance" (v. 32, "ἁμαρτωλοὺς εἰς μετάνοιαν"). In other words, Luke tells us that Jesus, who acts as a physician, warns Levi to repent his immorality of exploitation, which is not corrected by the emperor's *auctoritas*. In the Bible, repentance is typically understood as "a turning away from sinful ways," such as exploitation with the case of the tax collectors, and 'back toward God'.[134] Through this account, Luke aims to show that 'development occurs in the characterization of Levi, from an unscrupulous tax collector to a happy follower of Jesus'.[135] Through this development, Luke seems to differentiate Jesus' concern with morality from the emperor's lack of moral *auctoritas*. Therefore, Luke not only criticizes tax collector's corruption, but his critique of them also implies that Jesus' authority is superior to the emperor's moral *auctoritas*. He implicitly shows that Jesus is capable of doing what the emperor's moral *auctoritas* has failed through Levi's story.

Zacchaeus (Luke 19:1–10)

The story of Zacchaeus provides us with an excellent summary of many of Luke's major themes, since his story can be interpreted in various ways.

---

132. Luke 7:34; 15:1–2; 19:1–10; cf. Matt 11:19; also see Burridge, *Imitating Jesus*, 275–76.

133. Harrison, "Pharisee and Tax Collector," 110–11, focuses on tax collectors' willingness to receive Jesus' message as opposed to those who reject his message. He notes: "Rhetorically in this story, Luke is leading us to identify with the sinners, and with this hated tax collector, in hopes that we too will be inclined to make a choice to align ourselves with God by humbling ourselves in a social way, by physically moving from our own 'centers' of power and privilege towards the margins of society in order to demonstrate God's mercy"; also see next chapter.

134. Harrison, "Pharisee and Tax Collector," 104; for the significance of the relationship between "repentance" and "salvation" in tax-related accounts, see Ch.4.

135. Okorie, "Characterization of Tax Collectors," 28; later development occurs through the change of his name (6:15).

For example, some tend to read it in connection with the Travel Narrative.[136] Others understand it as a conversion story or vindication story.[137] With the help of the discussion of conversion or vindication interpretation, my focus in this account is on the Roman taxation and on those who collected taxes from their people. In other words, my argument takes into account Zacchaeus' role as a chief tax collector under the Roman Empire, since he stood in the centre of Roman taxation. In doing so, two main issues are to be examined as with Levi's account: Zacchaeus' economic status and his economic wrongs in terms of his occupation.

Interpretation of the story of Zacchaeus must begin with the fact that it occurs only in Luke's Gospel. This offers us an indication of Luke's special interest in tax-related issues. Along with other tax-related stories (such as census, Jesus' dispute over tribute, and Jesus' trial), this particular Lukan story is helpful in understanding the emperor's failure to correct tax collectors' corruption. As already discussed in the story of Levi, Luke, although it is not directly stated, aims at devaluing the emperor's moral *auctoritas* by expressing Zacchaeus' continuous immorality. In line with the story of Levi, the story of Zacchaeus plays a major role in Luke's implicit critique of the emperor.

A general characterization of Zacchaeus is not really a far cry from that of the earlier Levi, a lower level tax collector 'sitting at the tax office' (Luke 5:27). For me, the story of Zacchaeus re-emphasizes and maximizes the negative characterizations of the tax collectors expressed in the earlier stories, despite some differences between Levi and Zacchaeus. In this story, Luke provides us with more detailed information about the chief tax collector. What I wish to stress is that Luke describes Zacchaeus not only as a chief tax collector but also as a rich man. It is highly important to analyze Zacchaeus' economic status in connection with his occupation "chief tax collector." Also, it is necessary to discuss how he accumulated his wealth in this story.

The status of tax collector was not the same as that of chief tax collector (ἀρχιτελώνης), such as Zacchaeus. The chief tax collectors, who held a supervisory office, "had the opportunity for personal gain."[138] To put it differently, the chief tax collector (e.g. Zacchaeus), as a superinten-

---

136. E.g., O'Hanlon, "Story of Zacchaeus," 2–26.

137. For the bibliography, see the discussion below.

138. Harrison, "Pharisee and Tax Collector," 103 n12; it is also assumed that Zacchaeus accumulated his wealth by farming the tolls in the region of Jericho (a main centre of commercial activity).

dent of tax collectors, responsible for supervising other tax collectors, had more opportunities to obtain his wealth than the lower level tax collectors (e.g. Levi). Of course, the ordinary tax collectors probably had small opportunities to collect 'more than the amount prescribed' (Luke 3:13). However, due to their position, the ordinary tax collectors had less opportunity to amass wealth. As Corbin-Reuschling rightly states, the chief tax collectors had more power as well as more wealth than other ordinary tax collectors.[139]

Luke directly mentions that Zacchaeus was wealthy (πλούσιος) in connection with his occupation as a chief tax collector in v. 2.[140] Verses 2 and 3 are very important when we interpret the relationship between the occupation and its economic status in verses 7 and 8. In order to link his exploitation to the failure of the emperor's *auctoritas*, it is necessary to specify in detail how Zacchaeus obtained his wealth.

Even though many scholars admit that Zacchaeus was rich as a tax collector, there are contrasting views on his cheating in relation to his occupation. It has been debated whether or not he was morally wrong. Alan C. Mitchell suggests the theory of vindication, asserting that the story of Zacchaeus reflects a vindication of his job as a tax collector not a change of direction.[141] According to Mitchell, Zacchaeus offered to give back to anyone if he had cheated (Luke 19:8), implying the possibility that he had not cheated anybody in the collection of taxes. For him, Zacchaeus' statement in v. 8 had nothing to do with his moral wrongs, first because he was already doing good works of justice and generosity, and second because Jesus recognized him as a true son of Abraham on the basis of his good works. In other words, Zacchaeus, for Mitchell, was already "converted" in that he was declared righteous by Jesus and was already doing what was required as a son of Abraham.[142] Similarly, Richard C. White maintains that the story tells of a man who was stereotyped by his job, resented and wrongly accused by his neighbors, who defended himself

---

139. Corbin-Reuschling, "Zacchaeus' Conversion," 72.

140. The Greek word "πλούσιος" (rich) occurs more often in Luke. While the word occurs twice in Mark and three times in Matthew, there are eleven occurrences in Luke but none in Acts.

141. Mitchell, "Zacchaeus Revisited," 153–76.

142. Mitchell, "Zacchaeus Revisited," 162, notes: "To that end Luke 19:1–10 should be understood as a story about Zacchaeus, a rich toll collector, a Jew to whom Jesus came to bring salvation because he was a son of Abraham."

against the false charge, and whose good name was finally vindicated by Jesus.[143]

From the perspective of the vindication theory, Zacchaeus was not a sinner as a tax collector, for Luke's purpose in vindicating him was to serve "the underlying purpose . . . to make acceptable in the Christian community the presence of those who, although having socially despised occupations, were faithful believers."[144] Thus, for the supporters of this theory, any critique of Zacchaeus' wrongs relating to his occupation is not found in the story. For them, there is no room for the view that Luke intends to stress the failure of the emperor's moral *auctoritas* to correct Zacchaeus' extortion, simply because he was not morally wrong.

Their reading of the story, however, should be criticized for several reasons. It is very inconceivable to say that the tax collectors did not defraud others, even though the theory of vindication is not completely wrong. As mentioned above, it is better to think that the tax payers had an economic burden due to various taxes and tax collectors' exploitation. For me, Luke's general picture of ordinary tax collectors corresponds to his characterization of the chief tax collector, Zacchaeus. Regardless of the fact that he defrauded others, verse 8 functions as emphasizing what the tax collectors of the empire normally did. In other words, they were considered morally wrong in contrast to the vindication theory.

Moreover, it is wrong to connect the idea that Zacchaeus remained a tax collector or that Luke's Jesus did not tell Zacchaeus to stop his occupation in the conclusion that he was not morally wrong. As Luke's Jesus was not in opposition to paying taxes to the emperor,[145] he was not telling Zacchaeus to quit his job. What Luke attempts to criticize through this story is his extortion, not his job itself. That is why Luke's Jesus did not ask him to stop his occupation.

More critiques are found in an alternative theory suggested by Fernando Mendez-Moratalla, arguing that the story of Zacchaeus clearly points to his salvation and conversion.[146] For him, the vindication theory goes against the thrust of the passage, and it fails to show Luke's purpose to portray the immediacy of salvation and his changes in attitude toward wealth and possessions. In line with Mendez-Moratalla's assertion, my

---

143. Richard C. White, "A Good Word for Zacchaeus," 89–96.

144. Mitchell, "'Zacchaeus Revisited," 163.

145. See above.

146. Mendez-Moratalla, *Paradigm of Conversion*; also see Corbin-Reuschling, "Zacchaeus's Conversion," and Green, *Luke*

focus is on Zacchaeus' changes in attitudes toward wealth and on the question whether Zacchaeus consequently converted when he met Jesus: these two are correlated.

An important question arises: Can we find any evidence of Zacchaeus' conversion? Green, although he is in favor of the theory of conversion, claims that we ought to be cautious in reading this narrative as a "story of conversion" since Luke "mentions nothing of Zacchaeus' need for repentance, act of repentance or faith, nor of Jesus' summons to repentance . . ."[147] It is true that, when going into Zacchaeus' house, Jesus did not make any prior demands for repentance or changes in attitude. Green is correct in arguing that we, at a glance, cannot find Jesus' direct reference to repentance as opposed to Levi's story (Luke 5:32). But there are several inherent indicators of Zacchaeus' repentance in relation to his wrongs.[148]

First, the crux of the matter is how to interpret Zacchaeus' remark in v. 8.[149] Scholars who support his conversion tend to take the word δίδωμι in 19:8 as futurist present, emphasizing immediacy or certainty[150], and thus expressing Zacchaeus' repentance from a former way of life, evidenced through generosity and restitution. Conversely, those who reject the idea of Zacchaeus' conversion maintain that the word δίδωμι might be considered an iterative present, serving as an *apologia* against his critics (19:7) by pointing to his continuous generosity and integrity in contrast to their stereotypical assumptions.[151] To me, the conversion theory is more plausible than the vindication theory, since it is more likely that the word δίδωμι should be interpreted as futurist present. Verse 8 seems to imply Zacchaeus' return from his wrongs, as indicated in Luke 5:27–32;

---

147. Green, *Luke*, 672.

148. This point re-appears in next chapter in connection with other stories.

149. Concerning the meaning of his name, O'Hanlon, "Story of Zacchaeus," 12, holds that Zacchaeus (Hebrew, *Zakkay*, Neh 7:14; 2 Macc 10:19) means "the clean one." It is a thoroughly Jewish name. In contrast to the meaning of his name, his job is considered impure in his society. Here, it seems to me that Luke maximizes his wrongs/exploitations in spite of the meaning of his name.

150. E.g., Wallace, *Greek Grammar*, 535–36; Hamm, "Luke 19:8," 431–37 and his other article, "Zacchaeus Revisited," 248–51; Hays, *Luke's Wealth Ethics*, 178; cf. Tannehill, "Story of Zacchaeus," 203–10; Nolland, *Luke*, 3:906; Parsons, "Short in Stature," 57.

151. E.g., Fitzmyer, *Luke*, 2:1120–22; Mitchell, "Zacchaeus Revisited," 19–32; Gerard, "Les riches dans la communauté lucanienne," 98–101; Marshall, *Luke: Historian and Theologian*, 681.

15:1–32.¹⁵² That is, the three accounts focus on a lost sinner. For instance, as in the story of Levi (5:31), the mission of Jesus is summarized in 19:10 ("For the Son of Man came to seek out and to save the lost"). This verse re-affirms that Zacchaeus defrauded others by using his position. Jesus' understanding of Zacchaeus as the lost (v. 10) corresponds to people's identification of him as a sinner (v. 7).¹⁵³ Both Jesus and the people were aware that he was a sinner as well as a chief tax collector.¹⁵⁴ In connection with Zacchaeus' remark in v. 8, Luke's Jesus is also critical of his unjustly gained wealth by regarding him as the lost.¹⁵⁵

Second, Zacchaeus' encounter with Jesus functions symbolically as repentance. Mendez-Moratalla, arguing that the story of Zacchaeus does contain evidence of conversion, defines conversion "as starting with divine initiative and the desire to seek Jesus resulting in a life-changing encounter."¹⁵⁶ He goes on to maintain that this life-changing encounter provides a clue to the question of how Zacchaeus obtained his wealth and what he resolved to do with it in the future.¹⁵⁷ What we can know from the story is that Luke seems to emphasize Zacchaeus' eagerness and immediate response to Jesus as he ran ahead and climbed a tree to see him (Luke 19:4).¹⁵⁸ Also, Luke reports that, when Jesus called him, 'he

---

152. Hamm, "Luke 19:8," 436–37; Petracca, *Gott order das Geld*, 227.

153. *Contra.* White, "A Good Word," 89, argues that the theory of conversion is "overly dependent upon the final comment in which Luke tells us the meaning of the story."

154. *Contra.* White, "A Good Word," 91, asserts that Zacchaeus does not defer to Jesus' power and beg divine aid. (see Luke 9:37; 17:13; 18:13) His saying "I give half . . . I repay fourfold" implies confession and petition. He, "A Good Word," 91, goes on to argue that "it speaks only of restitution, and not (as is typical of forgiveness accounts) of confession and petition."

155. Cf. O'Hanlon, "Story of Zacchaeus," 18, relates this verse with the messianic shepherd of Ezekiel: "I will seek the lost, and I will bring back the strayed, and I will bind up the crippled, and I will strengthen the weak" (Ezek 34:16; also see Luke 15:4).

156. Mendez-Moratalla, *Paradigm of Conversion*, 159; according to Green, *Luke*, 672, "Zacchaeus joins the growing rolls of persons whose 'repentance' lies outside the narrative, who appear on the margins of the people of God, and yet who possess insight into and a commitment to the values of Jesus' mission that are exemplary." In a similar line, Corbin-Reuschling, "Zacchaeus's Conversion," 78, claims that Zacchaeus had "an encounter with Jesus that elicited a response that could be interpreted as repentance; and with the result of the inclusion of Zacchaeus into the people of God." Also see Ch. 4.

157. Mendez-Moratalla, *Paradigm of Conversion*, 160–78.

158. Cf. Tannehill, *Narrative Unity*, 1:122.

hurried down and was happy to welcome him' (Luke 19:6). His immediate response symbolizes his repentance, which evidences his wrongs as a chief tax collector. Hays rightly points out, "His behavior evokes the dramatic commitment of Levi, Peter, James, and John, and contrasts with the failings of the would-be disciples (Luke 9:57–62) and the Rich Ruler (Luke 18:23)."[159] Besides, after welcoming Jesus in his place, something changed for Zacchaeus. His giving back of unjustly obtained possessions could be regarded as an act of repentance for past actions which would have implications for any future actions related to the obtaining and use of wealth and possessions.[160] This means that, after acknowledging Jesus as Lord (Luke 19:8), he sought to make things right by rectifying the economic wrongs he had done.[161] In this respect, Corbin-Reuschling defines conversion as "an ongoing socialization and formation by and into a Christian narrative for all dimensions of life."[162] His definition of conversion seems to highlight the aspect of social value or morality in relation to one's occupation. Likewise, O'Hanlon underscores that "[it] is packed with language and moral theology that is typically Lukan."[163] It is therefore highly possible that Zacchaeus experienced a profound change in attitude and behavior after his encounter with Jesus.[164]

Third, we need to take a look at the Greek word, σήμερον ("today"), twice in vv. 5 and 9.[165] Even though the word is not exclusively a Lukan word,[166] it is important to note that the word "today" can function as an indicator of Zacchaeus' wrongdoings in relation to his job.[167] Right

---

159. Hays, *Luke's Wealth Ethics*, 176. As Hays (178) correctly argues, "In contrast the Rich Ruler, Zacchaeus becomes a positive behavioral exemplar."

160. Mendez-Moratalla, *Paradigm of Conversion*, 160–78.

161. On the contrary, White, "A Good Word," 91, argues Zacchaeus' addressing Jesus as "Lord" should be seen as "petition," not as repentance. He goes on to claim that Zacchaeus "does so in reaction to the crowd's accusing him, rather than as a spontaneous response to Jesus' presence and the awareness of his sin." For White, he does not patently ask for forgiveness; he does not appeal to Jesus.

162. Corbin-Reuschling, "Zacchaeus's Conversion," 80.

163. O'Hanlon, "Story of Zacchaeus," 2.

164. Corbin-Reuschling, "Zacchaeus's Conversion," 74.

165. According to Loewe, "Towards an Interpretation," 326, v. 9 recalls the angel's message to the shepherds: "to you is born this day (σήμερον) in the city of David a Savior, who is the Messiah, the Lord" (2:11).

166. It occurs eight times in Matthew, once in Mark and twenty times in Luke–Acts (eleven times in Luke) and eight times in Hebrews.

167. See Hamm, "Luke 19:8," 431–37; and Tannehill, "Story of Zacchaeus," 203.

after Zacchaeus' remark in v. 8, Jesus declares, "*Today* (σήμερον) salvation has come to this house, because he too is a son of Abraham" (v. 9). By adding the word 'today' into the sentence, it seems to highlight that Zacchaeus did not receive salvation from his exploitation relating to his job until he met Jesus.[168] In Luke's Gospel, the term σήμερον often "heightens the immediacy of the salvation which becomes effectively present with Jesus."[169] For example, in Luke 23:43 Luke uses the word when Jesus promises the criminal crucified with him: "*today* (σήμερον) you will be with me in Paradise." Thus, Zacchaeus' encounter with Jesus led him immediately to change his attitudes toward wealth so that he gave up such wealth which had been accumulated through his extortion.

Lastly, let us focus on Zacchaeus' physical description. In contrast to his identity as an important citizen (a chief tax collector) from the perspective of Rome, Luke describes Zacchaeus as the one who is short in stature in 19:3 (τῇ ἡλικίᾳ μικρὸς ἦν). He is the only evangelist who refers to one's stature in a non-metaphorical physical sense.[170] Along with Luke's description of Zacchaeus' occupation and riches (19:2), such a physical description is of high significance. Why does Luke describe that Zacchaeus is short in stature? One of the plausible and straightforward reasons could be that Luke's mention of his physical stature is somewhat linked to his subsequent action of climbing a sycamore tree in order to see Jesus. But this assumption is not helpful in analyzing Luke's reference to Zacchaeus' stature in relation to his occupational wrongs.

Some scholars have attempted to analyze why Luke refers to Zacchaeus' physical description. Among them, Fitzmyer maintains that "small in stature" is "a mere physical description of the man. We are not to conclude from the episode that Zacchaeus finds real 'stature' through the welcome extended him by Jesus. The Greek ἡλικίᾳ nowhere bears the connotation that the English word has in that understanding."[171] On the contrary, Nolland states that Luke's reference to Zacchaeus' 'littleness in the eyes of others' is to be considered "more than physical."[172] In a

---

168. Marshall, *Luke: Historian*, 697, asserts that σήμερον should be taken quite literally in v. 5. At the same time, he cautions that "it may convey the idea that the time has come for the fulfillment of God's plan of salvation" not only in view of 19:9 but also in view of the Lukan usage as a whole.

169. Loewe, "Towards an Interpretation," 325.

170. See Luke 2:52 and, for a didactic usage, 12:25; cf. Matt 6:27.

171. Fitzmyer, *Luke*, 2:1223.

172. Nolland, *Luke*, 3:905.

different way, Green, acknowledging some significance of the reference, asserts that ἡλικίᾳ in 19:3 is "better represented with a reference not to his shortness of stature but to his relative youth."[173] But we cannot find any source indicating that the reference involves his relative youth in the account itself. Rather, it should be analyzed in what ways the physical descriptions function in the ancient writings in connection with Zacchaeus' occupation and his economic wrongs.

Mikeal C. Parsons' analysis of the ancient rhetoric is helpful in identifying Zacchaeus' characterisation. His book, *Luke: Storyteller, Interpreter, Evangelist*, underscores the importance of physical description in the ancient world.[174] Emphasizing Luke's rhetorical skills as a writer, Parsons holds that the rhetorical tradition which Luke uses is familiar with his audience, living in the Roman Empire in the first century. Among the Lukan rhetorical skills, he strongly argues that the "physiognomic consciousness" is clearly inscribed in Luke's writings.[175]

Given that "Luke and his audience lived in a world in which it was commonplace to associate outer physical characteristics with inner qualities," according to Parsons, "the study of the relationship between the physical and the moral was known as 'physiognomics' and was widely practiced in late antiquity by philosophers, astrologers, and physicians."[176] In *Physiognomonica*, it is written:

> The Physiognomist takes his information from movements, shapes, colors, and traits as they appear in the face, from the hair, from the smoothness of the skin, from the voice, from the appearance of the flesh, from the limbs, and from the entire stature of the body.[177]

---

173. Green, *Luke*, 669.

174. Parsons, *Luke*; the same point is also made in his article and book, "Short in Stature," 50–57; *Body and Character*.

175. Parsons, *Luke*, 63. Parsons' study is based partly upon the early analysis of Evans, "Physiognomics in the Ancient World," 5–101, highlighting a widespread use of physiognomy in the Greco-Roman world. For the pervasiveness of physiognomy in the ancient world, see a third-century BC document, *Physiognomonica*, *On Physiognomy*, a work by the second-century AD rhetorician Polemo of Laodicea, two later documents from the fourth century CE, *Physiognomonica* by Adamantius the sophist, and an anonymous Latin handbook, *de Physiognomonica*.

176. Parsons, "Short in Stature," 51.

177. *Physiogn*. 806a, quoted in Parsons, "Short in Stature," 51. Parsons' suggestion is that "Luke's knowledge of the rhetorical devices" is "drawn primarily from the *progymnasmata* of Aelius Theon of Alexandria (50–100 AD), the only textbook roughly

In the ancient world, the physical descriptions contained, to some extent, a person's information. Parsons maintains that "smallness in physical stature was generally seen in physiognomic terms as reflective of 'smallness in spirit,'" by taking an example of Pseudo-Aristotle: "These are the marks of a small-minded person. He is small-limbed, small and round, dry, with small eyes and a small face, like a Corinthian or Leucadian" (*Physiogn.* 808a.30).[178] In doing so, Parsons connects Zacchaeus' smallness of physical stature with his small-mindedness.[179] As mentioned, Zacchaeus' occupation had a negative impression among people due to nationalistic and religious reasons and, more importantly, due to his extortion. Relating to his occupation, Parson draws a conclusion that Zacchaeus' smallness should be interpreted first as his "small-mindedness," and second as his "greediness."[180] On the basis of Parsons' physiognomic analysis, I wish to heighten "greediness," first because it is consistent, to a large extent, with my argument that Zacchaeus was viewed negatively, and second because he accumulated his wealth at the expense of others.[181] His greediness for riches through exploitation makes him a sinner. It is clear that Luke, along with the portrayal of his occupation and riches, depicts Zacchaeus in a negative tone by using the expression, τῇ ἡλικίᾳ μικρὸς ἦν. As with the case of Levi, Zacchaeus' wrongs were corrected by Jesus, not by the emperor's moral *auctoritas*.

Summary

This chapter has examined the extent to which Luke can be shown as comparing Jesus to the emperor (as seen in Luke's parallelism between Jesus and John) on the topic of taxes. Luke draws special attention to the

---

contemporary to Luke" (*Luke*, 19).

178. Parsons, "Short in Stature," 53; he contrasts this smallness with "greatness of soul" of great physical stature (cf. Aristotle, *Eth. nic.* 4.3.1123b.7; 4.8.1128a.8–13).

179. Parsons, "Short in Stature," 53.

180. Ibid.

181. In spite of Parsons' helpful analysis, he pays little attention to relating the physical description of Zacchaeus to Luke's critique of his morality. Although he rightly asserts that Zacchaeus is a sinner on the basis of his occupation and that the physiognomic analysis provides a valuable clue to a person's inner state in the Greco-Roman world, he does not take into account Zacchaeus' corruption in relation to the Roman taxation system and the emperor's emphasis on morality. Moreover, he ignores why Zacchaeus is viewed as a sinner in a concrete way.

tax-related issues through Jesus' birth, teaching, and trial, in Luke 2:1:2, 20:19–26, and 23:3, respectively. Such accounts implicitly heighten Luke's intention that tax was inseparable from the Roman power. In this regard, it is very important to distinguish Augustus' *imperium* and moral *auctoritas* although it is not easy to draw a clear distinction between them. *Imperium* was more concerned about his command of military force or about his governmental power, while his *auctoritas*, which sometimes helps to enhance his *imperium*, is based more upon his moral and social values.

Luke works within a wide frame of reference where there might be some implicit implication of the emperor's moral authority, though this is not explicitly mentioned in his Gospel. Luke implicitly blames the emperor's role as a supreme supervisor of morals through various accounts, while stressing that Jesus did not forbid the tribute itself. For Luke, corruption or abuse by tax-collectors can be explained in terms of a failure of the emperor's moral *auctoritas*. I have taken two examples which signify tax collectors' extortion: both Levi and Zacchaeus were rich. Luke regards both as sinners because they accumulated their wealth at the expense of others. He hints at Zacchaeus' extortion in more detail than that of Levi by describing him in three ways: he was a chief tax collector, he was wealthy, and he was small in stature. For Luke, all these three elements function as representing Zacchaeus' immorality under the Roman taxation system. What is noticeable is that Luke takes two examples (Levi and Zacchaeus) in order implicitly to stress the emperor's failure to correct their prior extortion, which finally contrasts with Jesus' successful correction. It is therefore implied that, while the emperor's moral *auctoritas* is devalued, Jesus' authority is heightened through Luke's tax accounts.

3

Benefactor: Who is Greater?

A dispute also arose among them as to which one of them was to be regarded as the greatest. But he said to them, 'The kings of the Gentiles lord it over them; and those in authority over them are called benefactors. But not so with you; rather the greatest among you must become like the youngest, and the leader like one who serves. For who is greater, the one who is at the table or the one who serves? Is it not the one at the table? But I am among you as one who serves' (Luke 22:24-27; 24Ἐγένετο δὲ καὶ φιλονεικία ἐν αὐτοῖς, τὸ τίς αὐτῶν δοκεῖ εἶναι μείζων. 25ὁ δὲ εἶπεν αὐτοῖς, Οἱ βασιλεῖς τῶν ἐθνῶν κυριεύουσιν αὐτῶν καὶ οἱ ἐξουσιάζοντες αὐτῶν εὐεργέται καλοῦνται. 26ὑμεῖς δὲ οὐχ οὕτως, ἀλλ' ὁ μείζων ἐν ὑμῖν γινέσθω ὡς ὁ νεώτερος, καὶ ὁ ἡγούμενος ὡς ὁ διακονῶν. 27τίς γὰρ μείζων, ὁ ἀνακείμενος ἢ ὁ διακονῶν; οὐχὶ ὁ ἀνακείμενος; ἐγὼ δὲ ἐν μέσῳ ὑμῶν εἰμι ὡς ὁ διακονῶν.)

IN THE PREVIOUS CHAPTER, we discussed Luke's emphasis on Jesus' superiority over the emperor's moral *auctoritas* through his accounts of tax collectors. Likewise, this chapter deals with Luke's depiction of Jesus' authority in comparison with the pagan kings' authority. In other words, it will focus on the question of how far the former is different from the latter. This will be analyzed on the basis of the title "benefactor" expressed in Luke 22:24-27.[1] It is highly important to look into this passage because Luke here seems to heighten Jesus' authority in comparison with that of the emperor. This chapter will also help understand another title "savior," which will be discussed in Chapter 4. I will challenge two contrasting views on the interpretation of Luke 22:24-27. In doing so, I will suggest

---

1. See par. Mark 10:41-45; Matt 20:24-28. But Luke is the only evangelist who refers to the dispute (φιλονεικία) over greatness among Jesus' disciples at the Last Supper. On the brief discussion of the usage of φιλονεικία both in the New Testament (1 Cor. 11:16) and in classical literature, see Nelson, "Flow of Thought," 121-22.

a new and more plausible interpretation based upon Luke's emphasis on Jesus' superiority over the emperor.

We can find two significant titles, king (βασιλεύς) and benefactor (εὐεργέτης), in Luke 22:24–27. It has been often interpreted that these two titles should be treated as one. As a result, this approach has led some scholars to draw the conclusion either that Luke critiques both benefactor-client relations and the pagan kings, or that he has a positive stance towards both. However, both claims fail to explicate Luke's way of highlighting Jesus' authority in connection with the Roman emperor. Such claims cannot explain why Luke intends to show that Jesus' authority is far greater than that of the pagan kings. Even though kings are often spoken of in the language of benefaction, it does not necessarily mean that benefactor is a synonym for king. We do not need to take the two titles as one; rather, we have to deal with them separately. Thus, we shall examine two titles individually in order to better understand Luke's attitude towards them in the context of the Roman Empire.

In order to decipher Luke's intention to critique the emperor's title as well as the authority which the title bears, it is necessary to investigate whether Luke's phrase, "the kings of the Gentiles" (v. 25; οἱ βασιλεῖς τῶν ἐθνῶν), includes the Roman emperor. In addition, how does Luke interpret the pagan kings' authority? I will explore the term 'benefactor' in association with the theme of authority to determine if Luke has a favorable attitude towards the title. To put it differently, given the assumption that he lives and writes under the Greco-Roman influence of the patron/benefactor-client relations, I will explore whether the relations influence Luke's view on the title "benefactor" negatively or positively. This will be answered in the light of the scrutiny of the ancient writers' understanding of ideal kings. In this regard, I have a further question. What are the main criteria for a true benefactor or an ideal king? This question will help us to analyze Luke's attitude towards the pagan kings called benefactors. Finally, I will focus briefly on the issue of authority which the title, benefactor, bears in connection with another title, savior.

The Identity of the Kings of the Gentiles

Let us first investigate the identity of the pagan kings. As discussed in the trial scene, there are contrasting views among scholars: on the one hand, some assert that Luke has a favorable stance towards the Roman Empire;

others, on the other hand, argue that he is very critical of the empire. Likewise, the account in Luke 22:24-27, in general, has been understood in relation to two different views on Luke's depiction of the Roman Empire. It is essential to define the identity of the pagan kings before moving on to explore the differences between Jesus' authority and the emperor's authority.

Christopher Bryan maintains that the account has nothing to do with anti-Roman attitude in particular, but it shows a general critique of pagan kings' abuse of their authority.[2] For him, Luke in this account does not portray the Roman emperor in an unfavorable sense. However, Bryan's idea that Jesus' teaching in 22:24-27 does not display Luke's anti-Roman attitude should be criticized for several reasons. First and foremost, a key question is whether the Roman emperor belongs to Luke's grouping of "the kings of the Gentiles (οἱ βασιλεῖς τῶν ἐθνῶν)" at v. 25. This question aids us to analyze his attitude towards the emperor. S. P. Freyne, attempting to identify who the kings of the Gentiles are, draws the conclusion that Luke intends to criticize, in particular, Herod Antipas because of his luxurious way of life and his elitist circle expressed in Luke 7:24-28.[3] Although Freyne's assertion that Luke's criticism is targeted at Herod Antipas is not completely incorrect, we need to consider other figures or groups whom Luke critiques through his account of Jesus' teaching. As Seyoon Kim rightly points out, it is almost impossible to assume that the phrase "the kings of the Gentiles" refers only to Herod Antipas simply because the phrase is used in a plural term (οἱ βασιλεῖς τῶν ἐθνῶν).[4] That is to say, it is more likely that Luke's criticism is targeted at Herod Antipas as well as other pagan rulers.

Then, who are the other pagan kings? Along with Luke's contrast between Jesus and the emperor in other places of Luke's Gospel, Kim asserts that Luke's criticism of the kings of the Gentiles includes the Roman emperor.[5] At least, there is no reason to remove the Roman emperor from

---

2. Bryan, *Render to Caesar*, 101.

3. Freyne, *Jesus, a Jewish Galilean*, 144–47.

4. Kim, *Christ and Caesar*, 90 n18; cf. Wengst, *Pax Romana*, 55–57. It seems probable that Herod Antipas would not have been pleased at being described as a pagan king because he saw himself as Jewish. But what should be noted is how Luke understands him on a literary level. For me, Luke describes him as a Gentile ruler because of his co-operation with the Roman power, or, at least, as a representative of the Roman power on the basis of Luke 3:1.

5. Kim, *Christ and Caesar*, 89, understands two accounts (Luke 2:1–4; 3:1–22) as Luke's contrast between Jesus and the emperor.

the grouping of the pagan kings. An important clue to the identity of the group is evident in Luke 3:1:

> In the fifteenth year of the reign of Emperor Tiberius, when Pontius Pilate was governor of Judea, and Herod was ruler of Galilee, and his brother Philip ruler of the region of Ituraea and Trachonitis, and Lysanias ruler of Abilene (Ἐν ἔτει δὲ πεντεκαιδεκάτῳ τῆς ἡγεμονίας Τιβερίου Καίσαρος, ἡγεμονεύοντος Ποντίου Πιλάτου τῆς Ἰουδαίας, καὶ τετρααρχοῦντος τῆς Γαλιλαίας Ἡρῴδου, Φιλίππου δὲ τοῦ ἀδελφοῦ αὐτοῦ τετρααρχοῦντος τῆς Ἰτουραίας καὶ Τραχωνίτιδος χώρας, καὶ Λυσανίου τῆς Ἀβιληνῆς τετρααρχοῦντος).

Here, two points are to be made. Concerning the language of βασιλεύς used at 22:25, the term βασιλεύς is not referred to in 3:1. Although it is true that the emperor is not depicted as βασιλεύς but as Καῖσαρ in 3:1, this should not lead us to conclude that Καῖσαρ in Luke 3:1 is not related to οἱ βασιλεῖς τῶν ἐθνῶν in 22:25. In Acts 17:7b, the emperor is implicitly expressed as a king: "They are all acting contrary to the decrees of the emperor (τῶν δογμάτων Καίσαρος), saying that there is another king (βασιλέα ἕτερον)." Here, Luke's expression of another king (βασιλέα ἕτερον) implicitly means that the emperor (Καῖσαρ) is also regarded as a king (βασιλεύς). Moreover, the Roman emperor (Καῖσαρ) is expressed as βασιλεύς more clearly in other books of the New Testament. For instance, in 1 Tim 2:2, it is reported: "For kings (βασιλέων) and all who are in high positions, so that we may lead a quiet and peaceful life in all godliness and dignity." Here, there is no reason to exclude the emperor from the grouping of "kings and all who are in high positions." Similarly, the emperor is once again referred to as βασιλεύς in 1 Pet 2:13 and 17: "For the Lord's sake accept the authority of every human institution whether of the emperor (βασιλεῖ) as supreme... Honor everyone. Love the family of believers. Fear God. Honor the emperor (τὸν βασιλέα)." Taken together, it is clear that the emperor (Καῖσαρ) in 3:1 is sometimes expressed by the language of βασιλεύς in the New Testament. That is, there is a strong link between Καῖσαρ and βασιλεύς in terms of the emperor's identity.

Another significant point which should be made is that Luke 3:1 shows a power relation of the Roman Empire. People mentioned in this verse can be understood as rulers who have authority/power given by the emperor, even though not stated directly. It is interesting to note that the emperor is the first person mentioned among the rulers in order to highlight his supreme power compared to other rulers as shown by the

Roman hierarchical system.⁶ As Luke lists the names of the people who have power/authority in Luke 3:1, it is more probable to include the Roman emperor than to exclude him from the grouping of the pagan kings. Thus, both Freyne and Bryan are incorrect. Luke's οἱ βασιλεῖς τῶν ἐθνῶν includes more rulers than Freyne supposes (Herod). Accordingly, Bryan's claim that the account has nothing to do with Luke's critique of the emperor is inconceivable. Luke is clearly critical of the emperor's authority.

Moreover, in order to draw a vivid picture of Luke's critique of the emperor, it is necessary to make a clear distinction between an anti-Roman attitude and an attitude towards an overthrow of the empire. All too often, several interpreters have tended to simply consider the former as the latter without noticing the differences between the two. Among them, Bryan seems to equate anti-Roman attitude with one's attempt to overthrow the imperial regime.⁷ As a consequence, he strongly argues that Luke's account at 22:24–27 is not specifically anti-Roman. He is right in claiming that Luke does not depict Jesus in Luke 22:24–27 as calling for his disciples and his followers to overthrow the Roman Empire. But the problem is that such a view leads him to draw a wrong conclusion that Luke's criticism is not targeted at the Roman emperor. The view of Luke's anti-Roman attitude is not the same as that of his attempt to overthrow the empire. It is incorrect to assume that one's anti-imperial stance is always rooted in his or her intention to remove a government. Thus, the implication of an anti-Roman attitude should not be over-interpreted; that is, Luke's anti-Roman view has nothing to do with his elimination or rejection of the Roman Empire. Even though he does not have Jesus command his disciples to overthrow the empire, Luke portrays the Roman Empire in a very negative light. As discussed in Ch.2, Luke explains that Jesus does not forbid his followers to pay taxes to the emperor although he is critical of tax collectors' extortion, and he contrasts Jesus' successful authority with the emperor's unsuccessful moral *auctoritas*. Moreover, as mentioned, Luke stresses that Jesus' attitude is very different from his contemporary revolutionaries who focus on the overthrow of the empire. For Luke, Jesus' position is not as radical as their outlook. Therefore, the fact that Luke has Jesus critique the Roman Empire (especially, the emperor) does not necessarily mean that he intends to build up an alternative world after overthrowing the current imperial regime. On the basis

---

6. See 1 Pet 2:17 for the emperor's supreme power/authority.
7. Bryan, *Render to Caesar*, 101f.

of Luke's anti-Roman stance, there is no reason to exclude the emperor from the grouping of οἱ βασιλεῖς τῶν ἐθνῶν.

Furthermore, the fact that the emperor belongs to the group is based on the description that the pagan kings are displayed as those who have dominion over their subjects (22:25).[8] According to Luke, these pagan rulers have authority/power to rule over them, and they are called benefactors. When Jesus talks about the greatest in connection with benefactor, it is evident that the emperor is generally expected to be recognized as one of the greatest benefactors among first-century people. The emperor himself advertised his great authority/power to his subjects, for example, through the imperial coins, inscriptions, and the like.[9] As the evidence shows, it is very natural for first-century people to view the emperor, along with other rulers, as having authority with the title "benefactor" when they listen to/read Jesus' teaching in v. 25. Therefore, it is almost impossible to assume that the emperor has been excluded in Luke 22:24–27. Given that Luke is implicitly critical of the emperor's authority in several ways, it is highly likely that the emperor is one of οἱ βασιλεῖς τῶν ἐθνῶν whom Luke has in mind when describing this phrase at 22:25. The pagan kings whom Luke criticizes are clearly inclusive of the Roman emperor.

Luke's Understanding of the Title "Benefactor"

Let us turn to the issue of the title, benefactor, given to the pagan kings in 22:25. What I wish to stress is that the term "benefactor" is related closely to rulers' authority. Prior to the analysis of the issue of rulers' authority, we need to discuss whether or not Luke understands the title, benefactor, in a negative light.

Patron/benefactor-client relations were regarded as one of the most important social constructs in the first-century world. Blok attempts to analyze patronage from the perspective of social science, noting:

> Patronage is a model or analytical construct which the social scientist applies in order to understand and explain a range of apparent different social relationships: God-man, saint-devotee,

8. Kim, *Christ and Caesar*, 90, seems to regard the pagan kings who lord it over their people as those who exercise their authority/power "in service of the devil's intention" on the basis of the temptation story. In other words, for him, Luke understands both the emperor and other pagan rulers exercising "their political authority in the Satanic way and for the Satanic purpose, i.e., for the kingdom of Satan."

9. See Ch.4.

godfather-godchild, lord-vassal, landlord-tenant, politician-voter, professor-student, and so forth.[10]

This system is also associated directly with the theme of authority/power and honor. In general, a patron or a benefactor in the system of hierarchy provides social, economic, and political resources to his or her client reciprocated by the latter's loyalty and honor to the former.[11] Green describes how the emperors attempted to conceptualize and organize the Roman society as a network of overlapping patron-client systems, regarding themselves as supreme benefactors.[12] In other words, according to the Roman hierarchical system, the emperor, placed on the top of the pyramid, is displayed as the greatest benefactor. When we talk about the title, benefactor, it is associated closely with patron-client relations in antiquity as well as with authority/power which the title conveys.[13] Without careful consideration of such relations, it is almost impossible to comprehend the importance of the authority which benefactors normally possess.

---

10. Blok, "Variations in Patronage," 366; see also Harland, *Associations*, 97.

11. For the discussion of the importance of patron-client relations from the perspective of cultural-anthropological analysis, see Blok, "Variations in Patronage"; Schmidt et. al., *Friends, Followers and Factions*; Gellner and Waterbury, eds., *Patrons and Clients*; Eisenstadt and Roniger, *Patron, Clients and Friends*; Moxnes, *Economy of Kingdom*, 40-47 and his article "Patron-Client Relations," 241-268; Elliott, "Patronage and Clientage," 142-56; Malina, "Patron and Client," 143-75; Neyrey, "God, Benefactor and Patron," 465-92; for the historical analysis of benefactor/patron and client relationships in the Greco-Roman world, see Danker, *Benefactor*; Saller, *Personal Patronage*, and his article "Patronage and Friendship," 117-35, esp. 128, describing the importance of loyalty/faithfulness in the patron-client relation; Wallace-Hadrill, *Patronage in Ancient Society*, 1-8.

12. Green, *Theology*, 191-21. Also, he (*Theology*, 191-92) further argues that the patron/benefactor relations were "extended beyond the sphere of humans so as to include the gods" in the empire. For the discussion of the patron/benefactor-client relations between divine benefactor and mortal clients, see Neyrey, "God, Benefactor and Patron," 465-492. In many cases, gods (and God) are expressed as a benefactor in the Roman Empire. In general, the title of God-as-benefactor is examined in the light of various kinds of benefaction. For instance, Philo (*Plant.* 90) calls attention to the benefaction of commitment that God cultivates: "He [God] shall no longer exhibit toward me the masterfulness that characterizes the rule of an autocrat, but the readiness to bless that marks the power that is in every way kindly, and bent on the welfare of men. He shall do away with the fear we feel before Him as Master, and implant in the soul the loyalty and affection that goes out to Him as Benefactor."

13. *Contra.* Winter claims that not all the benefactors are patrons, *Seek the Welfare*, 34-41.

Deissmann, contrasting Jesus' attitude towards the term εὐεργέτης and its common use in the papyri, argues that Jesus "mentioned the title not without contempt, and forbade his disciples to allow themselves to be so called: the name contradicted the idea of service in brotherhood."[14] Much the same point is made by Ahn, focusing on the servant-benefactor model of the Lukan Gospel. He puts it:

> Jesus criticizes both inequality and the reciprocity of the Roman client system. The reason is that Jesus in Luke does not exercise authority to establish his own leadership over people . . . [Luke builds] Jesus' authority against "unclean spirits" (Luke 4:36), "sin" (5:24), all demons (9:1), over all the "power of the enemy" (10:19), over death (12:5) . . . The "servant benefactor" model in Luke cannot be established without destroying the Roman patron-client system. Luke's criticism of the patron-client system would likely be understood as a disapproval of the way the empire is going on.[15]

Ahn therefore sees Luke's account of Jesus' teaching as a critique of the Roman patron-client system.[16] Both Deissmann's and Ahn's views are rooted in the assumption that Luke's Jesus, who is very critical of the empire, considers Roman values purely as evil things. In this respect, they seem to maintain that Luke is not favorable towards the Roman system of patron-client.

There are, however, some problems with their argument. It is less likely that Luke characterizes benefaction in a negative light. It is not true that Jesus is critical of those who offer benefaction to people throughout Luke–Acts. Nor does Luke reject the patron/benefactor-client system itself. Rather, Luke attempts to place the status of Jesus above the emperor by using the title "benefactor" as a positive title, as he does so in the use of the title, savior (see the next chapter). In doing so, Jesus' status is now understood as higher than the emperor's which was once expected to be regarded as the greatest by first-century readers.

More importantly, Luke places much emphasis on Jesus' benefaction to his people. According to Danker, Luke displays "Jesus as the benefactor par excellence" in his Gospel.[17] Throughout Luke–Acts, Luke

14. Deissmann, *Light*, 253–54.
15. Ahn, *Reign of God*, 166–67.
16. Ibid., 205; *contra*. Lull, "Servant-Benefactor," 289–305, and P. W. Walaskay, *"And so We Came": Political Perspective*, 36–37.
17. Danker, *Jesus*, 28; and his other book, *Benefactor*.

strives to depict Jesus, along with God, as a great benefactor.[18] A good example of Luke's positive stance towards the concept of the title is found in Luke 7:1–9. The centurion of Luke 7:1–9 can be seen as a benefactor since he builds the Jewish synagogue in Capernaum.[19] There is no doubt that Luke sees the centurion's benefaction to the Jewish society in a very favorable light.

In addition, the cognates relating to the honorable title "benefactor," such as εὐεργεσία and εὐεργετέω, are also used in a positive sense in Acts. For example, Luke records that the Jewish leaders arrested Peter and John, and that they put them in custody because of their preaching about Jesus (Acts 4:1–12). When their opponents inquired ("By what power or by what name did you do this?" in Acts 4:7), Peter said to them, "if we are questioned today because of a good deed (εὐεργεσίᾳ) done to someone who was sick and are asked how this man has been healed" (Acts 4:9). Also, although it is not directly stated, Barnabas' gift in Acts 4:36–37 can be understood as a way of benefaction to the Christian community: "[Barnabas] sold a field that belonged to him, then brought the money, and laid it at the apostles' feet (v. 37)." Besides, when preaching peace brought by Jesus (εἰρήνην διὰ Ἰησοῦ Χριστοῦ in Acts 10:36), Peter emphasizes Jesus' 'doing good' (εὐεργετῶν) to people (Acts 10:38) in a very favorable sense. What is more, as will be discussed, it is undeniable that Luke portrays Jesus as a great benefactor-savior who offers victory, peace, and salvation to his people. Thus, it is wrong to claim that Luke's stance towards the term εὐεργέτης has a negative connotation.

Another objection against the idea that Luke is very critical of benefactor-client relations is based upon the question as to what exactly he is criticizing if he is not critical of the title itself? In order to answer this question, we have to distinguish between *true* benefactors and *false* benefactors. This distinction helps understand why Luke, who is not in opposition to the benefactor-client relations, draws a negative picture of the rulers who are called benefactors (εὐεργέται καλοῦνται) in Luke 22:25. In other words, what Luke centers on is whether, or not, the pagan kings are the *true* benefactors. The fact that the term itself does not bear any negative implication should not lead us to conclude that Luke is not critical of the pagan kings. Put briefly, Luke aims to critique the false holders of such a title by using it. For him, they are not verified as a true

---

18. E.g., 4:18–19; 6:20–23; 7:22; 9:1–2; 10:17–20; 13:22:30; 19:10; 24:21, 49; Acts 1:8.

19. See Marshall, *Jesus, Patron, and Benefactors*, 235–36.

benefactor; that is, the problem lies in the holders of the title, not in the title itself. Danker argues that Jesus' saying is understood as a criticism "of petty tyrants who like to pass themselves off as benefactors," or, of "rulers who mask their tyranny with a flourish of public works."[20] As he rightly claims, the pagan kings who exercise oppressive power and authority disguise themselves as benefactors.[21] Luke stresses that they are not true benefactors, and that those false benefactors are not eligible to obtain the title "benefactor" through Jesus' saying. Thus, he strives to remove the title from them as a means of degrading their authority which the title bears. As the title was regarded as an honorable one in the ancient world, Luke also uses the title "benefactor" as a very honorable one in his Gospel, and he applies it to Jesus' authority.

Here, what is noticeable is that the theme of authority serves as an important marker for the title. To put it another way, the idea that the pagan kings are false benefactors becomes more evident when exploring the title in terms of the issue of authority. In my view, Luke aims to compare and contrast Jesus with the pagan rulers by illustrating two concepts, namely authority and benefactor. It is necessary to examine them in detail in v. 25: first, the pagan kings have authority (οἱ ἐξουσιάζοντες) to rule over their subjects; and, second, they are *falsely* called benefactors (εὐεργέται καλοῦνται).[22] As can be seen, two parts are interrelated, and accordingly, the verse can be understood as "the pagan kings called benefactors have authority to rule over their subjects." Linking rulers' authority to the title benefactor, Luke seems to attack their false authority to rule the subjects on the grounds of the subsequent verse. He reports that the one who serves is greater than the one who is at the table (the pagan kings) in v. 27.[23] Luke defines their authority as ruling over (κυριεύω)[24]

---

20. Danker, *Benefactor*, 324; see also Nock, *Essays on Religion*, 2:726 n27; *contra*. Lull, "Servant-Benefactor," 290, asserts that the usual negative interpretation of Luke 22:25 is not justified.

21. See Danker, *Jesus*, 222; and Danker, *Benefactor*, 294 and 324.

22. The verb καλοῦνται can be either passive (they are called) or reflexive (they call themselves). Only a few commentators take it to be reflexive. Cf. Plummer, *A Critical and Exegetical Commentary*, 501.

23. In v. 24 (τὸ τίς αὐτῶν δοκεῖ εἶναι μείζων) μείζων technically means "greater," but the context suggests that "greatest" is meant. For a discussion of the use of the comparative form for the superlative, see Turner, *Syntax*, 29.

24. Lull and Clark argues that κυριεύουσιν at v. 25 connotes not harsh or oppressive rule but mere rule. Lull, "Servant-Benefactor," 291 n17 and Clark, *Gentile Bias*, 207–12. Differently, Nelson, "Flow of Thought," 119 n3, argues that "the fact that oppressive

their subjects without caring for them; at the same time, he heightens that one's authority based upon service is far greater than theirs.

A key question should be answered in order to understand Luke's contrast between Jesus and the emperor. What are the criteria for true benefactors from the perspective of Luke? Or, in what ways does Luke's understanding of Jesus' authority sharply contrast with that of the pagan kings? Why does he regard them as false benefactors? According to v. 26, the true benefactors are expressed in the language of ὁ μείζων (the greatest), ὁ νεώτερος (the youngest) and ὁ διακονῶν (the one who serves).[25] Here, my argument centres on the relations between ὁ μείζων and ὁ διακονῶν. With respect to the term ὁ μείζων (the greatest), Luke links it to an authority-related issue on the grounds that the word 'greatest' is useful in the recognition of the title "benefactor" and "king" (βασιλεύς). Nelson, acknowledging the issue of authority in this passage, draws a sharp contrast between the greatest/leader/diner, which he names *Position A* (high status), and the youngest/servant/table-servant, which he names *Position B* (low status), and he argues that "Luke is commending these low-power, lower-status roles in some way."[26] He is correct in maintaining that Luke takes the Gentile rulers as negative examples. However, Nelson's attempt to categorize "greatest" into *Position A* is not conceivable because his categorization cannot explain why humble servants (ὁ διακονῶν) are to be considered great (ὁ μείζων). For me, Luke tries to describe the correct criteria for the greatness, rather than to consider the greatness as anti-thesis for service-oriented benefaction. In other words, Nelson's two contrasting positions should be modified because his analysis fails to understand the correlation between "service" (ὁ διακονῶν) and "greatness" (ὁ μείζων). Luke reports that Jesus in Luke 9:46-48 draws on a child as an example in order to give an answer to his disciples' argument about who among them is greatest (μείζων).[27] He refers to Jesus' saying in Luke 9:48:

---

rule is not in view by no means excludes an allusion to the 'high and mighty' standing of monarchs in antiquity." Even though the term does not connote any oppressive rule, it does not necessarily imply that the rule is based upon service. What Luke seems to underline is not κυριεύω itself, but κυριεύω based upon service. Luke highlights that the pagan rulers' ruling over (κυριεύω) is devoid of διακονέω in contrast to Jesus' authority. See below.

25. For the use of ὁ νεώτερος for those who perform basic service (cf. Acts 5:6, 10), see Marshall, *Luke*, 813.

26. Nelson, "Flow of Thought," 117; see also his monograph, *Leadership and Discipleship*, 117; cf. Rowe, "Luke–Acts and the Imperial Cult," 298–99.

27. See Moxnes, "Patron-Client Relations," 261.

"Whoever welcomes this child in my name welcomes me, and whoever welcomes me welcomes the one who sent me; for the least among all of you is the greatest (μέγας)." Taken with 9:46–48, it is very unlikely that Luke contrasts the greatest (ὁ μείζων) with servant (ὁ διακονῶν) in 22:26. What he stresses is that the true benefactor's greatness (or great authority) is based upon his service.

In terms of the relations between greatness and authority given to benefactors, Heinz Schurmann's view is more plausible than Nelson's categorization. Schurmann points out that the question about who is the greatest is interpreted as a question about how the greatest should behave.[28] In a similar way, as Lull correctly points out (even though mistakenly asserting that Luke opposes the Roman benefactor-client system), "it is better to say that behavior determines who 'the greatest' is."[29] To put it another way, those who have great authority can be determined by their action and behavior, not by the title itself.

In this regard, rulers' authority is considered great when their beneficent behaviors centre on service to their subjects.[30] For instance, Dio Chrysostom stresses what a great king should be like, suggesting that he

28. Schurmann, *Jesu Abschiedsrede*, 67–69.

29. Lull, "Servant-Benefactor," 295; similarly, Moxnes, "Patron-Client Relations," 260–61.

30. I have used several ancient materials from Lull's article. His main view, "Servant-Benefactor," 305, is that Luke–Acts focusing on "embody[ing] the ideal of the 'servant-benefactor,' well-known in the ancient Greco-Roman world." See also Dio (*Or.* 3.73–75; cf. also 3.55 and 81). Lull and Walaskay challenge the view that the "kings" and "those in authority" are presented as an antitype for the disciples, claiming that the rulers are depicted as positive models of "benefactors" worthy of imitation. (Lull, "Servant-Benefactor," 289–305; Walaskay, *"And so We Came,"* 36–37; it is interesting to note that, for both, Luke–Acts presents a generally favorable picture of Roman officials) For Lull, the saying about rulers who are called benefactors does not illustrate a form of "tyranny masked by public works," but the saying describes "an ideal well known in the Greco-Roman world and exemplified in Jesus," who is the "servant-benefactor par excellence." (Lull, "Servant-Benefactor," 295–96 and 303) Although I am in line with Lull's view that there are ideal characteristics of kings in the Roman Empire which also can be seen in Jesus' teaching on service, his argument that 'the pagan kings' are portrayed in a positive tone is not conceivable. Lull fails to distinguish the ideal kings who focus on service from the pagan kings (Luke 22:25) who do not. Dio's description of what the ideal kings should be like does not necessarily mean that the pagan kings in Luke are the ideal kings. It is therefore a mistake to conclude that those pagan kings are automatically interpreted as those who bear the characteristics of the ideal kings that Dio describes. For more critiques, see Moxnes, "Patron-Client Relations," 261; Nelson, "Flow of Thought," 113–23; and Nelson, *Leadership and Discipleship*.

"does not grow weary in ministering to us and doing everything to promote our welfare ... never grows weary in showering these blessing upon us ... endures servitude most exacting" (*Or.* 4.65–66). Dio rejects the idea that a king "exercises general control over human beings and gives them orders without being accountable to them," and he, at the same time, places much emphasis on kings' beneficence/service to their subjects.[31] He further maintains that a king, whose authority is greater than theirs, "must save the multitude of his subjects" on the basis of his beneficence.[32] Thus, Dio depicts an ideal and great king as one who not only exercises his great authority over the greatest number of people, but also exercises "care" for them.[33] His authority therefore signifies his attempt to reduce suffering and to improve the condition that his subjects live in. In contrast to Dio's portrayal of ideal/great rulers, the rulers' authority in Luke 22:24–27 is not rooted in true beneficence from the perspective of Luke.

Furthermore, Dio, contrasting the title "father," relating to a good king, with the title "despot" (*Or.* 1.22), asserts that a king's deeds must demonstrate character that "above all ... takes delight in bestowing benefits- a trait which approaches most nearly to the divine nature" (*Or.* 2.26). When linking Zeus to a great king, Dio notes: "In like manner do the gods act, and especially the great King of Kings, Zeus, who is the common protector and father of men and gods" (*Or.* 2.75; ὁμοίως δὲ καὶ οἱ θεοὶ καὶ ὁ δὴ μέγας βασιλεὺς βασιλέων, ὅτε κηδεμὼν καὶπατὴρ κοινὸς ἀνθρώπων καὶ θεῶν, Ζεύς). Thus, he describes the great king as a protector and father, suggesting the positive governance by benefaction.[34] In Dio's writing, greatness is emphasized in relation to the title of king and his behavior as a king. In a similar manner, when stressing the god's sovereignty and benefaction, Seneca notes:

> You may address this being who is the author of this world of ours by different names; it will be right for you to call him Jupiter Best and Greatest (*Optimum ac Maximum*), and the Thunderer and the Stayer ... Any name you choose will be properly

---

31. *Or.* 56.5; quoted in Lull, "Servant-Benefactor," 304.

32. *Or.* 2:71; quoted in Lull, "Servant-Benefactor," 305.

33. *Or.* 1.15–18; cf. also 3.39; also see Lull's analysis of Dio's description of a good king, "Servant-Benefactor," 297.

34. The title "king" is often expressed in connection with another title "father" in Dio's writing. See Dio, *Or.* 36.35–36. As we discussed, Augustus described himself as the *Pater Patriae*, stressing his great beneficence and his rule. See also D'Angelo, "Abba and 'Father,'" 611–30.

applied to him if it connotes some force that operates in the domain of heaven—his titles may be as countless as are his benefits (*beneficio eius*).³⁵

Also, Cicero's emphasis on the importance of service-related benefaction corresponds to both Dio and Seneca's comprehension of a king's beneficence. He writes:

> We may also observe that a great many people do many things that seem to be inspired more by a spirit of ostentation (*gloria*) than by heart-felt kindness (*ut benefici videantur*); for such people are not really generous but are rather influenced by a sort of ambition to make a show of being open-handed. Such a pose is nearer akin to hypocrisy than to generosity or moral goodness.³⁶

It is clear that the ancient writers, such as Dio, Seneca, and Cicero, describe what the great kings should be like in relation to their benefaction. A similar echo is also evident in the Old Testament. God is frequently portrayed as the one who cares for the weak. As Hays puts it, God is "the ideal King, the defender of the poor and oppressed; the prophet foretold God's redemptive action for the poor."³⁷

Luke's understanding of the true benefactor is not a far cry from that of other ancient writers. For him, the best benefit that Jesus teaches is to serve others (even his enemies without the use of coercive power- see the next chapter), rather than simply to rule over them. In this sense, Luke underscores that Jesus' authority whose benefaction is rooted in service is far greater than the pagan kings who lack "meaningful beneficence" because Jesus' beneficence "derives from a service oriented frame of mind," such as caring for their subjects and service-based benefaction.³⁸ In other words, what Luke has in mind is that his categorization of the pagan kings is not the same as ideal kings, since the so-called benefaction provided by them in v. 25 is not inspired by "heart-felt kindness."³⁹ In Luke's view, they are not eligible to be called true benefactors. Thus,

---

35. Seneca, *Benefits* 4.7.1.

36. Cicero, *Duties*, 1.44.

37. Hays, *Luke's Wealth Ethics*, 108, who also holds that in the Psalms particularly the poor become a rhetorical foil to the wicked rich, ciphers for righteous people. (108–9); see also Nolland, *Luke*, 1:89 and 282.

38. Danker, *Benefactor*, 324; also see below, for the greatness of altruistic beneficence.

39. For the phrase of "heart-felt kindness," see Cicero, *Duties*, 1.44.

Luke implicitly degrades their authority by re-defining them as pseudo-benefactors, as he regards the emperor as a false savior in Ch. 4. Without meaningful beneficence, their authority is not considered great, and they, accordingly, cannot be regarded as true benefactors.

In Luke–Acts, there are several examples which show the importance of a service-oriented mind in relation to the issue of authority. In Luke's unique parable of the Pharisee and the tax collectors, Jesus says, "for all who exalt themselves will be humbled, but all who humble themselves will be exalted" (Luke 18:9–14). For me, this verse implies that those who do not know how to serve, their authority will be humbled or devalued. This is consistent with the parable of the wedding banquet at Luke 14:7–11, where Jesus charges both Pharisees and scribes with choosing the best seats at the table. A similar example is found in Luke 11:43. Luke has Jesus criticize the Pharisees' love of seats of honor since they neglect God's love and justice (11:42), saying, "Woe to you Pharisees! For you love to have the seat of honor in the synagogues and to be greeted with respect in the market-places" (Luke 11:43).[40] Concerning the table places, Jesus tells his disciples to sit down at the lowest place so that their honor/authority might be exalted. The same point is made in Acts 6:1—7:60 that the "deacons" are commissioned to "serve" at tables to follow Jesus' example.[41] It is evident that Luke interprets the serving of others by humbling oneself as a way of elaborating one's authority. Thus, Luke rejects the idea that the pagan rulers are great, and accordingly, their authority which their title "benefactor" bears is to be removed or, at least, to be devalued.

Luke's focus on service-oriented benefaction can be also explained with the help of the characterizations of benefactor-client relations. Some scholars (e.g., Ahn), maintaining that Luke is critical of the Roman benefactor-client system, tend to draw little attention to its characteristics. On the basis of the previous scholarship, Neyrey notes that benefactor-client relations have several characteristics: asymmetrical relationship, simultaneous exchange of different types of resources, interpersonal obligation,

---

40. Similarly, Hays, *Luke's Wealth Ethics*, 181, claims that Luke's Jesus has a critical view on the garments by which the scribes show off their status, since the term στολαῖς often refers to longer gowns typical of higher status (cf. Luke 15:22; Rev. 6:11). See also Nolland, *Luke*, 3:976; Fitzmyer, *Luke*, 2:1318. On the correlation between garment length and social class, see Hamel, *Poverty and Charity*, 78.

41. Burridge, *Imitating Jesus*, 271.

favoritism, reciprocity, patron as father, and honor.⁴² Among these characteristics, I wish to highlight "reciprocity" since it is helpful in decoding Luke's emphasis on service.

Marshall Sahlins' view, rooted in the patron/benefactor-client relations, strives to categorize the types of reciprocity in antiquity, asserting that there are three kinds of reciprocity: "generalized reciprocity" (the solidarity extreme), "balanced reciprocity" (the midpoint), "negative reciprocity" (the unsocial extreme).⁴³ Among these different types of reciprocity, negative reciprocity is important for the comprehension of Luke's critique of the false benefactors in vv. 24–27. For Luke, the pagan kings, including the Roman emperor, who are called benefactors, seek self-interest at the expense of others.⁴⁴ As Brunt stresses, men of rank and wealth celebrated an empire "that maintained peace, peace which brought most benefits to those who with most to lose, and secured them in their property and local dominance."⁴⁵ The pagan kings at 22:25 pretend to be true benefactors, but Luke argues that their reciprocity is rooted deeply in exploitive nature by "concealing the rapacity of the ruling class and naturalizing fundamentally unequal relations through routines of highly theatrical reciprocity."⁴⁶ Due to their negative reciprocity (self-interest) not based upon service, they are not eligible to be called true benefactors; that is, they are not ideal benefactors. In contrast to Cicero's emphasis on justice, which "instructs us to spare all men, to consider the interests of the whole human race" (*Rep.* 3.15), the pagan kings fail to provide generalized reciprocity. From Luke's perspective, the ideology of the emperor's benefaction is characterized as negative reciprocity.

Conversely, Luke focuses Jesus' benefaction on generalized reciprocity rooted in service. Seneca, in line with Luke, stresses that divine benefaction is altruistic, claiming:

> God seeks no servants. He himself does service to mankind, everywhere and to all he is at hand to help ... a man will never make sufficient progress until he has conceived a right idea of God- regarding Him as one who possesses all things, and allots

---

42. For the detailed explanation of these characteristics, see Neyrey, "God, Benefactor," 467–68.

43. Sahlins, *Stone-Age Economics*, 185–230.

44. See Neyrey, "God, Benefactor," 469; cf. Luke 10:30 and 19:22.

45. Brunt, *Roman Imperial Themes*, 272–73.

46. Elliott, *Arrogance of Nations*,.29, but he does pay little attention to aspects of benefactor-client system.

all things, and bestows them without price. And what reasons have the gods for doing deeds of kindness? It is their nature.[47]

Again, Jesus in Luke does not seek servants whom he intends to rule over; rather, he is ready to serve his people. Therefore, in contrast with the pagan kings, Luke emphasizes 'generalized reciprocity' which connotes "altruistic interactions."[48] A good example of Jesus' altruistic interaction can be found here in Luke 22:24–27 and in the story of enemy love (Luke 6:27–38). As will be seen, Jesus does not command his disciples to give back negative reciprocity to their enemies, but he commands them to love their enemies. Jesus' altruistic interaction based upon love is expressed in serving others.[49] When the two accounts are taken together, it can be concluded that Jesus' reciprocal interaction even with enemies is rooted in his altruistic motivation. Thus, Luke seeks to describe Jesus as a true benefactor, who is greatest as opposed to the pagan kings, pseudo-benefactors.

Benefactor and Savior

Along with the title of king discussed earlier, other titles relating to benefactor provide clues to understanding the authority which they bear. As Neyrey rightly suggests, there were many synonyms for benefactor in antiquity.[50] Among the significant titles expressive of benefaction, the title "savior" had various meanings in antiquity.

In general, as Neyrey puts it, a savior is considered as the one who "rescues another from danger and peril, such as war, illness, judicial condemnation, floods and famines," who "protects and preserves the polis and its citizens," "inaugurates a golden age," and who "benefits others."[51] The holder of the title "savior" plays a role as a benefactor as well. The emperor, who is portrayed as savior, is also depicted as a benefactor who

47. *Ep.* 95.48–49; cf. Philo, *Plant.* 130.

48. Here I borrowed the term "altruistic interaction" from Neyrey, "God, Benefactor," 469.

49. See also 1 Pet 4:8–10, where the relation between love and service is emphasized: "Above all, maintain constant love (ἀγάπην) for one another, for love (ἀγάπη) covers a multitude of sins. Be hospitable to one another without complaining. Like good stewards of the manifold grace of God, serve (διακονοῦντες) one another with whatever gift each of you has received."

50. Neyrey, "God, Benefactor," 471.

51. Ibid., 472; for the detailed discussion, see the next chapter on Savior.

brought benefaction, such as victory and peace, to his subjects.[52] Plutarch relates the title "benefactor" to "savior," saying that "other persons publicly styled themselves Benefactor (Εὐεργέτας), Conquerors, Saviors (Σωτῆρας) or the Great (Μεγάλους)."[53] It is clear that the title "benefactor" is used as a synonym for another title "savior." In this respect, when talking about the pagan kings called benefactors at v. 25, we need to explore whether they are true saviors. As Luke strives to portray the emperor as a pseudo-savior,[54] he tells us that the kings of the Gentiles, including the Roman emperor, are false benefactors in Luke 22:24–27. That is, the same principle is applied: as Luke attempts to depict Jesus (Luke 2:11) as a true σωτὴρ, he also sees him as a true benefactor.

Moreover, as the title "savior" signifies a person's authority, the title "benefactor" bears a holder's authority and power.[55] Danker, who collects and analyses the ancient inscriptions, argues that honor and authority were given to benefactors/saviors.[56] Among the mortals, the emperor and rulers are placed on the top of the hierarchy, as their powers are extended to their territory and their subjects. As indicated in v. 25, the kings of the Gentiles called benefactors have authority/power to exercise rule over their subjects. Again, I read the account in Luke 22:24–27 as Luke's implicit critique of the pagan kings, especially the Roman emperor at the top of hierarchy. Thus, I argue that the dispute about the greatest can be interpreted as a sort of competition of authority/power between pagan

---

52. See the next chapter.

53. Plutarch, *On the Fortune of Alexander* 338C; see also Polybius, *Hist.* 9.36.5; for immortals, see Philo, *Leg. All.* 2.57; 3.137; *Spec. Leg.* 1.300; *Leg. Gai.* 118; and *Dec.* 41; Josephus, *War* 3.9.8, 459; *War* 7.4.1, 70–71; see also Nock, "Soter and Euergetes," 2:720–735.

54. On the discussion of how Luke re-defines the emperor as a pseudo-savior, see Ch. 4.

55. It is also associated with the theme of honor and shame. An aim of the systematic pattern of benefaction is to obtain honor (*philotimia*) and to avoid shame (*aischyne*), which were central cultural values in the ancient world; see Malina, *New Testament World*; Elliott, *What is Social-Scientific Criticism* and his essay, "Disgraced Yet Graced," 166–78; similarly, Harland, *Associations*, 98, argues, "shame might be viewed as analogous to impiety (*asebeia*) toward the gods (the ultimate benefactors)"; cf. Dio, *Or.* 31.57, 65, 80–1, 157.

56. Danker, *Benefactor*; see also Hands, *Charities and Social Aid*, 175–209; Lucian, *Apology* 13, "the king's most important reward is praise, universal fame, reverence for his benefactions, statues and temples and shrines bestowed on him by his subjects -all these are payment for the thought and care which such men evidence in their continual watch over the common weal and its improvement."

kings and Jesus through benefaction in Luke. In antiquity, the one who provided the most and best benefits was considered the *greatest*. For instance, Seneca speaks of a sort of authority-contest existent in the ancient world, characterizing it as the "most honorable rivalry in outdoing benefits by benefits."[57] Similarly, Plutarch, hinting at the authority-contest, reports that Mark Antony in 41 BC was praised as Διόνυσος χαριδότης and μειλίχιος (Joy-giver and Gracious) in Asia, especially at Ephesus and that he and his wife Octavia were later acclaimed as "divine benefactors."[58] After achieving victory over him, Octavian took over Antony's title and authority together from the east. This tells us that the victor can take over both the loser's title and authority. This is like a challenge-response game: the winner takes all or defends his honor/authority. The victor, Octavian, not only defended his authority, but also took over Antony's authority. On the basis of this game, Luke's critique of the pagan kings can be seen as Jesus' challenge by re-defining them as false benefactors in order to take their title and authority. As seen above, the emperor fails to correct tax collectors' immorality, and his benefaction, not based upon a service-oriented mind, is limited mainly to the elite class. According to Harland, "failure of the upper classes to provide appropriate benefactions was a threat to the position and status they strove to maintain within society."[59] The emperor's failure as savior and benefactor becomes the threat to his authority. Through the contest, Luke stresses that Jesus achieves victory over the kings and the emperor, since they are not inspired by service-oriented benefaction, but by their self-interest. Even though there is no direct contact between Jesus and the emperor in Luke–Acts, the readers/hearers probably have in mind Luke's conclusion that the one who serves is the greatest in v. 27 in connection with Jesus' victory over the emperor and other rulers.

Summary

The account in Luke 22:24–27 echoes the theme of Luke's implicit critique of the emperor's authority in the earlier chapters. Through his assessment of the emperor's authority, Luke also heightens Jesus' superiority

---

57. Seneca, *Benefits* 1.4.4; see Isocrates 1.26; see also Hands, *Charities and Social Aid*, 31.

58. Plutarch, *Antony.*, 24.3; 26.5; 60.4–5; Seneca, *Suas.* 1.6–7.

59. Harland, *Associations*, 98.

over him. As indicated, when interpreting Luke 22:24–27, we should discuss Luke's attitude towards kings and benefactors separately in order to compare and contrast Jesus' authority and that of the emperor. Unlike some scholars (e.g., Bryan and Freyne), it is very clear that the emperor belongs to the grouping of 'the kings of the Gentiles'. This inclusion serves as Luke's implicit critique of the emperor through the account.

Moreover, Luke, in contrast to Lull's claim, does not portray "the kings (οἱ βασιλεῖς) of the Gentiles" in a favorable tone. Rather, he takes them as negative examples. Although acknowledging the importance of serving others, Lull's view that Luke takes the kings as positive exemplars should be rejected. He fails to draw attention to the differences between ideal and non-ideal benefactors. In Luke Jesus' teaching serves implicitly as criticizing non-ideal benefactors. However, this does not necessarily mean that Luke is critical of benefaction itself; rather, his critique is targeted at the holders of the title.

With the focus on different kinds of reciprocity in the Roman Empire, it is clear that Luke utilizes the benefactor-client system, rather than completely rejecting it (e.g., Ahn). For him, the pagan kings in 22:25 are not true benefactors on the grounds that they neglect altruistic benefaction. Their self-interest, rooted in negative reciprocity, makes it impossible for them to serve their subjects. In contrast, Luke portrays Jesus, who emphasizes service-oriented benefaction (i.e., a criterion for true benefactors), as a true benefactor-savior. This serves as an identity marker between true and false benefactors. Accordingly, Jesus' saying ("But not so with you") in Luke 22:26 to his disciples can be interpreted that he urges them not to be benefactors who ignore meaningful beneficence. Furthermore, from all the evidence shown above, we can draw an important conclusion that the title 'benefactor' has something to do with "the greatest." Luke does not say that the pagan kings called benefactors are the greatest, but he says that the one who serves is the greatest. In contrast to Jesus, the pagan kings who are not great are not true benefactors.

4

Savior: Victory–Peace–Salvation

IN CHAPTER 3, WE discussed Luke's implicit critique of the emperor's authority on the basis of the title "benefactor." With the focus on the emperor's other title "savior" in relation to Jesus' salvation, this echoing chapter aims to explore how Luke demonstrates Jesus' authority. Prior to the discussion of the title "savior," I will deal with its connotations, victory and peace, since they are not isolated from it. As can be seen in Fabius' decree in the *Introduction*, Augustus is viewed as a certain savior figure in connection with the peace and victory he has brought to his people. In order to affirm a strong link between savior and its connotations, it is important first to examine how Augustus (and his successors), with reference to his military *imperium*, achieved peace in the Roman Empire. In this regard, I will present Jesus' attitude in Luke towards the use of coercive power through several accounts, because this analysis will enable us to consider another issue about how Luke compares and contrasts Jesus with the emperor's title of savior. In general, this chapter intends to show in what ways victory, peace and salvation are applied to Jesus' identity, highlighting his authority in Luke's writings with the help of two sociological theories, acculturation (assimilation) theory and contra-culture theory.

In the second part of this chapter, I will relate Jesus' interaction with tax collectors to his salvific activities in Luke's Gospel to stress his title of savior compared to the emperor's on the basis of the discussion in Chapter 2, where I assert that the latter's moral *auctoritas* failed to correct their immorality. With reference to tax collectors, I will explore the meaningfulness of Jesus' salvation which centers on his forgiveness of sins. Also, I will take the example of Zechariah's praise, which shows all the themes of savior: salvation, peace, and victory. Prior to arguing those issues, it is necessary to examine Augustus' identity (or, the emperor in general) as savior expressed in literary sources and inscriptions.

Augustus as Savior

In ancient societies, the title "savior (σωτήρ)" enjoyed wide currency. It was often given to several important figures in various ways. In many cases, the title was not reserved only for imperial use.[1] For instance, as Graeco-Roman sources indicate, it was used for gods like Zeus, Asclepius, Isis, and Serapis, and for heroes or various influential leaders.[2] Among several prominent Romans, Pompey, and Julius Caesar were also called savior. Moreover, the title is used both for God (e.g., Isa 45:15, 21) and for human deliverers, such as Othniel and Ehud (Judg 3:9, 15) in LXX.[3] Philo occasionally regards God as "savior of the world" (σωτήρ τοῦ κόσμου, *Spec.* 2.198) and "savior of all" (σωτήρ τοῦ παντός, *Deus* 156; ὁ πάντων σωτήρ, *Fug.* 162). It is thus evident that both various individuals and gods did bear the title "savior" in the Greco-Roman world.

However, the situation changed to some extent in the Roman Empire. Despite the fact that it had been used for various figures, the title "savior" had striking imperial connotations in the first century. As a general rule, after Augustus onwards, it is very likely that the title σωτήρ underlined the emperor's supreme authority/power in the empire. A wide variety of material shows that Augustus and his successors, namely Tiberius, Claudius, Nero, Vespasian, and Domitian, were all described as savior.[4] For instance, the decree of the provincial council eulogizes Augustus as the "savior of the whole human race."[5] Even the second-century

---

1. For the examples of the use of "savior" in the ancient world, see Wendland, "Σωτήρ," 335–53; Lietzmann, *Der Weltheiland*; Otto, "Augustus Soter," 448–60; Dolger, "Der Heiland," 241–72; Dornseiff, "Swthr," 1:1211–21; Nock, "Soter and Euergetes," 2:720–35; Foerster and Fohrer, "σωτήρ," 1003–23; Dibelius and Conzelmann, *Pastoral Epistles*, 100–103; Marwood, *Roman Cult*; Moralee, "For Salvation's Sake".

2. In the second century the orator Aelius Aristides referred to the god Asclepius as "savior of all people" (σωτήρ πάντων ἀνθρώπων) and "saviour (σωτήρ) of all."

3. Mordecai is also described as savior in the Greek additions to Esther (Add Esth 16:13; cf. Neh 9:27).

4. E.g., "savior (σωτήρ) and benefactor of the whole human race," *Select Papyri*, 76–79; "savior (σωτήρ) of the common race of men," (*TDNT* 7. 1012); "savior of the common human life," (*MM*, 621); also see the references in *PW* 3.A.1:1214; cf. Pliny, *Ep.* 10.52, 102; Statius, *Silv.* 3.4.20; 4.2.14–15; and Martial 2.91.1; 5.1.7; Bousset, *Kyrios Christos*, 314; Deissmann, *Light*, 363–65. On the discussion of savior in John, see Koester, "Savior of the World," 665–680, attempting to connect "he savior of the world" in John 4:42 to the imperial use of the title; also Barrett, *John*, 244; Haenchen, *John 1*, 226.

5. See my *Introduction* (*OGIS* 458.1.3–30; *SEG* 4.490); also see Danker, *Benefactor*, 215–22.

emperors, such as Trajan and Hadrian also adopted the title of savior as a formal designation of the emperors.[6]

In addition, the emperor in Josephus' writing was regarded as savior. Josephus reports that Vespasian arrived at the city of Tiberius during the Jewish revolt and "the population opened their gates to him and went out to meet him, hailing him as savior and benefactor" (*War* 3.9.8, 459). Later, when Vespasian returned to Rome as the emperor, the populace went out to hail him "as benefactor, savior, and only worthy emperor of Rome" (*War* 7.4.1, 70–71).[7] Therefore, the title "savior" became one of the chief designations of the Roman emperors. In order to highlight their superiority, few persons or even deities could compete with Augustus and his successors for being recognized as "saviors of the entire world."[8]

Moreover, according to Virgil, Augustus is celebrated as a savior figure by heightening his divinity:

> He shall have the gift of divine life, shall see heroes mingled with gods, and shall himself be seen of them . . . Enter on thy high honors . . . O thou dear offspring of the gods, mighty seed of a Jupiter to be.[9]

In this poetry, Augustus' authority is expressed and stressed by depicting him as the one who holds the divine honor. R. Jewett claims that "[t]his follows the pattern established by Augustus, who developed this masterpiece of propaganda, with the regent holding unlimited power and ostensibly resisting divinization while receiving divine honors as the humble Apollo who restores peace to the world."[10] In this regard, the depiction of the savior figure functions as emphasizing Augustus' power.

As the term "savior" itself implies, salvation is a key theme of the emperor's title. It became common for priesthoods and individuals to offer vows in relation to the emperor's salvation. A well-known example would be the Arval Brotherhood (*Fratres Arvales*) in Rome, which, by the time of Tiberius was offering prayers for the emperor's salvation every

---

6. Nock, "Soter and Euergetes," 2:727.

7. A similar reception was given to his son Titus (*War* 4.2.5; *War* 7.5.2–3).

8. Gilbert, "Roman Propaganda," at 238; Nilsson, *History of Greek Religion*, 2:184–85, 390–92.

9. Virgil, *Ecl.* 4.11.48. The title "savior" is often associated with the title "*theos*," *Syll3*. 760; see also Lintott, *Imperium Romanum*, 181. For a discussion of Horace's presentation of Augustus as savior in connection with his divinity, see Kiernan, *Horace*, 74–78.

10. Jewett, *Romans*, 49.

year on 3 January. Numerous individuals and cities extended similar expressions of piety and loyalty to the emperor. The emperor's salvation became part of a widely circulated imperial ideology that portrayed him "as the medium through whom imperial and local salvation was achieved."[11] In this process, the emperor's salvation is associated directly with his victory and peace.

Augustus' Victory and Peace Based upon His Military *Imperium*

We had a brief look at Augustus (and his successors), as savior, expressed in various literary sources and inscriptions. Now my focus is on the question as to how he achieved such a title. What made it possible for Augustus to achieve the title savior? This question is very helpful in comparing and contrasting the emperor and Jesus, who were both called saviors.

One of the most important titles of Augustus, savior, was based largely on his victory. In his position as savior, Augustus was understood to surpass not only everything human beings could do but also everything the gods could do. In this regard, his power is often expressed by his military victory. For instance, Velleius Paterculus describes Augustus' victorious return to Rome after the defeat of Antony:

> There is nothing that man can desire from the gods, nothing that the gods can grant to a man, nothing that wish can conceive or good fortune bring to pass, which Augustus on his return to the city did not bestow upon the republic, the Roman people, and the world.[12]

Similarly, emphasizing his own victorious achievements, Augustus himself records, "the whole of Italy swore allegiance to me and demanded me as the leader in the war in which I was victorious at Actium" (*RG.* 25). His victorious return after war made a considerable contribution to his role as savior. Thus, it can be said that his title of savior is based largely upon his victory.

Also, an important point I wish to make is that Augustus' victory over enemies is linked directly to his emphasis on peace which he brought to the Roman Empire. Among many benefactions associated with Augustus and other Roman emperors, the ability to establish peace

---

11. Gilbert, "Roman Propaganda," 239; see also Marwood, *Roman Cult*, 10; Price, *Rituals and Power,* 51 and 54, and his article, "Gods and Emperors," 79–95.

12. Velleius Paterculus 2.89.

and security was considered highly significant. Velleius lists Augustus' great achievements, including restoration of the laws, re-establishing the dignity of the Senate, respect to religion, and the like. By regarding him as a peace bringer in his lists, Velleius notes: "The civil wars were ended after 20 years, foreign wars suppressed, peace restored, the frenzy of arms everywhere lulled to rest" (2.89). Later, he refers explicitly to the *Pax Augusta*: the universality of peace "spread to the regions of the east and of the west and to the bounds of the north and of the south, preserv[ing] every corner of the world" (2.126). Likewise, the elder Pliny also speaks of "the immeasurable majesty of the Roman peace."[13] As Wells rightly puts it, "the idea of the empire as the model of peace and stability became a commonplace."[14] Therefore, it is highly likely that peace, along with victory, cannot be separable from Augustus' title, savior.[15]

A range of sources, including literary texts, inscriptions, and coins, highlights "the Roman world with evocations of and tributes to peace."[16] For instance, Epictetus emphasizes the emperor's ability to establish great peace, saying: "there are neither wars nor battles, nor great robberies nor piracies; but we may travel at all hours, and sail from east to west" (Epictetus 3.13.9). In this respect, it is interesting that peace is understood as the situation without war.

Ironically, however, the peace and stability of the empire depended largely on the exercise of the emperor's military *imperium*, the army.[17] Roman military power, along with the emperor's other power sources, played a vital role in ceasing war as a means of achieving peace.[18] The

---

13. Pliny, *NH*, 27.3.

14. Wells, *Roman Empire*, 244.

15. cf. Velleius Paterculus 2.131: *hanc pacem, hunc principem*.

16. Gilbert, "Roman Propaganda," 240; Weinstock, "Pax and the 'Ara Pacis,'" 44–58; Wengst, *Pax Romana*, 6–54.

17. See Wells, *Roman Empire*, 133.

18. We can add more elements to Augustus' accession, as Lintott, *Imperium Romanum*, 14, rightly suggests: "Other important works are devoted to Roman strategy, military techniques and the vast reservoir of Italian manpower." In addition to Lintott's suggestions, Augustus' substantive power stemmed from financial success and resources gained in conquest or through tax, the building of patron-client relations, the concept of honor and shame, as well as accumulation of the various offices. Besides, Clifford Ando, who centers his argument on the stability as the result of genuine consensus, asserts that the Roman Empire was successful in winning the hearts and minds of at least some of its subjects (Ando, *Imperial Ideology*). He takes an example of Tacitus' writing: Tacitus recognizes that Augustus' position became unshakable, because it was rooted in genuine gratitude and in a general recognition of everyone's interests,

army was essential for Augustus and his successors because it was responsible for the frontiers as well as internal security.[19] Rome's military might was hymned by an unknown poetess, Melinno, who depicts Rome as the offspring of Ares (Mars) whose own progeny were the finest spearmen; that is, Rome's home was a peaceful Olympus on earth.[20] Cicero also emphasizes the importance of military achievement in connection with divinity, saying: "In the case of certain supreme individuals, they have a sort of good fortune divinely implanted in them that brings them greatness, fame, and mighty achievement."[21]

In the process of victory, the army played a key role in making Augustus a victor. Lintott cites:

> It was only the armies that could hold the empire together, and in fact the corruption of the military worked in the opposite sense towards disintegration. Augustus and certain of his successors had tried to create an integrated whole, but this integration was essentially a matter of armies and taxation, never the creation of society.[22]

"He seduces the army with bonuses, and his cheap food policy was a successful bait for civilians. Indeed, he attracted everybody's goodwill by the enjoyable gift of peace . . . Opposition did not exist." (Tacitus, *Ann.* 1.2) However, Ando tends to minimize the aspect of Rome's coercive power. One of the main problems with his argument is that he takes elite sources at face value without considering them critically. We have to analyze the elite sources very carefully and critically in order to decide whether they are biased. It is true that we cannot explain Rome's peace and stability by appeal to the emperor's coercive power alone. But, at the same time, it is very unlikely that his military might does not play a crucial role in achieving victory over his enemies. For that reason, here, I wish to focus primarily on military images of the empire in order to demonstrate a strong link between peace and military power.

19. According to Wells, *Roman Empire*, 133, the army also played "an important social and economic role, as an agent of social mobility among its recruits and its offices, as a powerful influence for Romanization, as an economic stimulus to the areas in which it was stationed." Also, Lintott, *Imperium Romanum*, 125, maintains that Augustus "made the army professional in another sense by requiring long service-a minimum of sixteen years from legionary infantry-and apparently forbidding Roman soldiers to marry" (Dio, 54.25.5-6; 55.23ff.; for the evidence for the ban on marriage, see Dio 60.24.3).

20. Cited in Lintott, *Imperium Romanum*, 177; also see Stobaeus, 3.7.12.

21. Cicero, *On the Command of Pompey*, 47.

22. Lintott, *Imperium Romanum*, 190-19; in a similar vein, Strabo (17.3.25) talks of becoming "lord of peace and war" by virtue of his people awarding him supreme power over the empire. On the discussion of taxation, see Ch. 2.

All the remarks shown above affirm that Augustus used his military *imperium* in order to obtain peace and stability in the empire. What is noticeable is that war was followed by peace. In the empire, victory in war was essential for achieving peace and stability. For instance, in 6 AD the Pannonian revolt, which spread into Illyricum, required military strength for three years to suppress it.[23] Also, Fabius' decree and the explanation of the provincial council refer more explicitly to Augustus' peace in connection with the war, depicting him as the savior "who has made war to cease and who shall put everything in peaceful order."[24] As plenty of materials indicate, it is evident that Augustus, as a savior, achieved peace through military victory.

Furthermore, all too often, Augustus' military glory and victory are emphasized in the language of his virtues. A good example is that his victory is viewed as one of his main virtues, *Victoria* (Nike).[25] Victory and *pax*, from the beginning of Augustus' reign onwards, were to become strictly complementary conceptions. As Wells rightly points out, "the emphasis is on the victories that had secured peace, not just on peace itself" on the basis of "the connotation of peace and pacify (*pax, pacare*)."[26] Augustus, from the very moment of his victory at Actium, had claimed *Pax* and *Victoria* as his special supporters and twin enablers, whose power and virtue were thereafter to be recognized inherently in his power.[27] Only victory could precede peace, and no peace could endure without the future guarantee of victory. Thus *pax* and *victoria* achieved a primary status among the Augustan "virtues": "without them no *sovereignty* could stand firm and no empire survive."[28] In doing so, Augustus is often depicted as a victor. Cassius Dio, who is well aware

---

23. Lintott, *Imperium Romanum*, 13. Concerning the coins illustrating the emperors' military victory, see Friesen, *Imperial Cults,* 30, such as British Museum, Mysia 139 #242, pl.28 for Augustus; the coins of the Tiberian (BM Mysia 140 #256, pl.28); *RPC* 1, 1.2372 (pl.105) for Neronian periods; Domitian (BM Phrygia 307 #181–182); Domitia (BM Phrygia 308 #187–88).

24. EJ, 82–83 no.98; see also my *Introduction*. More examples can be seen in Fishwick's work, *Imperial Cult,* 11–12, 27, 48, and 50.

25. Brent, *Imperial Cult,* 64–67.

26. Wells, *Roman Empire,* 84.

27. Sutherland, *Coinage* = Sutherland, *Roman Imperial Coinage,* vol. 1, 97.

28. Sutherland, *Coinage,* 29; italics mine.

of the relationship between *pax Augusti* and *victoria Augusti*, describes Augustus "as perpetual victor over his enemies and savior of his citizens" when honoring him.[29]

What is more, many writers speak well of Augustus' warlike images in connection with victory. Among them, Virgil, stressing the peace Augustus brought, records that the Romans remained a nation devoted to military glory, as the monuments of the imperial city show.[30] Augustus' supremacy is frequently expressed in accordance with his military power, which enabled him to become a guarantor of peace and security.[31]

Finally, Augustus himself advertised his role as the author of peace in the *Res Gestae*, where he bragged that on three occasions he shut the doors of the temple of Janus in Rome.[32] This symbolized that peace had been achieved throughout the Roman world, emphasizing his feat accomplished only twice in the entire preceding history of Rome.[33]

Therefore, it is almost impossible to separate peace from victory when discussing the emperor's power in terms of his identity as savior. It is also impossible to describe Augustus as savior without considering his military *imperium*. The fact that his victory was rooted in his coercive power should not be under-estimated since it is related directly to his power which enabled him to obtain accession or to be called *imperator*. That is, Augustus' rule marked *Pax Romana* because his power was established, to a large extent, through his military *imperium*. As a result, the emperor, who brought victory and peace, was called savior. What is noticeable is that there is a significant pattern; that is, Augustus (and also his successors) is described

---

29. Dio, 53.16.4. On the discussion of *victoria* on the coins, see Sutherland, *Coinage*, 29; see also *RIC*, Mattingly, Sydenham etc. (London: 1923–), i, Augustus, nos. I, 2, 4, 7, 26–29, 32. On the discussion of *pax* on the coins, see Sutherland, *Coinage*, p.30; *RIC*. i, Augustus, nos. 3, 4, 6, 7, 25, 30, 31; *RAI*, p.17f.

30. Cf. Virgil, *Aen*. 1.278–279; also see *Ecl*. 1.6–8; cf. Horace, *Carm*. 3.5.1–4. Jewett, *Romans*, 48, maintains that Augustus was called the "son of the Divine Savior," and that he was initially depicted as a military redeemer, in nude pose, with his foot resting on a globe as universal ruler of the world. Also see Friesen, *Imperial Cults*, 61–62, for the descriptions of the various coins, which bear the military images.

31. Eck, *Age of Augustus*, 52–54.

32. *RG*. 13; cf. Virgil, *Aen*. 1.291–296.

33. Gilbert, "Roman Propaganda," 240, suggests that the emphasis on peace as a prominent benefit of the *imperium Romanum* continued through the first and second centuries. The doors to the temple of Janus were again shut during the reigns of Nero and Vespasian (see Suetonius, *Nero* 13.2; Josephus, *War* 7.158; Dio Chrysostom 66.15).

as a victor, peace-bringer, and savior. These titles are all intertwined on the grounds that they represent his supreme authority.

Two Theories

As seen above, the Roman emperors' peace is not separable from their victory over enemies. They are called savior owing to the peace they bring to their subjects. This pattern is also found in Luke's Gospel when he describes Jesus as savior. But it is wrong to assume that Jesus as savior is on a par level with the emperor. Based on that assumption, this subchapter will explore in what ways the emperor is described in connection with the title savior. Luke does not attempt to critique the emperor in a direct way. Instead, he chooses a different method in order first to highlight Jesus' authority by using existing imperial ideology, and second to stress the differences between Jesus and the emperor. Roman political propaganda frequently uses rhetorical strategies. Likewise, Luke not only adapts the rhetoric that legitimated Roman political authority but does so in order to stress Jesus' identity as savior.

Luke's strategy in terms of his use of the existing title can be explained in two ways. Sociological theories, acculturation (assimilation) theory and contra-culture theory, will be used as heuristic tools for understanding how Luke struggles to elevate Jesus' power. First, the former is very useful in identifying the issues of why Luke uses the imperial title to Jesus. This involves only the outward format of the imperial cults, victor/peace-bringer/savior. And second, the latter explains how Luke differentiates Jesus' role of savior from the emperor's through the critiques of tax collectors' corruption in Luke's Gospel. In this respect, the question as to how Jesus and the emperor obtained peace respectively will be answered. I will briefly explain the two theories before applying them to Luke's Gospel.

Assimilation and Acculturation

We have discussed that there is a clear pattern in the imperial ideology: victories, peace, and salvation. The link creates a sort of formula, victory–peace–salvation (or victor/peace-bringer/savior). Again, such a formula is also found in Luke's Gospel where Jesus is described as savior. Given the fact that the imperial cult was pervasive in the Roman Empire, the meaningfulness of savior, given to the emperor, was acknowledged among first-century people. Luke, who was also one of them, probably was well aware of it. My scenario about Luke's strategy is, therefore, based largely upon the view that he attempts to portray Jesus in existing imperial language. In this regard, for him, the emperor's title, which signifies his power/authority, is a very efficient method of describing Jesus' power without explaining further in detail to his audiences/readers who already knew the significance of the title of savior. To put it differently, Luke intends to advertise who Jesus is to them simply by applying the existing title to him. Along with this advertisement, they had probably in mind that Jesus was a figure with a certain power/authority similar to the emperor.

Assimilation (acculturation) theory will support my argument with some modifications. I use this theory only for identifying the similarities between the emperor and Jesus in terms of the shared pattern of victory–peace–salvation.[34] In my opinion, sociological insights of assimilation are useful in examining how Luke aims at stressing Jesus' authority in comparison with that of the emperor by using the same title "savior." Among the scholars, J. Milton Yinger emphasizes assimilation when two different cultures meet, defining it as "a process of boundary reduction that can occur when members of two or more societies or of smaller cultural groups meet."[35] In a similar vein, Harland's study of assimilation has made a valuable contribution to the identity of the early Christians. He asserts:

> [A]cculturation refers to the phenomena which result when groups of individuals having different cultures come into continuous first-hand contact, with subsequent changes in the original cultural patterns of either or both groups.[36]

34. Similarly, Rowe, "Luke–Acts," 285, acknowledging the differences between Luke's Gospel and *pax Romana*, asserts that the well-known similarities such as peace and savior languages, to some extent, "provide the touchstone for argument about Luke's Christianized version of *pax Romana*."

35. Yinger, "Toward a Theory," 249; on the discussion of usefulness of the assimilation (or acculturation) theory, see also Kim and Gudykunst, *Cross-Cultural Adaptation*; Elise, "Cultural and Structural Assimilation," 275–78; Harland, *Associations*, 195–200. Harland distinguishes acculturation from accommodation. He, *Associations*, 301 n12, argues that, when this approach is applied to ancient societies, we need to bear in mind that "[t]he processes of assimilation and acculturation are to be clearly distinguished from common value-laden terms such as 'accommodation;'" the former are not concerned with evaluating whether specific developments are "good" or "bad."

36. Harland, *Associations*, 196; also see Klauck, *Religious Context*, where he centers on the background of the early Christianity.

Thus, this theory stresses how one culture, such as the Roman Empire or the imperial propaganda, can influence other cultures, namely Luke's Gospel, when they meet together.

According to this theory, given that human beings are conveyors of socio-cultural values, individuals, who belong to a given ethnic, cultural, or religio-political group, can interact with other people from different cultural groups through personal social network connections.[37] When a person enters into a certain group or association, he or she has much contact with the values or ideology of that group. A good example is the Jewish or Christian individual's multiple memberships or interactions within other institutions and sub-groups of society, including occupational associations. Yinger maintains that such occupational connections of Jews or Christians are important for incorporation within occupational networks, and that they "almost certainly lead to at least some acculturation, identification [i.e., psychological identification with occupation or fellow workers], and amalgamation [e.g., intermarriage]."[38] Luke's readers/hearers were not an exception. Their double identity should not be overlooked when discussing Jesus as savior in connection with the emperor. They were a minority group, but at the same time were very familiar with the characteristics of the host group, the Roman imperial ideology; they perceived the emperor as savior since he brought peace to them after achieving victory over their enemies. It is very likely that they were affected by the contacts with socio-cultural institutions, conventions, practices, and values of the dominant Roman culture and ideology.[39] They were related closely to the Roman imperial culture. They already knew the title applied to the emperor, when they entered into Luke's religious community. Under such circumstances, it is very likely that Luke applies the existing imperial orders to his writing.[40]

---

37. E.g., Yinger, "Toward a Theory," 254; Elise, "Cultural and Structural Assimilation," 275; Harland, *Associations*, 196.

38. Yinger, "Toward a Theory," 254; cf. Harland, *Associations*, 197.

39. See Harland, *Associations*, 197–99; for this reason, he considers religious groups as minority cultural groups.

40. Harland, *Associations*, 198, points out: "Assimilation is a complex, two-way process that works at both the individual and group levels in the ancient context. The entrance of a new individual member (e.g., a Gentile or a Jew) into a group with a distinctive cultural complex could be part of this cultural exchange. All individuals, social-scientific studies emphasize, are culture carriers who bring with them a set of cultural traits pertaining to a particular way of life and worldview."

When two different cultures meet, the assimilation theory aids us to identify the similarities between the emperor and Luke's Jesus. Luke does not completely separate his "savior" from the imperial one in order to make use of the title. Based on this theory, Luke, who knew that his readers/hearers had two different cultures (Christian culture and Roman imperial culture), needed to bridge the gap between imperial ideology and his own theology. It would be very probable to claim that he attempts to borrow the imperial images in the process of assimilation. Luke, belonging to two different worlds and acknowledging the importance of the imperial title, applied the same formula (victor-peace bringer-savior), used for the emperor, to Jesus. For him, more important was to advertise who Jesus was *in comparison with* the emperor. By assimilating the formula to his writing, Luke was able to advertise Jesus' identity and his authority. To put it another way, Luke's contact with the imperial images offered him a strategic method concerning the advertisement of Jesus' authority/power in comparison with the emperor. When taking into account the fact that his readers are, to some extent, the Gentiles, Luke's method of using the existing imperial images seems to help assimilate imperial culture into his community.

Another point I wish to make is that my use of this theory focuses only on the very basic contents which are evident in the title of savior. That is, the theory used here is concerned only with the application of the emperor's title to Luke's writing on the grounds that a similar pattern is shown with both the emperor and Jesus. It aids us to explore in what ways Luke highlights Jesus' authority simply by using the title. However, when borrowing this title, Luke does not intend to apply all the values, which the title bears, to Jesus' power. It is wrong to assume that, although applying the same pattern "victory–peace–salvation" to Jesus, he copies all the concepts and methods evident in the imperial ideology. Even though Luke's use of the pattern is very similar to the emperor's pattern, he intentionally distinguishes the method of achieving each element from the emperor's method. Therefore, it is a mistake to argue that Luke is not critical of the imperial cults or the emperor as savior.

Again, what I am trying to say is that Luke just borrows the title and its basic contents, recognizing the importance of the title by taking only the outward format of the imperial ideology in his societies. Thus, even though Jesus was called savior as the emperor was, it does not mean that Jesus' power was on a par level with the emperor's. The inner-concepts and methods of achieving victory–peace–salvation are very different from each other. The assimilation theory does not provide a plausible scenario of the differences between the two figures, while useful in analyzing the similarities.[41] The main differences can be explained with the help of the contra-culture theory.

Contraculture Theory

In order to understand the differences between savior in Luke and that in the imperial cult, we need to answer several questions. What are the important contents of savior in both contexts? How far are they different? How was the title "savior" achieved? What values need to be reconstructed and what system of privilege and honor needs to be reversed? If there are any rejections of the source of the emperor's peace, how does Luke describe Jesus' peace in contrast to the emperor's *pax*? In order to answer these questions, the contra-culture theory will be used as an analytical tool.

At a glance, the contra-culture theory is somewhat similar to Wayne Meeks' portrayal of Jewish/Christian groups as sectarian, as they both centre on differentiating a society from the other societies.[42] It was common for several scholars to depict Jewish groups of the diaspora as iso-

---

41. Of course, scholars, who support the assimilation theory, admit that some selections or dissimulations, to some extent, occur in the theory. For instance, Harland, *Associations*, 196, argues that assimilation can "involve the selection, adoption, and adaptation of a variety of cultural traits including language, dress, religion, and other cultural conventions, beliefs, and values that make up the way of life and worldview of a particular cultural group." John W. Berry, "Acculturation as Varieties of Adaptation," 13, also stresses that culture contact takes various forms of adaptation, sometimes involving a twofold process that entails the "maintenance of cultural integrity as well as the movement to become an integral part of a lager societal framework." In addition, Yinger claims that the processes of dissimilation can occur at certain points in a group's history, maintaining: "powerful assimilative forces are matched by renewed attention to socio-cultural differences" ("Toward a Theory," 257; see also 257–61). They are right in asserting that there are selection, adoptions, and adaptation in the process of assimilation theory. However, their assertion is not sufficient to explain in what ways Luke attempts to differentiate Jesus as savior from the emperor as savior. The assimilation theory does not specifically explain which concepts and methods are different between Luke's Jesus and the emperor. In this respect, contra-culture theory is more useful in explaining how far Jesus' power is different from the emperor's. The selective and transformative character of intercultural transmission should be strongly emphasized in this case. To put it differently, the assimilation theory does not draw careful attention to the question as to what degree Jesus as savior in Luke's Gospel is distinctive.

42. Meeks, *First Urban Christians*.

lated and introverted communities living in hostile environments, largely alien to the institutions, conventions, and values or society in the Roman Empire. According to Meeks, this depiction of Jewish groups as sectarian has continued to have a huge influence on discussions of Christian congregations in the same setting.[43] Meeks, drawing attention to the surrounding background, is right in asserting that Christian and Jewish groups were not isolated from the dominant Roman culture. However, he draws little attention to the importance of positive influence of the Roman Empire on Christian values. It is wrong to assume that the Christian movement should be regarded purely as sectarian, evaluating that all the things of the Roman Empire were evil. It is not the case, at least, with Luke's Gospel, as discussed in the section on assimilation theory. Moreover, Meeks' analysis lacks the explanation of the imperial cult/ideology, which functions as the background for Luke's Gospel. Luke not only accepts the imperial images, though borrowing the basic concepts of the titles (as the assimilation theory indicates), but also attempts to differentiate Jesus from the emperor in order to highlight Jesus' superiority. It is unlikely that Christian groups, including Luke's community, were purely sectarian.

Allen Brent, recognizing the significance of the imperial cult, applies the contra-culture theory to his analysis of the relationship between Luke's Gospel and Roman propaganda.[44] He points out that the Christian social constructions of reality are formed in interaction with their pagan and imperial counter-parts.[45] He goes on to argue that "the development of early Christian church order is understood as the development of a contra-culture."[46] In brief, according to Brent, the contra-culture theory shows that "a group, deprived of status and significance by the wider culture, sets up its own contra-culture that mirrors and reverses the values of the former, granting the status and significance to its members that the former has denied them."[47]

---

43. See Meeks, *First Urban Christians*; and Elliott, *A Home for the Homeless*.

44. Brent, *Imperial Cult*.

45. Ibid., XXI.

46. Ibid., XXI and Ch.1.

47. Ibid., XXI, his concept of contra-culture is based on the argument of S. Leventman, ed., *Counterculture and Social Transformation*. Brent, *Imperial Cult*, 7, notes: "Part of the parallelism between imperial and Christian cults was the issue of the *pax deorum*. Augustus as augur had extraordinarily succeeded in securing this ritual and metaphysical *pax* in the wake of the failure of Republican magistrates. The superior

The contra-culture theory is useful for the analysis of the differences between the two cultures, since it shows how the relations between Jesus' authority and the emperor's authority are reformulated and reconstructed in Luke's writings. As Brent puts it, "the contra-culture was produced by an interaction that redefined the demands of the host culture, accepting some of them and reformulating others."[48] Here, I wish to highlight "reversing the values of the wider culture." Again, what should be kept in mind is that the contra-culture theory will be used only for identifying the differences between the innermost concepts of Jesus as savior and those of the emperor. This theory will provide a significant insight into the themes of Jesus' title, savior.

Taken together, my argument is that two contrasting characteristics exist in Jesus' title "savior": on the one hand, the similarities (victor, peace-bringer, and savior) are expressed by acculturation theory, and, on the other hand, the contra-culture theory provides the differences between Jesus and the emperor in order to critique the emperor's authority and to stress Jesus' superiority.

Jesus as Victor: His Victory over His Enemies

Let us first explore in what ways Luke expresses Jesus' victory over his enemies. When attempting to describe Jesus' identity in his writings, Luke follows the formula applied to Augustus' case, victor/peace-bringer/savior, which enabled him to elevate his own status. Augustus' power, as savior, is based firstly on victory over his enemies by using his coercive power. In brief, he defeated his enemies and accordingly achieved victory and brought peace to his people. This basic pattern is utilized by Luke in his Gospel. As Augustus and his successors achieved victory over his enemies, Luke's Jesus did the same.

Christian *pax dei* was secured by Christ and perpetrated through the cultic acts of the Christian community and its ministers according to the Luke–Acts, Clement Corinthians, and Ignatius of Antioch. The Christian cult was thus the rival means for obtaining the cultic objections of the imperial cults, and represented a denial of the claims of the latter to have achieved such objections"; see Rowe's critique, "Luke–Acts," 284–85. Rowe ("Luke–Acts," 285), who follows S. Sandmel's argument, "Parallelomania," 1–13, maintains that common peace and savior languages "reflect mutual cultural-linguistic imbeddedness rather than 'influence,' 'a reaction to' and so forth."

48. Brent, *Imperial Cult*, 11.

In order to evaluate the importance of victory in terms of Jesus' authority, some questions need to be answered. Who are Jesus' enemies in Luke's writings? What does Jesus use in order to achieve victory over them? How does Luke describe Jesus' victory in relation to peace? And, does Jesus' victory over enemies symbolize his power/authority? As a whole, Jesus' enemies in Luke's accounts can be divided into two groups: the first group is a non-human being, namely Satan, and the second group consists of human beings who exercise authority over their subjects. Interestingly, the two groups are sometimes intertwined when Luke addresses Jesus' authority versus his enemies' authority. Let us first explore non-human being as Jesus' enemies.

Non-Human Being: Satan and His relationship with the Roman Empire

It is not surprising that, as other evangelists report, Luke frequently depicts Satan/devil as one of Jesus' main enemies. Given that Jesus rejects Satan's power, Luke suggests that Jesus achieves his victory over Satan/devil. A well-known example is found in the temptation story. Satan appears in this narrative for the first time in Luke's Gospel. This temptation narrative is important because it alludes to the identity of Jesus' enemies. As both Mark and Matthew place Jesus' temptation by the devil before Jesus' mission, Luke does too. The main difference is that, while Mark very briefly reports that Jesus is tempted by the devil in the wilderness (Mark 1:12–13), both Luke and Matthew report it in more detail (Luke 4:1–13; Matt 4:1–11). In other words, while Mark does not specify in what ways Jesus is tempted, the other two evangelists elaborate on the temptations.[49] However, it is wrong to assume that the account of Matthew is identical with the Lukan account.[50] Although both Luke and Matthew report that Jesus was tempted by the devil in three ways, the order of the temptations is slightly different.[51] In both cases, the temptation of bread comes first, but the other two temptations have different orderings. While Luke puts

---

49. For a detailed discussion of the synoptic temptation accounts, see Gibson, *Temptations of Jesus*, 25–118.

50. Although the comparison between Mark and Luke is not helpful here because of Mark's very short report, the comparison between Luke and Matthew aids us to analyze the importance of the theme 'authority'.

51. On the differences, see Hays, "Liberation of Israel," 9.

the temptation of "worshipping Satan" right after the first temptation, Matthew places it after his second temptation of "jumping."

Here I wish to focus mainly on the second temptation in the Lukan account (the third temptation in the Gospel of Matthew), since this temptation is related both indirectly to the Roman emperor and directly to Jesus' authority/power (and/or his victory). These two aspects are very useful in the discussion of Luke's interest in heightening Jesus' authority. First and foremost, it is very noticeable that the phrase, πάσας τὰς βασιλείας τῆς οἰκουμένης (Luke 4:5), is used in this temptation. In a somewhat different vein, Matthew uses πάσας τὰς βασιλείας τοῦ κόσμου (Matt 4:8). The notable difference between the two phrases is that, while Matthew uses the term κόσμου, Luke uses another term οἰκουμένης. Why did Luke use οἰκουμένης unlike Matthew who uses κόσμου? What are the differences between κόσμου and οἰκουμένης in the first century?

It is worth noting that Luke's use of οἰκουμένη is reminiscent of the earlier one in Luke's census narrative (Luke 2:1; different case, here accusative). When speaking of the Augustan census, Luke relates it to Augustus' world (the empire), πᾶσαν τὴν οἰκουμένην. Along with its case, the structural difference between the two narratives is that τὰς βασιλείας is added to the temptation narrative. However, the meaning is not significantly different. In both narratives, it means the Roman Empire,[52] signifying the world under the emperor's power/authority. In my opinion, Luke, who is keenly interested in Jesus' power in comparison with the emperor's power, uses the term, οἰκουμένη, rather than κόσμος, in order to highlight the theme of authority in his Gospel.[53]

Another difference between Luke and Matthew involves the devil's remark after he shows all the kingdoms to Jesus. There is no reference to

---

52. For the meaning of the term οἰκουμένη as "an inhabited world" or "the Roman Empire," see Bock, *Luke*, 1:375; Theissen, *Gospels in Context*, 213. Fitzmyer, *Luke*, 1:400, argues that the term οἰκουμένη, which means "inhabited world," "was often used with hyperbole in the official rhetoric of decrees and inscriptions for the Roman Empire itself." In a similar vein, Marshall, *Luke*, 98, points out the exaggeration of equating the empire with the whole world. According to Johnson, *Luke*, 74, Luke's κόσμος implies the natural created order (Luke 9:25; 11:50; 12:30; Acts 17:24), while his οἰκουμένη refers to the socio-political order (Luke 2:1; 21:26; Acts 11:28; 17:6; 19:27; 24:5) with the only exception of Acts 17:31. He, *Luke*, 74, further claims, "The vision is of an empire with suzerainty over kingdoms (*basileia*) which in turn control cities, exactly Luke's perception of imperial arrangements."

53. The term οἰκουμένη is used fifteen times in the New Testament (Matt 24:14; Luke 2:1; 4:5; 21:26; Acts 11:28; 17:6, 31; 19:27; 24:5; Rom 10:18; Heb 1:6; 2:5; Rev 3:10; 12:9; 16:14) Only Luke uses οἰκουμένη in association with πᾶς as in 2:1 and 4:5.

authority in Matthew, just saying "All these I will give you" (Matt 4:9). But Luke refers clearly to "authority" and "a giver of such authority." In Luke 4:6, the devil said to Jesus, "To you I will give their glory and *all this authority* (τὴν ἐξουσίαν ταύτην ἅπασαν); *for it has been given over to me, and I give it to anyone I please.*" In this respect, Hays rightly argues that these additional clauses give us an important clue to the relationship between the Roman Empire and the devil, emphasizing that the devil gives the authority to the emperor and all the kings.[54] In doing so, Luke intends to differentiate Jesus' authority from the emperor's authority by refusing the devil's offer of authority.

When his additional clauses are taken together with his intentional use of οἰκουμένη, it becomes more evident that Luke attempts to distinguish Jesus' authority from the emperor's authority. What Luke intends to highlight is not only the relationship between οἰκουμένη and the emperor's authority, but also Jesus' rejection of such authority. By refusing the devil's proposal, Luke's Jesus also refuses to be equated with the emperor's authority which is limited only to the Roman Empire (οἰκουμένη). Thus, the former is not identical with the latter in Luke's Gospel even though he uses the same pattern found in Roman propaganda. On one level, Jesus achieves victory over the devil by rejecting and reproaching him, saying that "Worship the Lord your God, and serve only him" (v. 8). Luke deliberately contrasts the devil's authority with Jesus' authority, "received from God, his divine son-ship to represent the Kingdom of God" (Luke 3:22; cf. 22:29).[55] On another level, Luke also contrasts Jesus' authority given by God with the emperor's authority given by the devil. With the focus on the fact that Jesus' authority is not the same as that of the emperor, it seems to me that Luke underscores Jesus' superiority; that is, Jesus triumphs both over Satan and the emperor's authority through the second temptation story. Therefore, we can conclude that Jesus' en-

---

54. Hays, "Liberation of Israel," 9. Cf. Jervell, *Theology of Acts,* 106; Walton, "State They Were in," 27–28; Kim, *Christ and Caesar,* 88–89; Yamazaki-Ransom, *Roman Empire,* 90–97. Although these scholars do not deal with the theme of authority in connection with the title "savior," their argument is very useful in the analysis of the identity of Jesus' enemy in the temptation account.

55. Kim, *Christ and Caesar,* 89; he further points out: "This interpretation is supported by the contrast between the messianic kingship of Jesus and the reign of Tiberius Caesar, Pontius Pilate, Herod, and Philip, which Luke presents . . . by dating Jesus' messianic inauguration to the reign of these rulers (3:1–22), immediately before this account of his temptation by Satan." Also see Yamazaki-Ransom, *Roman Empire,* 93–97.

emy is first Satan, and that, second, he rejects the emperor's authority of οἰκουμένη given by Satan.

Along with the temptation story, Jesus' victory over the devil is found in various stories of exorcism. Among many examples, the Beelzebul controversy would be helpful in stressing the theme of Jesus' victory over Satan (Luke 11:14–23) in connection with the emperor's power. When Jesus casts out a demon that is dumb, some of the people say that he casts out demons by the power of "Beelzebul, the prince of demons" (v. 15). Unlike the Markan account (Mark 3:22–27), Luke explains that Jesus' opponents seek 'from him a sign from heaven' (v. 16). Such a sign from heaven can be explained as authority/power from God. In other words, Jesus' opponents test whether Jesus' authority has derived from God.[56] Ironically, their intention of seeking Jesus' authority functions as proving that his authority is more powerful than the devil's power in the following story. In Luke's Gospel, the remarks of Jesus' opponents often serve as indirectly vindicating Jesus' authority through the conflict; that is, Jesus' authority in Luke is sometimes highlighted from the lips of his opponents.[57]

Luke stresses that Jesus' power is from God by insisting that it is not from the power of Beelzebul.[58] In v. 20, he says, "But if it is by the finger of God that I cast out the demons, then the kingdom of God has come to you."[59] For me, Luke intends to indicate two key points relating to Jesus' authority through this story. First, his power is not from the demons as he rejected the demon's offer in the earlier temptation story. In this regard, Luke's readers/hearers might re-affirm that the source of power within Jesus is not identical with the source of the demon. Luke emphasizes that God's finger/power is with Jesus when casting out demons. Luke's emphasis on the source of power is also found in Jesus' followers' healing (Acts 14:10–18). After healing the crippled man, Paul and Barnabas are called Hermes and Zeus, respectively (v. 12). After watching the miraculous healing, the crowds say, "The gods have come down to us in human form" (v. 11). Luke strives to underline that the crowds, ascrib-

---

56. According to Goulder, *Luke*, 2:504, Luke's use of διαμερισθεῖσα (4:17) has "a hostile sense, just as he uses the similar διανοίᾳ καρδίας in a hostile sense at 1:51." Also see the LXX, Ezek 14:3–4.

57. For more examples, see below.

58. For the discussion of the name of Beelzebul, see Evans, *Luke*, 490.

59. God's finger is translated as the symbol of his action in Exod 8:19 and Deut 9:10, Goulder, *Luke*, 2:504.

ing the source of power to the gods of imperial cults, fail to comprehend where the power comes from. Paul and Barnabas strongly claim: "We are mortals just like you, and we bring you good news, that you should turn from these worthless things (e.g., the gods of imperial cults, probably, including the emperor) to the living God, who made the heaven and the earth and the sea and all that is in them" (v. 15). They stress that the source of power derives from God, not from other gods or other things.

Second, Luke seems to highlight that Jesus' power given by God is more powerful than that of the demon. This is explained in the subsequent verses of the strong man (11:21–23). By referring to several images relating to the Roman Empire, Luke offers a more detailed account than Mark. In 11:21 Luke records, "When a strong man, fully armed (καθωπλισμένος), guards his castle (φυλάσσῃ τὴν ἑαυτοῦ αὐλήν), his property is safe (in peace; ἐν εἰρήνῃ)." It is noticeable that Luke depicts him as the one who is fully armed (καθωπλισμένος) and guards his castle, which can be interpreted that one achieves peace and security through his coercive power. In addition, Luke adds "armor" (πανοπλία) to his account when depicting the strong man (v. 22), while there is no mention about military language in Mark 3:27. The Greek term πανοπλία includes shield, sword, helmet, breastplate and the like. In this regard, Luke seems to say that the strong man is *in peace* (ἐν εἰρήνῃ) due to his military power. The aim of a standing army is to keep his territory in peace. Such a description is very similar to the way in which the emperor is portrayed as a military redeemer. In other words, Luke's description of the strong man is not isolated from his understanding of the Roman coercive power in relation to the emperor's peace.

As Luke relates Satan to the Roman Empire by the implication in the story of temptation, he does so here in the story of the strong man. The main difference between the two stories is that the former does not refer to military power, but the latter does. It is true that the emperor is often displayed as the one with armor, which signifies his military *imperium*. By linking Beelzebul's story directly to the strong man with "armor," Luke seems, again, to associate the power of Satan with the emperor's military power. In doing so, he heightens that such power is defeated by Jesus who is more powerful than the strong man with armor. Luke's Jesus says, "when one stronger than he attacks him and overpowers him, he takes away his armor in which he trusted and divides his plunder" (v. 22). Luke reports that Jesus, stronger than the strong man (Satan/emperor), achieves victory over him. Besides, Luke's addition in v. 23 indicates the identity of Jesus' enemies: "Whoever is not with me is against me, and whoever does not gather with me scatters." From Luke's perspective, those who are not with Jesus are the same as those who hate him. Thus, Luke attempts to plant the theme of Jesus' victorious conflict with Satan into the story of exorcism. At the same time, he is critical of the emperor who uses coercive power in order to achieve peace because such peace is temporary. The peace based upon coercive power will be taken away by the one who is stronger. Luke highlights that Jesus' peace is not based upon such power, and that his peace, accordingly, is not temporary. It is clear that exorcism itself stresses Jesus' superiority over both Satan and the emperor.

Another exorcism story in association with Jesus' authority is found in the story of the Gerasene demoniac at Luke 8:26–39, where both salvation and the concept of authority are strongly emphasized. Luke explains again in this story the conflict between Jesus and the demon. Jesus meets a demon-possessed man who wears no clothes and who lives among the tombs.[60] What is interesting is that he cries out and falls down before Jesus when he sees him (v. 28). This implies that the demon exactly acknowledges Jesus' authority, saying, "What have you to do with me, Jesus, Son of the Most High God? I beg you, do not torment me" (v. 28). Both his action and remark apparently indicate that Jesus' power/authority is superior to the demon's power. First, his action of kneeling to Jesus entails his acknowledgement of Jesus' power which is superior to his. Second, his remark of 'Jesus, Son of the Most High God' involves his understanding of Jesus' status with power conferred on him as well as the source of his power.

What is more, concerning the identity of the demon, he replies that he is "Legion" when Jesus asks his name (v. 30).[61] It seems to me that his name "Legion" alludes to his relationship, to some extent, with the Roman Empire. According to Evans, legion (λεγιών) is a Latin loan word (*legio*) "for a body of front line soldiers in the Roman army, generally 6,000 strong, and often with the same number of auxiliaries attached."[62]

---

60. While Luke reports that the man has demons (δαιμόνια) in Luke 8:27, Mark depicts him as the one who is with an unclean spirit (ἐν πνεύματι ἀκαθάρτῳ) in Mark 5:2.

61. There is an alteration between the singular "he" of the man and the plural "they" of the possessing demons.

62. Evans, *Luke*, 386; cf. Matt 26:53; Mark 5:9, 15. Legionaries were Roman citizens, auxiliaries usually not. "In the West, in the first century, most legionaries came from Italy or increasingly, as the century went on, from the more Romanized

Both Mark and Luke include his name in the story, while Matthew does not. While Luke follows the Markan account, Matthew omits the conversation about the name between Jesus and the demon-possessed man. In my view, Luke, who has a deep interest in Jesus' authority in comparison with the emperor's, does not omit such an account in order to make his accounts consistent with the other accounts such as Jesus' temptation and Beelzebul controversy. In other words, taken with those accounts together, the Gerasene demoniac account functions as supporting details, that is, the relationship between the demon and the emperor's military *imperium*. Luke shows that the demon, which is linked to the Roman Empire, is fully armed, and therefore he is called "Legion." The terms used here and in the other two accounts are related closely to the Roman emperor, especially, his coercive power. Thus, it becomes more evident that Luke, first, implicitly shows the relationship between the demon and the emperor, and that second, he emphasizes Jesus' superiority over both the demon and the emperor. Through his exorcism, Luke shows that Jesus is successful in obtaining victory over his enemies. Jesus' exorcism is also directly related to his saving activity in the following verses. The demon-possessed man has been saved (ἐσώθη in v. 36: Luke's addition) and sits at Jesus' feet as a disciple (v. 35; cf. 10:39).

Human Being

As far as the identity of Jesus' enemies is concerned, there are, along with non-human beings, mortals in Luke.[63] First, the Jewish leaders are frequently depicted as Jesus' opponents in his missionary accounts and even in his trial scene. They attempted to remove Jesus many times. Their hatred appears for the first time in Luke 4:28. It is noteworthy that their hatred comes with Jesus' first mission at Nazareth. It seems to me that Luke strives to give his readers or hearers a negative impression of the Jewish leaders who hate Jesus by placing their first anger in the account of Jesus' first mission. When this is compared to Mark's account, it is clear that Luke seeks to portray them as those who hate Jesus. While Luke describes that they are against Jesus at his first mission and at his

---

provinces, especially southern Gaul and Spain. The eastern legions recruited heavily in Asia Minor, especially in Galatia. East and West alike found likely recruits among soldiers' and veterans' sons" (Wells, *Roman Empire*, 136).

63. See the chapter on Jesus' Trial. For the discussion of ὄχλος and λαός in relation to Jesus' enemies, see Zechariah's praise below.

first contact with them, Mark does not. Mark reports their first anger in 3:5–6, not at Jesus' first mission (his first mission already started in ch.1): "The Pharisees went out and immediately conspired with the Herodians against him, how to destroy him" (v. 6).[64]

In Luke, right after reading the scroll of the prophet of Isaiah, Jesus refers to a widow at Zarephath and Naaman the Syrian. When hearing this, the Jewish leaders were "filled with rage."[65] Then, they drove Jesus out of the town and plotted to "hurl him off the cliff" (Luke 4:29). This story clearly indicates that the Jewish leaders hate him. Another instance is found in Luke 6:11 (see above; par. Mark 3:1–6). As in 4:28, the scribes and the Pharisees "were filled with fury and discussed with one another what they might do to Jesus" (6:11), when Jesus healed a man whose right hand was withered on the Sabbath. In addition, the highlight of their hatred is seen in Jesus' trial scene. As discussed in the chapter of Jesus' trial, they put Jesus to death with false charges.[66] It is clear that the Jewish leaders (but not all of them) were enemies who hated Jesus, and that Luke is more concerned with the relationship between Jesus and the Jewish leaders than Mark is.

Along with the Jewish leaders, Herod is also portrayed as the one who is not favorable towards Jesus. As already discussed, Herod is depicted in a negative tone in the Lukan account. He is also responsible for Jesus' death. In addition, Pilate, a Roman governor, is the one who opposes Jesus because he is responsible, to a large extent, for Jesus' death.[67] Thus, the people who are responsible for Jesus' death (Jewish leaders, Herod, and Pilate) can be seen as Jesus' enemies. They appear again as the enemies of his followers in Acts. In Luke-Acts, they are those who hate Jesus and his followers. Luke not only stresses that they are Jesus' enemies; but he

---

64. Here in Mark, Jesus' opponents are identified with the Pharisees and the Herodians.

65. Even though Luke does not specify here the identity of "all in the synagogue," it is evident that the Jewish leaders are Jesus' opponents throughout Luke-Acts.

66. See also Luke 11:53–54; 13:14; 19:47; 20:19; 22:2.

67. It is not easy to say that Pilate hates Jesus in the passion narrative. Nonetheless, there are several indicators of negative portrayal of Pilate, such as his action and verdict as well as his friendship with Herod. Even though Luke does not express that Pilate hates Jesus in a direct way, we can suppose that he, at least, is not favorable towards Jesus through the passion narrative. Besides, Luke seems to describe Pilate's violence, reporting that Pilate mingled Galileans' blood with their sacrifices in 13:1. See the chapter on Jesus' trial.

also attempts to show that Jesus triumphs over those enemies through his crucifixion and resurrection in his later chapters and in Acts.

Jesus as Peace-Bringer

Prior to the discussion of Jesus as savior, we need to analyze Jesus' peace in comparison with Augustus' peace, as Luke is interested in the theme of peace in his Gospel, along with victory. We have already discussed the importance of peace in the Roman Empire in connection with the emperor's title, savior. Peace is a forceful vehicle which ultimately gives the emperor such a title. It is thus evident that "peace" is a key theme in the formation of the emperor's power/authority. This echoing significance of peace is also assimilated into the Lukan accounts as the assimilation theory suggests. Gilbert asserts that Luke is well aware of the ideology that claimed "an inseparable bond between peace and imperial rule."[68] As Augustus' peace is related to his title (savior), peace in Luke's Gospel is also connected with the theme of "savior."

First, let us very briefly look at Zechariah's praise.[69] His praise plays an important role in explaining the basic concept of peace: "By the tender mercy of our God, the dawn from on high will break upon us, to give light to those who sit in darkness and in the shadow of death, to guide our feet into the way of peace" (Luke 1.78–79).[70]

Second, along with Zechariah's song, Luke strives to portray Jesus as a peace bringer elsewhere in his writings in the process of depicting him as savior. For instance, in the angels' song to the shepherds, peace is announced "on earth peace among those whom he favors" (Luke 2:14).[71] It seems that bringing peace is Jesus' major act of benefaction in

---

68. Gilbert, "Roman Propaganda," 240; when Tertullus, for instance, addresses the Roman procurator Felix at Paul's trial in Jerusalem, he begins with customary words of praise, "Because of you we have long enjoyed peace" (Acts 24:2).

69. For the detailed discussion of this praise in terms of victory–peace–salvation, see below.

70. On the basis of the Fabius' decree (EJ, no.98 (a) line 6 and 1B 4), Brent, *Imperial Cult*, 94, argues that "setting right" is associated conceptually with Augustus' augural act in producing an extraordinary *pax deorum*. In Luke 1:79 there is a similar "setting right" in connection with εἰρήνη or *pax* in the description of John as "guiding our feet into the way of peace." In addition, when she is healed, for Brent, the crippled woman is described as "being set right (or stood upright = ἀνωρθώθη), uniquely in the New Testament, in Luke 13:13."

71. See also Acts 10:36.

Luke. As found in Roman propaganda, Luke links bringing peace to the savior's activity.[72]

Third, the same point is also made in Simeon's praise. Simeon links his departure "in peace" with "your salvation" (2.29–30). Here, "peace" is related directly with "salvation" in Luke.[73] By stressing peace established through Jesus, Luke alludes to the theme of savior. Concerning ἐν εἰρήνῃ which appears in 2:29, Farris relates its root to the Old Testament and Rabbinic usage, emphasizing that it indicates the eschatological salvation of the whole man which signifies God's power.[74] It is true that peace is an essential characteristic of the Messianic kingdom as shown in the Old Testament, such as Ps 72:7; Zech 8:12; Isa 9:6. However, its use of ἐν εἰρήνῃ can be also associated with imperial ideology as shown above. The emperor's emphasis on peace heavily influences Luke's composition of the writings because he uses "the language of imperial authority and applies it to Jesus."[75] As Gilbert rightly puts it, peace, the related concept of salvation, presents a fascinating example of the intersection between Luke's Gospel and Roman political ideology.[76] Both the emperor and Luke's Jesus are portrayed as the ones who brought peace to their people.

---

72. See Gilbert, "Roman Propaganda," 242, arguing that "Readers of Luke–Acts would likely hear an echo of Roman political ideology." However, like other proponents of assimilation theory, Gilbert pays little attention to the differences between the contents of peace by Jesus and that by the emperors. He simply argues that Luke uses Roman propaganda. Gilbert ignores how tactfully Luke differentiated them from each other.

73. See Borgman, *Way*, 123–45.

74. Farris, *Hymns of Luke's Infancy Narratives*, 147.

75. Gilbert, "Roman Propaganda," 242; *contra*. Swartley, "War and Peace," 2339–41, offers an interpretation of the theme of peace in Luke–Acts that rejects the connection with Roman political ideology.

76. Gilbert, "Roman Propaganda," 239. Salvation is referred to in 2:30, but this time it is not the usual feminine noun, while the feminine is used in Zechariah's praise. It is σωτήριον, the neuter adjective used. This occurs only four times in the New Testament and three times in Luke–Acts, here and at Luke 3:6 and Acts 28:28. In this respect, Farris argues, *Hymns of Luke's Infancy Narratives*, 147: "It is possible that there is in this word a deliberate etymological allusion to the Hebrew root of the name Jesus." He goes on to assert that salvation here is a reminiscence of Isa 40:5, "all flesh shall see salvation, σωτήριον, of God" (147–78). According to Marshall, *Luke*, 120, the neuter σωτήριον is not only salvation itself, but also the one who brings salvation.

Sword/Violence

As assimilation theory shows, Luke uses the similar Roman formula applied to the emperor, victor/peace-bringer/savior. However, this should not lead us to the assumption that there are no differences between Jesus' peace and the emperor's peace. With the use of contra-culture theory, it will be analyzed how Luke rejects the innermost values of the emperor's peace. Let us see in what ways Jesus' peace in Luke differs from the emperor's peace in terms of the use of coercive power.

Jesus' peace is not identical with the emperor's; that is, the source of the former is completely distinguished from that of the latter. As discussed above, the source of the emperor's peace is based largely on his military *imperium* which enables him to achieve peace. There is no peace without military victory over enemies. However, Jesus' attitude towards coercive power in Luke is completely different from the emperor's. Luke stresses that Jesus does not accept the use of violence as a means of securing peace. To validate the differences between the two, we shall look at several passages in Luke's Gospel.

Jesus' Rejection of the Use of Sword (Luke 22:35–38 and Luke 22:47–53)

First, let us turn to the account immediately before Jesus' trial scene. The account of the Last Supper in Luke 22:35–38, at a glance, could be seen as Jesus' positive attitude towards the use of coercive power because of Jesus' reference to "sword." But this account affirms that he rejects the use of such power which is used for enhancing the emperor's power. In v. 36, Jesus says to his disciples, "the one who has no sword must sell his cloak and buy one." Even though there are very few theories clearly accounting for the reference to "sword," it is generally accepted among modern scholars that Jesus' admonition to buy a sword is not to be taken literally.[77] Nolland, among them, asserts that "the sword is thought of as part of the equipment required for the self-sufficiency of any traveler in the Roman world. Nothing more than protection of one's person is in

---

77. E.g., Fitzmyer, *Luke*, 2:1432; Green, *Luke*, 774–75; Hays, *Moral Visions*, 333; Marshall, *Luke: Historian*, 825. For exceptions, see e.g., Loisy, *L'Evangile selon Luc*, 524; Leaney, *Commentary*, 271, who connects this account with Isa 53:12, arguing that Luke in this passage attempts to reconcile the way that Gospel traditions include unsavory accounts of violence in the Garden of Gethsemane (Mark 14:47; Matt 26:51) with Luke's non-violent Jesus who loves enemies and rejects violent Messianism.

view."⁷⁸ He thus understands Jesus' reference to swords as implements of self-defense.⁷⁹

In a different vein, Hays suggests that the reference to sword has a figurative purpose. According to him, the disciples, who fail to understand Jesus' "figurative warning," take his reference to the sword literally-⁸⁰on the basis of their reply, "Lord, look, here are two swords" (v. 38a). For Hays, Jesus' response vindicates that they do not comprehend what Jesus really means: "It is enough" (v. 38b). Similarly, Fitzmyer argues that 'the irony concerns not the number of the swords, but the whole mentality of the apostles. Jesus will have nothing to do with swords, even for defense'.⁸¹ Cassidy, in line with Fitzmyer's view, concludes that "Throughout Luke's gospel, Jesus' teaching and actions relative to violence are thoroughly consistent. In particular circumstances Jesus acts and speaks aggressively, but he always does so without doing or sanctioning violence to persons, and he continually witnesses to overriding love and forgiveness."⁸² As Hays summarizes:

> Jesus' response "it is enough" to the disciples' announcement that already have two swords indicates that Luke is not concerned about real military violence or preparation for extended persecution. First, if Luke's Jesus were telling them to prepare for war or persecution, why would he instruct them even to sell their cloak to acquire the sword (22:36)? . . .To sell a cloak is not evidence of a long-term plan to survive the rigors of persecution . . . If this kamikaze mission were violent, then two swords would hardly be "enough." Second, if Ἱκανόν is to refer to the two μάχαιρα, why is it singular in form? The only reasonable answer is that something besides the number of swords is "enough."⁸³

78. Nolland, *Luke*, 3:1076.

79. Ibid.. Also see Conzelmann's view, *Theology*, 80–82, that Jesus' reference to sword is to be interpreted as a symbol of the disciple's preparation for the persecution they will face. However, one of the biggest problems with Conzelmann's argument is that, as Hays, *Luke's Wealth Ethics*, 95, claims, he fails to "account for the manner in which the Sermon on the Plain includes ethics of generosity and open vulnerability to the attacks of enemies."

80. Hays, *Moral Visions*, 333; see also Fitzmyer, *Luke*, 2:1428.

81. Fitzmyer, *Luke*, 2:1434.

82. Cassidy, *Jesus, Politics*, 47.

83. Hays, *Luke's Wealth Ethics*, 97; also see Minear, "Notes on Luke," 131, asserting that Jesus' response indicates that the swords are not for battle, but the fulfillment of the prophesy of Isaiah; cf. Tannehill, *Narrative Unity* 1:267; Petracca, *Gott oder das*

The account in Luke 22:35–38, therefore, has nothing to do with the use of coercive power. Jesus' reference to the swords does not mean that he supports the use of coercive power. As Rowe rightly suggests, the disciples' incomprehension has nothing to do with what Jesus meant.[84] In contrast to the disciples' misunderstanding, Jesus' attitude towards swords is not disposed favorably throughout Luke's Gospel. This view can be explained in connection with the story of Jesus' arrest scene in Luke 22:47–53. This subsequent story will support the idea that the issue of "the sword" in Luke 22:36–38 is not to be taken literally because it functions as implying Luke's contrast between Jesus' objection to the use of violence and the emperor's military *imperium*.

The theme of Jesus' non-violence is more apparent in the scene of Jesus' arrest. As in the previous account (22:35–38), Luke seeks to tell us something about the relationship between Jesus' interpretation of coercive power and that of the emperor through the story in 22:47–53. Like Mark and Matthew, Luke tells of the cutting off of the ear of the high priest's slave (22:50).[85] While Mark does not show any dialogue between Jesus and his disciples, Luke reports it. In Luke, the disciples asked Jesus before one of them struck the slave and cut off his right ear: "Lord, shall we strike with the sword?" (Luke 22:49). It is interesting to note that they had already struck and cut off the slave's ear even prior to Jesus' answer. Their action can be related to their misunderstanding of the sword in vv. 36–38.[86] Their understanding of the sword is very similar to the emperor's understanding in which coercive power is used as a means of achieving victory. However, Jesus rebuked, "No more of this!" (v. 51). His answer signifies the disciples' incomprehension of the use of the sword. This echoing theme is also found in Luke 9:52–56, and is unique to Luke. Jesus' disciples ask, "Lord, do you want us to command fire to come down from heaven and consume them?" As in 22:51, Jesus in 9:55 reprimands his disciples because they misread Jesus' power/authority. The theme that Jesus' power is not based upon destruction re-appears in the passion

---

Geld, 109–10; Evans, *Luke*, 807.

84. Rowe, *Early Narrative Christology*, 180.

85. Only Luke specifies it as the right ear.

86. Similarly Rowe, *Early Narrative Christology*, 180, emphasizing the importance of Jesus' title "Lord" in Luke's Gospel, maintains: "The focus upon the misuse of the μάχαιρα, Jesus' rebuke, and the disciples' Κύριε address clearly parallel the end of the Last Supper. In Luke's Gospel, the incident of 22:49–51 serves to complete the disciples' misinterpretation of Jesus' words in 22:36."

narrative. By embracing the process that leads to the crucifixion, Jesus involves the suffering and death of his passion although his disciples do not yet understand.[87]

Furthermore, it is noticeable that only Luke's Jesus heals the man (Luke 22:51) while the other Gospel writers do not report it. As Swartley observes, "His healing the high priest's slave's ear demonstrates his mission and manner of ministry. Put sharply, Jesus came to heal precisely what the sword devastates."[88] In doing so, Luke's description of Jesus' non-violent action, healing, and acceptance of his arrest and his passion and death, "provides the narrative within which the various teachings about peace and violence are to be understood."[89]

More importantly, Luke contrasts Jesus' rejection of the use of coercive power and his healing with the use of swords and clubs as a means of bringing opponents into submission (22:52). That is, Luke implicitly criticizes the emperor's victory and peace based upon his military *imperium*. He portrays Jesus as the one who deconstructs the association of the emperor's power with violence. As Rowe aptly states, "The nature of Jesus' *power* is radically misunderstood if interpreted as the power to destroy opponents by means of the sword."[90] Luke's Jesus does not employ violence in defense of peace. As the contra-culture theory shows, Luke changes the innermost concept of peace by degrading the value of coercive power.

The Cleansing of the Temple (Luke 19:45-48)

In the echoing sequence, Jesus' rejection of the use of coercive power is found in Luke 19:45-38 (par. Matt 21:12-13; Mark 11:15-19). Regarding the significance of this passage, Theissen argues that Jesus' temple action in Luke (along with its parallel texts) has nothing to do with his "attempt to incite a political revolt," but it is associated with the theme of Jesus' "prophetic symbolic action" for the destruction of the temple and building a new temple.[91] I do agree with Theissen's view that Jesus' action

---

87. Rowe, *Early Narrative Christology*, 181-82.

88. Swartley, *Covenant of Peace*, 132; see 121-51 for his treatment of peace in Luke's Gospel and 152-76 for Acts; also see Burridge, *Imitating Jesus*, 270.

89. Burridge, *Imitating Jesus*, 270.

90. Rowe, *Early Narrative Christology*, 181; italics mine.

91. Theissen, "Political Dimension," 225-50.

cannot be regarded as political revolt. But I wish to focus more on the way in which Jesus rejects violent resistance in the Lukan version than on his prophetic symbolic action. It is highly important to compare Luke's account with his material, Mark's account.[92]

Luke's account of the cleansing of the temple is somewhat different from Mark's version. While Mark makes entry into city and temple a single act (Mark 11:11, 15), Luke separates city (Luke 19:28ff.) and temple (Luke 19:45ff.). Luke does not refer to any entry of the city as such. He omits the stories about Jesus' preliminary inspection (Mark 11:11) and his cursing of the fig tree (Mark 11:12–14).[93] Above all, compared to Mark's account, Luke offers a very short version of the cleansing of the temple.[94]

In order better to clarify Luke's attempt to remove Jesus' activities relating to the violent images, we need to take a careful look at what significant elements are missing in Luke's version. First and foremost, while Mark records that Jesus "overturned (κατέστρεψεν) the tables of the money-changers and the seats of those who sold pigeons" (Mark 11:15; Matthew also reports this, 21:12), Luke omits such an account. He does not specify in what ways Jesus was angry at those people. An important question arises here. Why does Luke omit such an account? If the omission is intentional, what is he attempting to tell us through this story? In my view, the possible answer is that he seeks, at most, to remove Jesus' violent activities clearly expressed in Mark's version in order best to stress Jesus' non-violent character. Perhaps, Luke worries that Jesus' action of overturning both tables and seats would be seen as an act of violence by his audiences/readers. For that reason, Luke does not follow Mark's account. Instead, he simply tells us that Jesus drove out those who sold without any mention of violence-related activities (Luke 19:45) unlike Mark's account.[95]

---

92. Theissen pays little attention to the differences between Luke and other Gospels. When discussing Jesus' temple action, he tends to take all the versions as a single story with a single theme. This tendency leads him to ignore the differences between the Lukan version and the Markan account. In my view, a marked different conclusion can be made by taking into account the differences between two versions.

93. A similar account of fig tree was already supplied in Luke 13:6–9.

94. Mark's 42 words are reduced to 19 words in Luke.

95. In the case of Mark, Jesus drove out both those who sold and those who bought in the temple. However, Luke's Jesus drove out only sellers without any hint of what they were selling there. Luke omits purchasers, money-changers, dove-sellers, passers-by, Gentiles, and the like. Concerning the "Gentiles," in Mark 11:17, it is recorded, "My house shall be called a house of prayer for all the nations." But, both in Matt 21:13

My argument that Luke intends to highlight Jesus' non-violence by omitting some elements of the Markan version becomes more conceivable when taking a look at verse 47. As Mark does, Luke describes Jewish leaders' reaction to Jesus' reproach, reporting that they want to kill Jesus.[96] Concerning the Jewish leaders' reaction itself, there are no significant differences between Mark and Luke. However, when this verse is taken together with v. 45, it is interesting to note that Luke seems to draw a sharp contrast between Jesus' non-violence and his enemies' (Jewish leaders) violence by omitting the Markan account of "overturning the table and the seats." On one level, Luke re-emphasizes Jesus' rejection of coercive power by omitting Mark's account. On another level, such a description contrasts sharply with the Jewish leaders who want to kill him.[97]

Therefore, Luke's short version of the account, ironically, is long enough to highlight Jesus' attitude towards violence. Although Luke's version is much shorter than Mark's, it seems to me that the former places more emphasis on Jesus' non-violence than the latter does through this account. In other words, Luke tends to diminish any violent images of Jesus' activities by reducing the words relating to violence. His abbreviation

---

and Luke 19:46, the phrase "all the nations" is omitted. In this regard, Hays, *Moral Vision*, 334 n49, argues that "this is presumably because both of them, writing after the destruction of the Temple, want to avoid tying the Gentile mission to a particular vision of restored Temple worship."

96. Even though there is no account of how to kill Jesus, it is clear that their plot can be regarded as a way of violence which results in destruction. As seen in Jesus' trial scene, they come to Jesus to arrest him with the officers of the temple police (swords and clubs) in Luke 22:52.

97. Furthermore, when we consider the place of this event, we can affirm that the Jewish leaders lost their control. It was happening in the temple, the place of the Jewish religion, where the Jewish leaders were expected to control the situation. However, by showing what happened in the temple, Luke seems to show the fact that the Jewish representatives lost their control. That is, their authority is severely damaged. The one who attempts to control the situation is Jesus, not the Jewish leaders. In doing so, Luke's hearers/readers probably recognize that Jesus' authority/power, which enables him to hold the control of the place of Jewish leaders, is superior to his opponents' authority through this story. Also, it is noticeable that in vv. 47–48, there is another contrast between people and leaders of the people. Although in both verses the term λαός is mentioned, their attitude to Jesus is completely different. While the people (ὁ λαός; v. 48) are those who favor Jesus by listening to him, the leaders of the people (οἱ πρῶτοι τοῦ λαοῦ; v. 47) look for a way to kill him. More importantly, Mark does not refer to the leaders of the people, but he mentions only chief priests and scribes. Luke's addition functions as drawing a sharp contrast between the leaders of the people and the people.

serves as meeting his goal that his Jesus rejects the use of the coercive power in Luke 19:45–48.

Love Your Enemies (Luke 6:27–38)

More broadly, it is necessary to consider Luke's view on the use of coercive power in relation to one's enemies in his other account. The account in Luke 6:27–38 (par. Matt 5:38–48; non-Markan material), which refers directly to the enemies, shows his view on violence, although there is no reference to a sword. This account will help us to consider whether or not Luke interprets violence as a way of defense of justice.

In brief, Luke focuses Jesus' teaching on love and enemy in 6.27–38, as verse 27 clearly indicates: "Love your enemies." Prior to exploring the theme of love in this context, we need to analyze the identity of the enemies. Richard Horsley, attempting to examine their identity, associates "enemies" only with personal enemies within the Palestinian village setting.[98] According to Horsley, Jesus' saying, "love your enemies," "pertains neither to external, political enemies nor to the question of non-violence or non resistance."[99] In other words, in his view, the term "enemy" refers only to "personal enemies" on the ground that other residents of small Palestinian villages were set in opposition with one another for scarce economic resources.[100] He goes on to argue that, as they cannot express resentment against "the dominant system . . . subject peoples tend to vent their frustration in attacks against one another."[101] According to his argument, Jesus' teaching centers on the poor peasants by encouraging them to cooperate for their mutual economic benefit and by telling them to stop fighting/hating one another. In doing so, Horsley concludes that the exhortation to "love your enemies" cannot be construed as a general ethical principle, nor can it be applied directly to issues of war and enmity between nations.[102] Moreover, he rejects the view that Luke 6:27–38 is

---

98. Horsley, *Jesus and the Spiral of Violence*, 272–73; also see his article, "Ethics and Exegesis," 3–31.

99. Horsley, "Ethics and Exegesis," 3.

100. Horsley, *Jesus and Spiral of Violence*, 255.

101. Ibid.; also see "Ethics and Exegesis," 17, where he holds that the enemy is "a local adversary, e.g., one who sabotages a farmer's crop by sowing weeds among the grain."

102. Horsley, *Jesus and Spiral of Violence*, 255–73.

related to the theme of non-violence, stating that "non-violence is not the issue or the message in these texts."¹⁰³

Horsley's argument, however, should be criticized for his misunderstanding of the scope of enemies in Jesus' teaching. Based upon Sherwin-White's view that there were poor masses in Palestine,¹⁰⁴ Horsley too quickly concludes that the enemies are only personal ones without considering any possibility of other aspects of enemies.¹⁰⁵ It is right that the vast majority of people were oppressed by a small minority of the extremely wealthy upper class. But, unlike his assertion, Luke's Gospel does not contain any kind of social situation that Horsley suggests (nor does Matthew). There are no accounts concerning village conflicts in Luke.

Moreover, as Hays correctly points out, Horsley's view on the term ἐχθροί "cannot be supported by lexicographical evidence" because it is "generic."¹⁰⁶ It is not questionable that the term often refers to national or military enemies. For instance, in Deut 20:1: "When you go out to war against your enemies [LXX: ἐχθρούς], and see horses and chariots, an army larger than your own, you shall not be afraid of them, for the Lord your God is with you, who brought you up from the land of Egypt."¹⁰⁷ Another example is found in Luke 19:43: "Indeed, the days will come upon you, when your *enemies* (οἱ ἐχθροί) will set up ramparts (χάρακα) around you and surround you, and hem you in on every side." The enemies here have nothing to do with the conflicts which result from scarce economic resources among peasants. The word χάραξ (19:43) provides a hint of national enemies, rather than peasant conflicts. The term is not found elsewhere in the New Testament. But we can, at least, find the meaning of the word on the basis of its references in the LXX. For example, the χάρακα in Isa 37:33 does not refer to social conflicts among peasants, but it is associated closely with military/national enemies: "Therefore thus says the Lord concerning the king of Assyria: He shall not come into this city, shoot an arrow there, come before it with a shield, or cast up a siege ramp against it."¹⁰⁸ As in Deut 20:1, it is wrong to claim that the term ἐχθροί in Luke 19:43 refers only to "personal enemies" (also see 19:27);

103. Horsley, "Ethics and Exegesis," 14.

104. Sherwin-White, *Roman Society*, 139–42.

105. For Horsley ("Ethics and Exegesis," 22), the poor peasants are "hating, cursing, and abusing" one another under such desperate economic circumstances.

106. Hays, *Moral Vision*, 328.

107. Ibid., 328.

108. Cf. Deut 20:19; Isa 29:3; 37:33; Ezek 4:2.

rather, it is also used for national or military enemies. Thus, it is a mistake to argue that the term implies only "personal enemies."

In addition, when Luke's Jesus teaches the theme of "love your enemies," he takes several examples of love in connection with sinners. Given that sinners are considered as socio-cultural outcasts in that society, it is unlikely that Jesus' teaching on love is restricted only to personal enemies.[109] That is, his teaching has a political implication in a broad sense.

Furthermore, Jesus' trial provides a significant clue to his enemies' identity even though Luke does not refer to the term ἐχθροί in this account. As discussed in Chapter 1, Luke describes those who attempt to put Jesus to death in a very negative tone; accordingly, they can be seen as his enemies.[110] They include the Jewish leaders, Herod, and Pilate. Are they portrayed only as Jesus' personal enemies for economic benefit as Horsley argues? It is doubtful that they imply only Jesus' personal enemies because of scarce economic resources. There are more aspects than Horsley supposed. Their behavior against Jesus should not be limited to "personal enemies" on the grounds that they are all religious or political leaders in Palestine. The scope of "enemy" is therefore inclusive of various enemies, such as personal, social, military, religious, and political enemies. As Heinz-Wolfgang Kuhn correctly notes, "The directive is without boundaries. The religious, the political, and the personal enemy are all meant."[111] It is highly likely that the enemies in Luke are identified with those who hate (μισοῦσιν), curse (καταρωμένους), and abuse (ἐπηρεαζόντων) religiously, socially, and politically (vv. 27–28).[112]

Let us turn to another theme, love. Many scholars argue that the command of love is one of the most important themes in the New

---

109. Burridge, *Imitating Jesus*, 269, notes: "The group chosen as a contrast to the behavior of Jesus' followers is interesting: while Matthew suggests that Gentiles' greet their brethren, Luke says that even 'sinners lend to sinners' and love those who love them' (Luke 6:32–35; cf. Matt 5:47); Matthew's low expectations of Gentiles' behavior would not be appreciated by Luke's wider audience!"

110. This is implied in Zechariah's praise. See below.

111. Kuhn, "Das Liebesgebot Jesu als Tora." The English translation here is from Klassen, "Love Your Enemies," 11; similarly, Theissen, "Political Dimension," 233–34, emphasizes that the identity of enemies include national enemies as well as personal enemies; cf. Wengst, *Pax Romana*, 68–72.

112. In Luke, the ἐχθροί are expressed as those who stand against Jesus and persecute him without any implication of fighting for economic benefit among peasants. They are also those who do not favor God (Luke 2:14). On the meaning of μισέω, see Zechariah's song.

Testament. For instance, Furnish claims that "for most of the New Testament writers the love command is . . . *decisive* and *central*."[113] Similarly, Blank states that "the commandment to love provides the fundamental unity in the New Testament ethics and . . . *the centre of Christian ethics*."[114] Then, what significance does Jesus' love command in terms of the use of coercive power (i.e., the exercise of the Roman emperors' power) bear? In Luke 6:27-28, Luke's Jesus takes several examples of how to love enemies. As a whole, he commands his readers/audiences to "do good to those who hate *them*, bless those who curse *them*, pray for those who abuse *them*" (vv. 27b-28) by using three imperative verbs such as do good (καλῶς ποιεῖτε), bless (εὐλογεῖτε), and pray (προσεύχεσθε).[115] The phrase "do good" refers to beneficent actions towards those who hate, and concrete examples of this are shown in vv. 29-31[116]. What is noticeable is that Luke's Jesus does not command his followers to do good only to his friends or neighbors in this story. Rather, his exhortation includes their enemies. The popular idea about love in the first century world is somewhat different from what Jesus in Luke says. Jesus says in Matthew 5:44, "You have heard that it was said, 'You shall love your neighbors and hate your enemies'" which represents a sort of popular idea of love among first century people. Klassen, who analyses Matthew's account of enemy love, notes:

> The formula "Be good to [or love] your friends and hate your enemies" was widespread in the ancient world and occurs in many layers of documentation. Rather than look in vain throughout Jewish sources, including Qumran, for example, for these exact words, we should simply treat them as part of the general folk

---

113. Furnish, *Love Command*, 200; his italics.

114. Blank, "Unity and Plurality," 70; his italics. Also see Hays, *Moral Vision*, 19–36, on Paul, 196-98 on the rest of NT, where he seems to place more emphasis on "cross, community and new creation" than on the theme of love.

115. Matthew's account is slightly different in specifying the identity of enemies. He, giving a double command in Matt 5:44 ("Love your enemies and pray for those who persecute you"), identifies them with those who persecute without any reference to the verbs such as "to hate," "to curse," or "to abuse." Compared to Matthew's account, Luke's account provides a specific explanation of the identity of enemies. See also Schottroff, "Non-Violence," 9–39; Swartley, ed., *Love of Enemy*; Theissen, "Non-Violence," 115–57.

116. "If anyone strikes you on the cheek, offer the other also; and from anyone who takes away your coat do not withhold even your shirt. Give to everyone who begs from you; and if anyone takes away your goods, do not ask for them again. Do to others as you would have them do to you."

wisdom that Jesus' listeners had heard -words that were well known to Matthew's audience as well.[117]

It is interesting to note that Jesus' love is not limited only to "friends" or "neighbors" in contrast to such a pervasive idea of the ancient world. In Luke, Jesus' expansive love includes even the enemies.

Besides, when talking about physical maltreatment in v. 29, Luke reports, "if anyone strikes you on the cheek, offer the other also." This means that he does not agree with the use of coercive power.[118] In this regard, it is implied that Luke strategically contrasts Jesus' love, which renounces violence, with the emperor's use of coercive power. While the emperor conquers his enemies by his military troops, Jesus does not. According to Luke, Jesus' way of victory over enemies is not based upon the use of violence, but upon love, drawing a sharp contrast between Jesus and the emperor. The point I wish to make here is that when talking about the theme of non-retaliation and love in connection with enemies, Luke does not focus Jesus' teaching on the use of violence in connection with his victory over enemies, but on love of enemies as a way of victory.[119]

For Luke, Jesus, when defending the outcasts, does not organize armed resistance against the Roman Empire or against the Jewish elites in collaboration with Roman authority. Rather, his activity consists of healing/exorcism and proclamation of the kingdom of God. To put it another way, he does not follow the Roman use of violence for promoting peace and security. It is clear that there is no foundation for the notion that violent action is justifiable in defense of Jesus himself or his followers.[120] Again, his death is consistent with his teaching on non-violence, and on love of the enemies by submitting to being persecuted and killed.[121]

---

117. Klassen, "Love Your Enemies," 12; in Matthew such a formula is mentioned, but Luke does not refer to it. See also Lev 19:18.

118. *Contra.* Horsley, "Ethics and Exegesis," 18, claims that "there is only insult and no damage to person"; similarly, Perrin, *Rediscovering*, 147.

119. Piper, *Love Your Enemies*, 56 and 58; Furnish, *Love Command*, 56 and 61; Caird, *Saint Luke*, 104; Hays, *Moral Vision*, 329; *contra.* Horsley, "Ethics and Exegesis," 14–5.

120. Hays, *Moral Vision*, 324; and he notes, "The transcendence of violence through loving the enemy is the most salient *feature of Luke's community* . . . Instead of wielding the power of violence, the community of Jesus' disciples is to be meek, merciful, pure, devoted to peacemaking . . ." (322; his italics)

121. Furnish, *Love Command*, 89–90 notes: "Luke views Jesus' whole ministry as a mission to the world's needy, as the effective presence of the gospel of peace. The command to love is given special prominence in the Sermon of the Plain, and its practical

Luke struggles to tell us that the hope of justice is not based upon coercive power, but upon God's love by including even the ungrateful and the wicked (6:35; also see vv. 27–28, those who hate, curse and abuse). The Greek word ἐπηρεαζόντων (abuse/insult) in v. 28 is referred to only in 1 Pet 3:16, apart from here in v. 28 and in Matthew 5:44, in the New Testament.[122] It is written, "Yet do it with gentleness and reverence. Keep your conscience clear, so that, when you are maligned, those who abuse (οἱ ἐπηρεάζοντες) you for your good conduct in Christ may be put to shame" (1 Pet 3:16). In this verse, those who abuse them are interpreted as the enemies of Christians as in Luke 6:27–28.[123] What Luke stresses is that Jesus' love includes even his (and his followers') enemies identified with the ungrateful and the wicked in v. 35.[124] In Luke, Jesus' rejection of vengeance upon his enemies is based upon his teachings on love and forgiveness.[125] Kim rightly puts it:

> his teachings on forgiveness and love, and his definition of lordship in the Kingdom of God in terms of humble service- the Lucan contrast between Jesus and Caesar in the *inclusio* of Luke 2:1–14 and Acts 28:30–31 makes it clear that Jesus' *authority/ power* is not a militaristic one like that of Caesar, and his peace and salvation is not a product of subjugation of *his enemies* like that of the Roman Empire, but is rather a fruit of his humble service for humankind symbolized by the manger and the cross. So Jesus brings salvation to Israel not in the Roman way, i.e., not by doing vengeance upon her enemy, the Roman Empire, or

---

implications for the Christian life are constantly emphasized. It means the compassionate serving of whoever stands in need, active 'doing good' even to one's enemies, restraint in judging others, forgiveness, reconciliation, and sharing one's resources with all the brethren in the Christian *koinonia*."

122. Horsley ("Ethics and Exegesis," 17), again, asserts that "those who mistreat you" would have to be local.

123. See Evans, *Luke*, 334.

124. See also Rom 12:14, 16a, 17–21: "Bless those who persecute you; bless and do not curse them . . . Live in harmony with one another . . . Do not repay anyone evil for evil, but take thought for what is noble in the sight of all. If it is possible, so far as it depends on you, live peaceably with all. Beloved, never avenge yourselves, but leave room for the wrath of God; for it is written, 'Vengeance is mine, I will repay, says the Lord.' No, 'if your enemies are hungry, feed them; if they are thirsty, give them something to drink; for by doing this you will heap burning coals on their heads.' Do not be overcome by evil, but overcome evil with good."

125. See Kim, *Christ and Caesar*, 104–5, who focuses on Jesus' rejection of the idea of vengeance upon Gentile enemies in connection with the account in Luke 9:51–56; on the discussion of forgiveness, see below.

subjugating her military to Israel, but in the way of the Kingdom of God: forgiveness and love.[126]

Thus, Jesus' victory over his enemies through love is not the same as the emperor's victory through his military power. With the focus on love, Hays underlines that Jesus' non-violence "may not only confound the enemy, but also pose an opportunity for the enemy to be converted to the truth of God's kingdom."[127] The disciples of Jesus reflect the character of God, who also offers mercy to the righteous and even to enemies by loving their enemies.[128] That is why those who sit in darkness and in the shadow of death (Luke 1:79; as well as the ungrateful and the wicked in 6:35) can be saved through Jesus (God's love).

As he rejects the use of violence as opposed to the Roman Empire, Luke contrasts Jesus' view on coercive power with some of the Jewish revolutionaries around his time. There are several examples which describe the Jewish revolutionaries. They include the Jewish revolt against Herod's appointment by Rome as "king of the Judeans" in 40 BC, the first Jewish-Roman War in AD 66–73, and Bar Kokhba's revolt in AD 132–135.[129] According to Horsley, such revolutionary resistance to foreign rule and domestic oppression is not isolated from the essence of Israel's tradition from the Exodus, the prophetic movements, and the Maccabean revolt.[130] They all advocated a violent revolt against their enemies.[131]

Stressing such Jewish resistance movements, Horsley goes on to argue that Jesus' movement has two major themes: proclamation of God's judgment both on the Roman Empire and Jewish rulers[132] and "a mission

---

126. Kim, *Christ and Caesar*, 105; italics mine.

127. Hays, *Moral Vision*, 326.

128. Ibid., 327.

129. For the discussion of the militaristic Messianic hopes prominent in certain first-century Jewish groups, see Freyne, "Herodian Period," 36–41.

130. Horsley, *Jesus and the Spiral of Violence*, esp. 28–145.

131. Horsley, based upon Josephus' works, *Jewish War* and *Jewish Antiquities*, presents several types of resistance and revolutionary movements. As a whole, he categorizes five types of resistance movement, namely, "the scribal resistance" (the fourth philosophy), "the *Sicarii*" (another scribal resistance), "popular resistance movements," "popular prophetic and messianic movements" (the three peasant revolts in Galilee, Judaea, and in Perea), "popular prophetic movements of Theudas."

132. Horsley, *Jesus and Empire*, 79–104.

of social renewal among subject peoples."[133] In terms of the first theme of Jesus' movement, he notes:

> Jesus of Nazareth belongs in the same context with and stands shoulder to shoulder with other revolutionary leaders of movements among the Judean and Galilean people, and pursues the same general agenda in parallel paths: independence from Roman imperial rule so that the people can again be empowered to renew their traditional way of life under the rule of God.[134]

When talking about the second theme of Jesus' work, he summarizes:

> Convinced that Roman rulers and their Herodian and high-priestly clients had been condemned by God . . . Jesus acted to heal the effects of empire and to summon people to rebuild their community life. In the conviction that the kingdom of God was at hand, he pressed a program of social revolution to re-establish just egalitarian and mutually supportive social-economic relations in the village communities that constituted the basic form of the people's life.[135]

In this regard, such views lead Horsley to define Jesus' work as "Jesus' alternative to the Roman imperial order."[136] For him, there is no big difference between Jesus movement and his contemporary revolutionary movements.

However, Horsley's understanding of Jesus' movement has some problems. While he is successful in analyzing some similarities between Jesus and his contemporary revolutionaries, he draws little attention to the differences between the two.[137] Several scholars, such as Wright and Theissen, strongly argue that Jesus is severely critical of his contemporaries' violent revolution.[138] For instance, Wright asserts that Jesus is opposed to nationalistic exclusivists, and he commands his followers to be the light to the nations (Matt 5:14; Mark 4:21; Luke 8:16).[139] He goes on to

---

133. Ibid., 105–28.
134. Ibid., 104.
135. Ibid., 105.
136. Ibid., 126.
137. See Kim's critiques of Horsley, *Christ and Caesar*, 108–111.
138. Wright, *Jesus and the Victory of God*, 446–50; Theissen, "Political Dimension," 233–35. Also see Ch.2.
139. Wright, *Jesus and the Victory of God*, 595–96; in a similar vein, Theissen, "Political Dimension," 233–35, holds that Jesus' teaching about "enemy love' heightens his rejection of 'the politics of physical force."

claim that the Jewish national exclusivism and their military power were as much compromises with paganism as was the Jewish rulers' collusion with the Romans.[140] Luke critiques the violent revolutionaries that can result in hatred of enemies, and he accordingly emphasizes Jesus' teaching on love of the enemies in order to bring peace to them. Therefore, Luke, in contrast to those revolutionaries, stresses that Jesus' victory over his enemies has nothing to do with the use of coercive power. Instead of violence, he offers his own way of peace, which is re-defined as forgiveness and love for even Jesus' enemies. For Luke, Jesus' teaching on mercy/love (Luke 6:36) makes both him and his disciples distinct from the emperor; that is, the Lukan Jesus as victor and peace-bringer is not identical with the emperor.

Jesus as Savior

We discussed the emperor's formula of victory and peace reconstructed in Luke's Gospel. Now we shall discuss the title "savior." As the emperor is portrayed as savior, Jesus is also expressed as such in Luke 2:11. Along with Luke's Gospel, Luke refers to this title again in Acts 5:31 and 13:23. Even though the title itself occurs only three times in Luke–Acts, the use of its cognates further heightens Jesus' identity as savior. Luke frequently describes Jesus as the one who brings peace and salvation to people, emphasizing that his salvation activities are inseparable from savior. The key words, which signify the term "savior" (σωτήρ), are primarily "salvation" (σωτηρία, σωτήριον) and "to save" (σῴζω). Jesus as savior is explicitly described in the language of salvation.

140. Wright, *Jesus and the Victory of God*, 446–50, 596. In this respect, he (413–28) holds that Jesus warned Israel of God's impending judgment in the form of Rome's devastation, as Jeremiah warned Judah of God's judgment through Babylon's devastation (Mark 13; Matthew 24; Luke 21). For him, God's judgment is done through Rome. There are no reasons to deny that Jesus was very critical of violent revolution. However, Wright's view that Rome played a leading role in punishing Israel is not convincing. Even though it is true that Jerusalem was collapsed by the Roman troops, it does not necessarily mean that God used Rome as his instrument of punishing his peoples. In my view, Rome is used as a representative with coercive power, which should be overcome by God's love and forgiveness. The Roman Empire as the enemy of Jesus, since she does not favor God's word, is depicted as the entity to be loved in spite of her use of coercive power. Moreover, although the Roman Empire as a whole is considered as the enemy, the peace and salvation which will be brought by Jesus are still available to Jesus' enemies if they truly turn to God. That is why Jesus' preaching continues in Acts through his followers in the Roman Empire.

Concerning the debate of Luke's frequent use of salvation language, Conzelmann, drawing attention to the insignificance of the word statistics, asserts that "the special elements in Luke's Christology cannot be set out by a statistical analysis of the titles applied to Jesus."[141] In a somewhat similar way, Cadbury maintains, "An adequate explanation of the occurrences of *salvation languages* would be found in the author's own free and unconscious use of the term, rather than in any systematic derivation from sources."[142] Cadbury is right in asserting that Luke himself freely uses the languages or titles. However, his view that such occurrences are 'unconscious' should be reconsidered.[143] When compared with Mark and Matthew, it is clear that Luke uses salvation language more often than they do. The frequency in the occurrences of these cognates distinguishes Luke from them. Also, the author who uses σωτήρ, σωτηρία, and σωτήριον altogether is only Luke. His use of such terms is his comprehensive narrative strategy, making a conscious effort to heighten Jesus' identity as savior as opposed to Conzelmann's and Cadbury's arguments.[144] For instance, the angels in the birth narrative tell the shepherds, "to you is born this day in the city of David a Savior" (2:11), and Simeon says of the infant Jesus, "my eyes have seen your salvation" (2:30).[145] Also, in response

---

141. Conzelmann, *Theology*, 170. Along with σωτήρ (Luke 1:47; 2:11; Acts 5:31; 13:23), Luke's use of salvation languages, such as σωτηρία (Luke 1:69, 71, 77; 19:9; Acts 4:12; 7:25; 13:26; 16:17; 27:34), and σωτήριον (Luke 2:30; 3:6; Acts 28:28), are relatively frequent in his two-volume writings. Besides, the word "save" (σῴζω) in Luke's Gospel occurs seventeen times, referring twelve times to healing or some other temporal restoration (6:9; 7:50; 8:36, 48, 50; 9:24a; 17:19; 18:42; and the four insults aimed at Jesus at the cross in 23:35–39), and five times to forgiveness or some other eschatological restoration (7:50; 8:12; 9:24b; 13:23; 18:26). In this regard, Malherbe, "Christology in Luke–Acts 2," 115, suggests that "σῴζω" is "never used in a purely therapeutic manner when it is used in connection with healing. There is always a higher purpose, and this higher purpose is the reason why the healing is performed. It thus stands frequently with *pistis*, 'faith,' and its cognates, and with psyche, 'soul.'" "Saved by faith" brings temporal restoration four times in Luke (8:48, 50; 17:19; 18:42), and eschatological restoration twice (7:50; 8:12). For the further discussion of the meaning of "save" and "savior" in Luke, see Witherington, "Salvation and Health," 145–66.

142. Cadbury, "Titles of Jesus," 361; italics mine.

143. The same point is made by Rowe, *Early Narrative Christology*, 4 n14.

144. Alter, *Art of Biblical Narrative*, 113, argues that the "pervasive repetitions" in various sections of the Old Testament are constitutive of "the Bible's narrative art"; he explores the "[t]echniques of Repetition," stressing: "One of the most imposing barriers that stands between the modern reader and the imaginative subtlety of biblical narrative is the extraordinary prominence of verbatim repetition in the Bible" (88).

145. Also see the Zechariah's prophecy.

to a question posed by members of the high-priestly family, Peter stresses Jesus' salvation: "there is salvation in no one else (but Jesus), for there is no other name under heaven given among mortals by which we must be saved" (Acts 4:12).[146] In addition, when Paul and his followers met a slave-girl having a spirit of divination and prophetic abilities, she said that Paul proclaimed "a way of salvation" (Acts 16:17).[147] It is therefore evident that Luke's intention of depicting Jesus as savior is connected, to a large extent, with his frequent use of salvation language.

It is important to explore to whom salvation is offered in Luke's Gospel, and what the basis for salvation is. Luke describes how Jesus' salvation involves peace, restoration, healing, exorcism, and forgiveness.[148]

Jesus' Saving Activities in Relation to Tax Collectors

We have already discussed how Jesus offered salvation to the demon-possessed people with reference to his victory over enemies. In this respect, his victory can be interpreted as salvation. In this section, we shall focus on Jesus' salvation given to tax collectors. We have already analyzed that, on the one hand, Luke attempts to adopt, adapt and maintain values and conventions of the imperial ideas with reference to assimilation theory. On the other hand, as the contra-culture theory shows, he aims to differentiate the status of the emperor and that of Jesus by re-evaluating morality in his Gospel. Taken together with the previous chapter on Luke's implicit critique of the emperor's moral *auctoritas*, Luke implicitly shows that the emperor is to be seen as a pseudo-savior as opposed to Jesus as a true savior. Again, he does not reject the title of savior; rather, he utilizes the imperial pattern of victory–peace–salvation.

It is evident that Luke wishes to emphasize that Jesus' salvation is for all (Luke 2:31; 3:6; Acts 2:21) as the emperor's is intended to be. Concerning the recipients of salvation, Luke tells of various people who are real

---

146. In this respect, Malherbe, "Christology in Luke–Acts 2,"115, argues that Jesus himself is the salvation (Acts 13:26), and salvation is to be found only in him (Acts 4:12).

147. See Gilbert, "Roman Propaganda," 241.

148. Danker, *Jesus and New Age,* 28–46, holds that Jesus, as savior, is the one through whom God's mercy is extended to all (Acts 2:21; 10:36); he meets and surpasses society's expectations of a Hellenistic "benefactor" by bestowing such divine gifts as healing, peace, and forgiveness of sins (Acts 4:9–10; 10:38); on the discussion of benefactor, see Ch.3.

or potential recipients of salvation in his writings. As Luke's writing has a universal concern, he intentionally includes men and women, adults and children, Jews and Gentiles, and people representative of various social classes in his salvation accounts.[149]

Let us now analyze the accounts of tax collectors to show Jesus' salvation activities. A significant question arises. To what extent is Luke's Jesus as savior different from the emperor? Or, how does Luke associate Jesus' salvation with removal of sins? While in Chapter 2 I stressed tax collectors' immorality and the emperor's failure to correct it, in this part I intend to highlight Jesus' correction in relation to his provision of salvation and forgiveness of sins. My intention is to validate that Luke uses tax collectors in order to show the differences between Jesus and the emperor in terms of their salvation. In the light of the analysis of several accounts, we can affirm that Jesus' encounters with tax collectors point to his identity as savior. As McComiskey rightly suggests, Luke appears to "have repeated particular themes, words, and characters from one story to another" to form Jesus' saving activities.[150]

Let us consider the stories about forgiving sins and salvation. Tannehill demonstrates the correspondences of Jesus' "releasing sins" in four passages (Luke 5:17–32; 7:31–50; 15:1–32; 19:1–10).[151] Tannehill, stressing the unity in Luke–Acts, notes:

> Beginning in 5:17 the narrator demonstrates special interest in Jesus as the proclaimer of the release of sins by taking a diverse group of stories related to this theme and artfully connecting them, even though they are separated by other materials. The stories are connected because later stories repeatedly remind the reader of earlier, related stories. This contributes to the unity of the narrative *and to Luke's emphasis on Jesus' authority*. It also encourages a reading process of recall and comparison so that as

---

149. This contrasts with the scope of the emperor's salvation. As Jewett, *Romans*, 143, demonstrates, "in place of the salvation of the *Pax Romana*, based on force, there is the salvation of small groups cooperatively interacting with one another to extend their new forms of communality to the end of the world." But Jesus' salvation does include those considered as outcasts. This implies that Jesus with his power can save the outcasts while the emperor cannot.

150. McComiskey, *Lukan Theology*, 425–48.

151. Tannehill, *Narrative Unity*, 1:9, 103–109; also see McComiskey, *Lukan Theology*, 49–53. For direct thematic connections, see, e.g., Luke 2:11, 30: 19:9; Acts 4:12; 5:31; 13:32, 26; 16:17; 28:28 (σωτήρ); and Luke 5:20–24; 7:47–49; Acts 2:38; 5:31; 7:60; 10:43; 13:38; 22:16; 26:18 (ἁμαρτία).

SAVIOR: VICTORY–PEACE–SALVATION

each new episode is sounded, the related episodes resound with enriching harmonies.[152]

As Tannehill suggests, there are several accounts which are reminiscent of previous stories in Luke's Gospel. With the help of Tannehill's assertion, I wish to relate four stories indicated above to the theme of Jesus' forgiveness of sins, which signifies his saving activities in association with his title of savior.[153]

It is noticeable that the account at Luke 5:17–32, including the story of Levi, highlights Jesus' authority to forgive sins. As in other Gospels, Luke tells of Jesus' authority in terms of forgiveness of sins.[154] The theme is clearer when we look into vv. 20–21. When Jesus says, "Friend, your sins are forgiven you" (v. 20), the scribes and the Pharisees ask, "Who is this . . . Who can forgive sins but God alone?" (v. 21). Their questions are important for identifying the source of Jesus' authority. At a glance, it seems that their question functions as denying Jesus' authority. However, ironically, Luke alludes to the fact that their questions signify both the source of Jesus' authority and his identity.[155] It is interesting to note that this fact comes from the mouth of Jesus' opponents. The logic is very simple. Their remarks functions as affirming that Jesus' power, which comes from God, enables him to forgive sins after healing a paralyzed man with "the power of the Lord" (v. 17).[156] They continue by saying that only God can forgive sins (v. 21) after seeing Jesus' forgiveness of sins (v. 20). In doing so, Luke artfully and deliberately portrays Jesus' opponents as his witnesses who play a certain role in validating Jesus' authority in

---

152. Tannehill, *Narrative Unity*, 1:103–4; italics mine.

153. One of the Lukan favorite expressions "forgiveness of sins" is previously mentioned in Luke 1:77, and it occurs eight times in Luke-Acts (out of eleven times in the New Testament). This expression is linked directly to Luke 3:3: "a baptism of repentance for the forgiveness of sins."

154. For a discussion of 'forgiven' in this story see Bock, "Son of Man," 121 n37.

155. Similar functions can be found in Luke 11:14–23 and Acts 14:10–18. See above.

156. For the discussion of Jesus' identity of "Lord," see Rowe, *Early Narrative Christology*. His argument is that that Jesus and God share the identity as κύριος, which is used with reference both to Jesus and to God, in spite of Luke's intentional ambiguity in its use. One of the examples of such ambiguity is in the infancy narrative, when God has repeatedly been referred to as κύριος. The fetus in Mary's womb is suddenly called κύριος by Elizabeth (1:43). Rowe (78) goes on to assert that, "when Luke later in 2:11 brings together the two titles Χριστός and κύριος, he provides his interpretation of the Messiah-title. Jesus is a Messiah who is also Lord."

his writing. Like God as "savior" in Luke 1:47, who offers salvation (Luke 2:30, 31) to his people, Jesus is expressed as a savior who is also responsible for salvation by forgiving sins. That is, God's authority to save his people comes true through Jesus' activity.

Moreover, the subsequent account of Levi (vv. 27–32) serves to "confirm the extension of this forgiveness even to those considered unworthy by the scribes and the Pharisees."[157] When Jesus calls him, Levi "got up, left everything, and followed him" (v. 28). In v. 32, Jesus says, "I have come to call not the righteous but sinners to repentance." Matthew 9:13 and Mark 2:17 have the same line, but only Luke has the last two words, "to repentance," reminding readers of John the Baptist's warning in Luke 3.[158] Neufeld asserts:

> Our readers now know that Jesus calls sinners and has authority to forgive sins. The examples thus far are first Simon, James, and John, and then Levi. Each of these left all to follow Jesus, and this will resonate with our reader, who, with the Baptist's words still freshly in mind, quickly connects repentance with radically adjusting one's relationship to possessions, which people abandon when they come to Jesus. Once sinners leave all for Jesus, the text assumes they have repented and been forgiven by Jesus the forgiver.[159]

Thus, it is evident that Luke's Jesus has authority to forgive the sins of Levi, and that this can be seen as a way of salvation.

Concerning Luke 7:31–50, Luke's depiction of Jesus as a friend of tax collectors/sinners is reminiscent of the account of Levi.[160] Also, the next scene focuses on Jesus as the one who offers divine forgiveness to an unworthy woman (Luke 7:48). Both the tax collectors and the woman, regarded as sinners by Jesus' opponents, are forgiven and accordingly saved.[161] Here again, the question of Jesus' opponents functions as an

---

157. McComiskey, *Lukan Theology*, 50–51.

158. Neufeld, "Gospel in the Gospels," 286 n46; also see Ch. 2.

159. Ibid.

160. See Luke 5:30 and 7:34, in particular. McComiskey, *Lukan Theology*, 51; Tannehill's *Narrative Unity*, 1:105.

161. Burridge, *Imitating Jesus*, 52 (italics mine) notes: "No wonder that Luke depicts Jesus dying with such words of forgiveness for enemies and acceptance of sinners on his lips (Luke 23:34, 39–43) . . . [F]orgiveness is . . . another distinctive feature of Jesus' salvation activities"; see also Shriver, *Ethics for Enemies*, 33–45.

indicator of Jesus' identity: "Who is this who even forgives sins?" (v. 49) Their question validates Jesus' authority to forgive sins and to save.[162]

Luke's emphasis on Jesus' forgiveness of sins is also evident in 15:1–32. The story of Levi in 5:29–32 is linked to the parables in 15:1–32 on the grounds that there is a sharp contrast between the righteous and sinners in both accounts (5:32 and 15:7, 10). It is noticeable that both accounts seem to stress the theme of repentance by contrasting two groups. As mentioned above, this theme also corresponds to John the Baptist's emphasis on repentance in his preaching (3:8).[163] It is true that both Matthew and Mark also refer to "repentance" in their Gospels.[164] But Luke has John the Baptist elaborate on the theme of repentance while Mark refers to repentance only once without a vivid picture of John's preaching of repentance.[165] He says, "bear fruits worthy of repentance," because the axe is already at the root of the tree, and trees without good fruit will be thrown in the fire (Luke 3:8–9). The people ask how to be saved from this coming judgment, and John teaches the fruit of repentance to the crowds, tax collectors, and soldiers "in very practical terms like sharing food and clothing, and not extorting money" (Luke 3:7–14).[166] In each case, John requires "generosity and honesty regarding money and possessions," all related to morality as discussed in Chapter 2.[167] It is thus evident that 'to

162. In v. 50, salvation is linked to peace as shown in the imperial cults.

163. Also see Acts 3:19.

164. While John the Baptist's first direct speech in Matthew is, "Repent, for the kingdom of heaven has come near" (Matt 3:2), his first direct speech in Mark is not associated with repentance: "The one who is more powerful than I is coming after me" (Mark 1:7). John's first direct speech in Luke opens with "You brood of vipers! Who warned you to flee from the wrath to come?" (Luke 3:7; and this to all who come for baptism, not just leaders, as in Matthew) Luke's description seems more vivid and urgent than Mark's.

165. Sanders, *Jesus and Judaism*, 108–13, has doubts about claims that repentance is "central to Jesus' message." Although the word "to repent" may not be common in Jesus' preaching, Wright, *Jesus and the Victory of God*, 254, correctly asserts that in many of the parables and the rest of Jesus' teaching, the challenge of his "different values" and the call to discipleship all implied "a summons to repentance." Similarly, Burridge, *Imitating Jesus*, 70, claims: "There are Jesus' warnings about what might happen if people or towns do not repent (Luke 13:1–5; Matt 11:20–24/ Luke 10:13–15; Matt 12:41/ Luke 11:32). Thus it is clear that Jesus expects a total response, but, unlike John the Baptist, he does not give concrete instructions about how his followers are to demonstrate repentance."

166. Burridge, *Imitating Jesus*, 70.

167. Neufeld, "Gospel in the Gospels," 285; he goes on to argue that "God's wrath is coming, and to repent and be baptized will bring a merciful salvation, as long as it

be saved' is explained in accordance with "repentance" in Luke's Gospel. Thus, both accounts (5:29–32 and 15:1–32) contain the theme of repentance which corresponds to John the Baptist's preaching.

The main difference between Luke 5 and Luke 15 is that forgiveness of sins is not explicitly mentioned in 15:1–32. But this theme is implicitly implanted into the story. Tannehill argues that the demonstrated connections to Luke 5:17–32 import the theme into this chapter in the reading process, a suggestion certainly consistent with the father's reception of the prodigal son.[168] In other words, it is very probable that the father's reception can be interpreted as the forgiveness of his son's sin. Furthermore, Luke often makes a strong link between forgiveness and repentance in his writing. For example, Luke reports Jesus' last words summarizing the importance of two elements: "repentance and forgiveness of sins is to be proclaimed in his name to all nations, beginning from Jerusalem" (24:47).[169] Also, Luke links Jesus' forgiveness directly to repentance in Luke 17:4, stating: "And if the same person sins against you seven times a day, and turns back to you seven times and says, 'I repent,' you must forgive."

Lastly, Jesus' encounter with Zacchaeus (Luke 19:1–10) also contains a number of connections with the earlier accounts and, echoes the topic of forgiveness.[170] There is a statement of Jesus' mission (Luke 19:10), which is reminiscent of Luke 5:32. The concluding line in Zacchaeus is very similar in content to the ending of the call of Levi: "For the Son of Man came to seek out and to save the lost" and "I have come to call not the righteous but sinners to repentance." In this regard, Tannehill aptly states, ". . . the use of 'Son of Man' in 19:10 may relate this statement to

---

includes repentance fruit, particularly economic kindness and integrity" (285). Likewise, Evans, *Luke*, 49, generalizing from Luke 3:10–14, claims: "According to Luke, the evidence of true repentance is chiefly seen in the ethics of contentment and generosity"; see also Nolland, *Luke*, 1:149–50.

168. Tannehill's *Narrative Unity*, 1:106–7.

169. Burridge, *Imitating Jesus*, 69–73, asserts, forgiveness involves repentance; e.g., Luke 5:32; 13:3, 5; 15:7, 10; 16:30; see also Acts 26:20, where Paul calls for deeds "worthy of repentance." See also Dunn, *Jesus Remembered*, 498–99.

170. See Tannehill's *Narrative Unity*, 1:107–108. Also, Neufeld, "Gospel in the Gospels," 290, claims: "Loyalty to Jesus over possessions receives special association with salvation by John's focus on this at the start, and by the accounts of the rich ruler and Zacchaeus at the end of Jesus' public ministry."

the general statement about Jesus' authority to forgive in 5:24, where this title was also used."[171]

Also, the reference to the lost in the mission statement recalls the parables in Luke 15. As in 15:1–32, forgiveness of sins is not directly expressed in Zacchaeus' story. However, as it is implicitly articulated in Luke 15, the theme of forgiveness is implied in the salvation of Zacchaeus (Luke 19:9). Therefore, both stories in 15:1–32 and 19:1–10, in spite of the absence of a direct reference to forgiveness, have inherent messages of Jesus' authority to forgive sins in connection with Luke 5:17–32 which "is imported to these suitable locations."[172]

Furthermore, Luke links Jesus' forgiveness of sins directly to his salvific activity in Luke 19:9. Luke seems to stress that, when the one who is lost is sought out or his or her sins are forgiven, he or she is saved. As discussed in Chapter 2, Levi and Zacchaeus were regarded as a sinner since they exploited his people. Their immoral wrongs are cured by the physician, who is Jesus, and, therefore, they are saved. Luke underlines that Jesus is successful in correcting their exploitations. Jesus' correction of their wrongs is directly associated with their salvation: Jesus in Luke forgives their sins and saves them.

In spite of his attempt to restore morality, the emperor fails to correct tax collectors' wrongdoings. This means that he fails to offer them forgiveness of sins or salvation, and accordingly indicates that he is a pseudo-savior. In this way, Luke presents Jesus, not the emperor, as the true savior and bringer of peace (Acts 5:31; 13:23) and as the one who obtains victory over immorality. As in the angel's announcement at 2:11, Luke's Jesus is born a savior who forgives sins and brings salvation to people. The use of "savior" in Luke 2:11 contrasts Jesus, who has come to 'seek and save the lost' (19:10), with Augustus, who is mentioned in 2:1.[173] As Powell rightly asserts, "Through encounters with Jesus, people are set free from things that prevent them from living life as God intends,"[174] since they are forgiven and saved through Jesus. Therefore, with the help of the title "savior," Luke successfully advertises Jesus' superiority over

---

171. Tannehill's *Narrative Unity*, 1:107.

172. McComiskey, *Lukan Theology*, 53.

173. See Brown, *Birth of the Messiah*, 415–16.

174. Powell, "Salvation in Luke–Acts," 8; for him, in Luke 18:24–26, "entering the kingdom of God" and "being saved" are treated almost as synonyms (8). Participation in the kingdom of God involves liberation from anything that prevents one from living life as God intends (cf. 4:18–19).

the emperor to his readers/hearers who were probably familiar with the imperial propaganda.

Zechariah's Praise

On the basis of the application of the Roman imperial formula to Luke's writings, it is necessary to look at a specific passage which contains the formula (victory–peace–salvation). Zechariah's praise (Luke 1:68–79) would be a good example. Prior to the discussion of the pattern, we need to see whether the praise is related to the Roman propaganda.

Scholars have suggested that this praise is based upon the Old Testament. There are several plausible reasons. First, it begins with a familiar Old Testament formula (the word of praise).[175] Second, there is also reference to characters of the Old Testament: David (v. 69) and Abraham (v. 73), both considered as key figures in the salvation of Israel. Thirdly, Luke records that God has "a mighty savior for us" (Luke 1:69; "raised up the horn of salvation for us"; καὶ ἤγειρεν κέρας σωτηρίας ἡμῖν). The expression "a horn of salvation" (κέρας σωτηρίας) is found in the LXX only in the Song of David and the parallel Psalm 17.[176] It is plausible to argue that σωτηρία has an Old Testament background where "salvation from our enemies" (Luke 1:71), for instance, is derived from 2 Sam 22:3 and Ps 17:18–19 in the process of Luke's construction of Zechariah's hymn (Luke 1:71–72). In this respect, the Septuagint may have influenced Luke's application of the terms "savior" and "salvation" to Jesus.

Although the word "savior" appears often in the Septuagint, it refers almost always to God apart from a few exceptions.[177] I do not wish to

---

175. According to Goulder, *Luke*, 1:240, it becomes clear that the Song of David functions as Luke's model, in the same way that the Magnificat is based upon the Song of Hannah; see also Farris, *Hymns of Luke's Infancy Narratives*, 71–72 and 134, arguing that similar formulae are often linked with David or David's son (1 Sam 25:32; 1 Kgs 1:48; 8:15).

176. Here, Zechariah speaks of Jesus (the Lord in v. 76) as κέρας σωτηρίας. It is often interpreted as "a mighty/powerful savior." Evans, *Luke*, 183, maintains that "a Semitic expression in which the noun *horn*, a symbol of power derived from horned animals (cf. Ps 89:17), acts adjectivally, and *of salvation* = 'effecting salvation' acts as a noun."

177. Deut 35:15; 1 Sam 10:19; 1 Chr 16:15; Jdt 9:11; Add Esth 15:2; Pss 23(24):5; 24(25):5; 26(26):1, 9; 61(62):2, 6; 64(65): 5; 78(79):9; 94(95):1; Sir 51:1; Wis 16:7; Hab 3:18; Isa 12:2; 17:10; 25:9; 45:15, 21, 22; Bar 4:22; 1 Macc 4:30; 3 Macc 6:29, 32; 7:16. For a few exceptions, see n3 in this chapter. See also Fitzmyer, *Luke*, 1:204–5; Gilbert,

deny the fact that the praise is based partly upon the Old Testament background. It is true that the formula, victory–peace–salvation, is, of course, found in the Old Testament, often depicting God as a victor.[178] But, at the same time, what I intend to stress is that the praise can be interpreted in connection with the imperial ideology. When considering Luke's purpose for constituting a challenge to the imperial ideology, the pattern of victor/peace-bringer/savior is more applicable for the Roman emperor, rather than for the Old Testament. Also, while the Old Testament passages quoted in Luke–Acts highlight God's promise–fulfillment,[179] Luke's use of the pattern of the imperial ideology aids us to understand Jesus' authority and his identity as a savior in comparison with the emperor. When it comes to Zechariah's praise, I am not concerned entirely with such a theme of promise–fulfillment, rather with the theme of salvation coming true through Jesus.

Another significant point I wish to make is that, when the title of savior is used for Jesus, it is associated more with worldwide dominion, rather than with Jewish expectations. Luke underlines Jesus transcended national boundaries as the emperor is perceived as a figure of universal significance. Given that Luke's portrayal of Jesus has social and political implications, Jesus' identity as the universal savior who brings salvation to all humanity (Luke 3:6; 24:47) presents parallels with the claims for the Roman emperor.[180] It is probable to argue that Luke's salvation language is rooted more in the imperial cults than in the Old Testament or other sources. There are no references to Jesus as savior (σωτήρ) in Mark's Gospel, Q, or Matthew's Gospel, and none of these designate Jesus as victor/peace-bringer/savior in comparison with the emperor.[181]

"Roman Propaganda," 241 n9.

178. Some scholars argue that David is portrayed as a victor in the Old Testament. For instance, Benoit, "L'enfance de Jean-Baptiste selon Luc 1," 185, asserts that deliverance from enemies corresponds to the mention of David the warrior, the service of God to the possession to the land promised to the patriarchs; the same structure has been suggested by Brown, *Birth of the Messiah*, 381–82.

179. For the scholars who have recognized that there is the theme of promise and fulfillment in Luke–Acts, see, for example, Cadbury, *Making*, 303ff.; Conzelmann, *Theology*, 57–63; Wilson, *Gentiles and Gentile Mission*, 53–54; Franklin, *Christ the Lord*, 60 and 69ff., 119ff.; Minear, "Luke's Use," 111–30 and 117–20; Farris, *Hymns of Luke's Infancy Narratives*, 152.

180. Gilbert, "Roman Propaganda," 241.

181. It is likely that the identification of Jesus as savior reflects Luke's own redactional interests.

Furthermore, according to Gilbert, 'the Septuagint role does not undermine the view that Luke's selection of biblical themes and terms are influenced by contemporary political propaganda' on the grounds that the Septuagint usage of the term savior does "not explain why Luke would have selected this particular term as a designation for Jesus in the first place."[182] In a similar vein, as Brent claims, the sentiment that Augustus and his successors 'made war to cease and had adorned peace' is indicated in Luke 1:55, 71, 77, 79; 2:11, 14, 29.[183] As Augustus saved his people from their enemies, "a mighty savior" in Luke will save his people from their enemies. When discussing Luke's association of the divine plan with themes of σωτηρία and σωτήρ,[184] Brent asserts that there is "'a more direct connection with σωτήρ in the ideology of the imperial cult.'"[185] With an easy access to the imperial images applied to the emperor, Luke is able to use those images when depicting Jesus' authority. Therefore, it seems the theme of savior is assimilated into Luke's writing.

Again, the reason to pick up Zechariah's praise in Luke's Gospel is that it condenses the pattern which appears in the Roman propaganda. We can find all the things relating to the Roman formula, such as victory,[186] peace, and salvation. Luke clearly refers to "enemies," "peace," and "salvation" through the praise. The theme of salvation in this praise is best understood in connection with victory (enemy) and peace. Again, given that Luke's audiences were, to some extent, the Gentiles, it is probably more efficient for him to use an already existing formula in terms of the advertisement of Jesus' power and identity as a savior.

When he was filled with the Holy Spirit, Zechariah spoke the prophecy as follows[187]:

182. Gilbert, "Roman Propaganda," 242.

183. Brent, *Imperial Cult*, 105.

184. Salvation (σωτηρία) occurs three times in Zechariah's praise (Luke 1:69, 71, 77).

185. Brent, *Imperial Cult*, 92–93; also see above.

186. Although the term "victory" is not directly expressed in this praise, we can find "enemies" which hints at the theme of victory. Moreover, being saved from enemies can be interpreted as victory over enemies.

187. On the discussion of the structure of this praise, see Farris, *Hymns of Luke's Infancy Narratives*, 128–34 (particularly, 133), who outlines the structure of Zechariah's praise as follows: Word of Praise (v. 68a) - Motive Clause (v. 68b) - Statements amplifying the Motive Clause (vv. 69–75) - Prophecy concerning John (vv. 76–77) - Recapitulation (vv. 78–79). He also analyses whether this prophecy is a unitary composition or whether vv. 76–79 were added to the original psalm. See also Marshall,

Savior: Victory–Peace–Salvation

⁶⁸ Blessed be the Lord God of Israel,

for he has looked favorably on his people

and redeemed them.

⁶⁹ He has raised up *a mighty savior (a horn of salvation)* for us

in the house of his servant David,

⁷⁰ as he spoke through the mouth of his holy prophets from of old,

⁷¹ that *we would be saved from our enemies and from the hand of all who hate us*.

⁷² Thus he has shown the mercy promised to our ancestors,

and has remembered his holy covenant,

⁷³ the oath that he swore to our ancestor Abraham,

to grant us ⁷⁴ that we, *being rescued from the hands*

of our enemies, might serve him without fear,

⁷⁵ in holiness and righteousness before him all our days.

⁷⁶ And you, child, will be called the prophet of the Most High;

for you will go before the Lord to prepare his ways,

⁷⁷ to *give knowledge of salvation to his people by the forgiveness of their sins.*

⁷⁸ By the tender mercy of our God,

the dawn from on high will break upon us,

⁷⁹ to give light to those who sit in darkness and in the shadow of death,

to *guide our feet into the way of peace.* (Luke 1:68–79)

Enemy

Let us first begin by taking a look at the reference to enemies in vv. 71 and 74. It is noticeable that this praise gives some clues to the identity of enemies.[188] Luke takes an example of the characteristics of enemies in v. 71. It is correct that the salvation in vv. 68–69 consists of national redemption,

---

Luke, 87.

188. We already talked about the identity of non-humans being enemies and human-beings. The focus is on human beings in this section.

since God, for example, delivered the Israelites from Egypt (Ps 106:7–12). However, it is wrong to conclude that this praise emphasizes only such national redemption. When we think about the identity of enemies more carefully, the theme of Jewish national redemption is less important.

It is necessary to identify who "we" (v. 71; and "us") are in the praise. Literally, the first person plural pronoun "we" indicates Israel. There is no doubt that the enemies were those who hated Israel ("us" in Zechariah's praise) since Zechariah, as a Jew, talks first about what happened to Israel. Yet, it is not correct that "we" refers only to Israel in this praise. Luke's use of 'we' functions as synecdochism. In this respect, I interpret the enemies as those who oppose Jesus (and his followers); likewise Israel's enemies opposed God's will in the past. It is a mistake to argue that Zechariah's praise focuses only on God. His praise intends to show not only God's saving activity from enemies; but also does such activity continue through Jesus. Along with God, his praise emphasizes both John the Baptist and the Lord in v. 76 with the focus on the fact that the Lord Jesus is the one who will save his people.[189] The identity of enemies should therefore be interpreted more broadly in Zechariah's song. It seems unlikely that the enemies are purely Israel's national enemies.[190] They are not only Israel's

189. The identity of the κύριος of v. 76 has been disputed. Scholars who support the Baptist provenance of the praise argue that in Luke 1–2 κύριος, with the exception of 1:43 and 2:11, refers to God, not Jesus. They interpret the child of v. 76 to be Jesus, rather than John. See, e.g., Klostermann, *Das Lukasevangelium*, 28; Lagrange, *L'Evangile selon St. Luc*, 61; Schurmann, *Das Lukasevangelium*, 91. Evans, *Luke*, 186 (italic original), argues that in Luke 1:16–17 "the Lord before whom John goes is God, and the parallelism suggests that here it corresponds to *the Most High*, even if in between Jesus has already been called *the Lord*, at least by implication (v. 43)." But the κύριος in v. 76 is intended to be Jesus. Certainly for the Lukan readers, the Lord before whom John will go is Jesus; see Marshall, *Luke*, 28; Farris, *Hymns of Luke's Infancy Narratives*, 139; Rowe, *Early Narrative Christology*. The theme of Luke 1:76 is similar to that of 3:4. Similarly, the identity of κύριος in 3:4 was debatable. Although it is true that in the Isaiah quotation itself the κύριος of 40:3 refers to God, the κύριος clearly indicates Jesus on the grounds that John the Baptist prepares the way for Jesus. Most scholars view κύριος in 3:4 as Jesus. E.g., Green, *Luke*, 171; Schneider, "Gott und Christus als Kyrios," 167 n36; Evans, *Luke*, 106; Nolland, *Luke*, 1:143; Plummer, *Critical and Exegetical Commentary*, 87; Rowe, *Early Narrative Christology*, 71. A very few old scholars argued that it refers to God; e.g., Bleek, *Synoptische Erklarung*, 159; Zahn, *Das Evangelium des Lucas*, 190–91.

190. It is true that the tense of vv. 68–75 is aorist. It, at a glance, indicates what happened to Israel in the past, not what will happen to them in the future. However, given that what happened in the past is related directly to what will happen in the future throughout the Bible, this should not be restricted to past time. This is often found in salvation history. Salvation itself throughout history happens as it happened

Savior: Victory–Peace–Salvation

enemies but also Jesus' (and his followers) enemies.[191] This implies that they are those who are against God and Jesus.

Also, Luke's association of "enemy" with "the ones who hate" occurs elsewhere in his Gospel. As discussed earlier, the term "enemies" (ἐχθρός) is again linked to the verb "hate" (μισέω) in Luke 6:27 where Luke emphasizes love of one's enemies.[192] As in 1:71, enemies are characterized as those who hate in 6:27. In 6:27–28, Luke gives a more concrete description of the characteristics of enemies with the reference of three participles: hate (μισοῦσιν), curse (καταρωμένους), and abuse (ἐπηρεαζόντων). As in Zechariah's song, the pronoun "you" in Luke 6:27–28 is used for synecdochism. The accusative "you" should not exclude the addresser, Jesus. It should not be limited only to addressees, since Jesus is the one who first sets an example for his teaching. It includes both Jesus and those who follow him. Taken together with Luke 1, the enemies are both the ones who "hate" Jesus (Israel; "us" in Zechariah's praise) and those "who sit in darkness and in the shadow of death" (1:71 and 74; although they are later saved by Jesus).

Even though we have identified the characteristics of Jesus' enemies in Luke, it is not easy to classify who has such characteristics in this praise only. Who hates Jesus (or his followers)?[193] In spite of the fact that Luke does not specify who hates Jesus in this praise, we can find Jesus' enemies, at least, on the basis of the characteristics of his enemies. Luke hints at the answer to the question in various ways throughout his writings. In this case, Luke's account of Jesus' trial provides a valuable clue to the identity of Jesus' enemies. The enemies expressed in 1:71 and 74 can be interpreted as the Jewish leaders, Herod, and Pilate in the later chapters. Luke describes that they put Jesus into danger and ultimately to death, and he,

---

in the past although they are different in methods and persons. In this respect, the tense of vv. 68–75 is not really important when we apply it to Jesus' activities evident after Luke 2.

191. Farris, *Hymns of Luke's Infancy Narratives*, 137, claims that the enemies "who are doubtless both national and individual."

192. Borgman, *Way*, 199–200 (his italics) asserts: "The Greek word [μισέω] for 'hate' does not connote feeling at all ... The language of hatred as for love ... points to intention and will, no emotional state. *To hate* demands a thoughtful action, a formidable choice rather than a visceral reaction based on feeling"; similarly, Marshall, *Luke*, 592, defines hatred as "renunciation," not as "psychological hate."

193. We have discussed Jesus' enemies in terms of non-human beings, such as Satan relating to the Roman emperor, and human-beings. Here, I wish to focus Jesus' enemies as human beings. See above.

accordingly, views them as responsible for Jesus' death. To put it another way, they, sitting in darkness and in the shadow of death (1:79), are those who hate Jesus and his followers.

Along with those religious and political leaders as Jesus' enemies, another question might be answered. Who else are Jesus' enemies? Or, are people in Luke's writings portrayed in a favorable fashion? For example, in Simeon's praise, we can find a clue to the question of who are to be saved by analyzing Jesus' attitude towards people generally. The exploration of this identity aids us to understand Jesus' salvation and peace in relation to his victory over the enemies. Thus, an important question is: Who are the peoples in 2:31? This will be answered in comparison with Luke's use of "crowd" (ὄχλος).

As a whole, Luke mainly uses two different terms, ὄχλος and λαός, when referring to the people. Jesus teaches them, preaches his message of the kingdom (Luke 4:43–44; 7:22; 9:11; 20:1) to them, and tells them parables; they, in turn, are amazed at his words and hang on them. However, Luke's use of the two terms is not really uniform because he, at times, seems to use the terms interchangeably.[194]

Let us first begin by exploring the term, crowd (ὄχλος). Some scholars assert that, while the term "crowd" is a somewhat vague and general word indicating a large number of persons, another group "people" (λαός) bears a religious implication and refers to Israel as God's chosen nation.[195] For instance, Ahn attempts to distinguish Luke's use of "crowd" (ὄχλος) or "multitude" (πλῆθος) from his use of the "people" (λαός), arguing:

> The first two words just describe a largeness of number, regardless of its composition. The "crowd" includes some different groups such as people, the Jewish leaders (Luke 5:17–19; 19:39; 22:47; 23:4), tax collectors (5:29), and disciples (6:17). The 'multitude' includes the heavenly host (2:13), fish (5:6), disciples (19:37), the Jewish leaders (23:1), women mourning the crucifixion (23:27).[196]

---

194. See 6:17 with 6:19; 7:24 with 7:29; 9:12 with 9:13; 18:36 with 18:43; 23:4 with 23:13.

195. Kingsbury, *Conflict in Luke*, 29. See Minear, "Jesus' Audiences, 81–87; Kodell, "Luke's Use of Laos," 327–43.

196. Ahn, *Reign of God*, 170 n.65; cf. Ascough, "Narrative Technique," at 69ff. For Ascough, the crowds appear as the hearers of the stories and teachings and as witnesses of mighty deeds. However, Ascough neglects the differences between Luke's use of "people" (λαός) and "crowd" (ὄχλος).

In general, the crowds in the Gospel show their positive attitude towards Jesus (e.g., Luke 19:47–48; 20:6, 19; 21:38; 22:2, 6, 53). However, there is a dramatic change in their attitude towards Jesus in the trial scene.[197] They demanded Jesus' crucifixion in opposition to Jesus (Luke 23:13).[198] Concerning their negative attitude towards Jesus in his trial, Neagoe argues that "it would be wrong to assume that the friendly crowds of previous passages have been composed of the same individuals as the crowd (23:18) which now calls for his crucifixion."[199] The reason for such a view is based upon his assumption that Jesus is isolated from any human support and that "the opposition to him is stronger than ever in the Gospel."[200] It could be right, but we need to consider other elements which Luke has in mind. Another dramatic change in their attitude is found when Jesus is led to crucifixion. They are associated with the women who lamented over Jesus (Luke 23:27). Here what is important is that not all of them beat their own breasts. It seems to me that Luke emphasizes the demarcation between those who favored Jesus again and those who did not. In both cases, they hate Jesus by demanding his crucifixion before he is led to death. Both groups can be interpreted as those who hated Jesus and those who sat in darkness and in the shadow of death (1:79). But, after the scene of Jesus being led to crucifixion, some of them (women) changed their attitude to him favorably. While some remain as those who still hated him, others changed their attitude by giving up their hatred. In this respect, Luke seeks to associate 'those who hate and sit in the darkness and in the shadow of death' in Zechariah's song with the women who changed their attitude to Jesus favorably. In other words, Luke stresses that they who once hated Jesus and sat in the darkness have become God's people after changing their attitude. Although there is no mention of their repentance directly, we can assume that they actually repented: "among them were women who were beating their breasts and wailing for him" (v. 27). We have already considered the significance of

---

197. Bond, *Pontius Pilate*, 143; Neagoe, *Trial*, 85.

198. Bond, *Pontius Pilate*, 143, n.21, asserts that there is 'the urgency of the crowd's demand . . . intensified by Luke' on the grounds that "Mark's aorist imperative Σταύρωσον αὐτόν (Mark 15:13) has been converted to a more emotional present imperative and doubled for emphasis, Σταύρου, σταύρου αὐτόν (Luke 23:21)." Thus, according to her, the chief priests do not need to stir up the crowd in Luke's account unlike Mark 15:11.

199. Neagoe, *Trial*, 85; he also argues that Luke is not interested in differentiating between them or to indicate a coherent pattern in their attitude (ibid., 38).

200. Neagoe, *Trial*, 85; see also 23:5.

repentance in relation to salvation through the stories of John the Baptist and Levi. Thus, the women, who once were Jesus' enemies, have been saved. As indicated in Luke 1:79, Jesus has given light and peace to them.

Luke's other favorite term for Jesus' audience is "people" (λαός), which occurs thirty-seven times in the Gospel and forty-eight times in Acts.[201] Ahn points out:

> Contrary to "multitude" and "crowd," Luke mainly indicates with λαός the people of Israel, who are distinguished from the gentiles (2:31–32), from their leaders (7:29–30; 19:47, 48; 20:1, 6, 9, 19, 26, 45; 21:38; 22:2, 66; 23:5, 13, 14, 27, 35) and from the disciples (6:17; 9:13).[202]

In Luke's writing, people are generally portrayed as favorable hearers (3:21; 6:17; 7:1, 29; 18:43), responding to Jesus' salvation work. They are praying (Luke 1:10); John the Baptist comes "to make ready a people prepared for the Lord" (1:17); and they were later baptized by him (3:21); they "were filled with expectation" of Christ (3:15); they praise God as the response to what Jesus does (18:43). In this regard, they are positively depicted not only as those who listen to Jesus' word, but also as those who recognize Jesus' authority which comes from God.

However, it is not easy to identify who the people are in Luke's writings, since the term itself is often elastic. As Evans suggests, "it can be a general word for 'people', but is also a regular Old Testament designation of Israel as the people of God (cf. Acts 10:2; 21:28 of the empirical Israel)." Luke also uses it of the Christian community (Acts 15:14; 18:10).[203]

Let us explore Simeon's praise in order to examine their identity. In Luke 2:31, the question immediately arises: Who are the peoples? G. D. Kilpatrick points out that the word "peoples" in v. 31 refers only to the tribes of Israel on the basis of the only other occurrences of the plural of λαός (Acts 4:25, 27) in Luke's writings.[204] For Kilpatrick, the term should be distinguished from the Gentiles. But this view is flawed. First, Kilpatrick's interpretation is not conceivable because the use of λαός in Acts 4:25, 27 is heavily influenced by the language of Psalm 2. In other

---

201. Statistically speaking, Luke is by far the chief user of the term in the New Testament. The occurrences of "people" in other writings of the New Testament: only three times in Mark, fourteen (four in Old Testament citations) in Matthew, twice in John and ten times (all from the Old Testament) in Paul.

202. Ahn, *Reign of God*, 170 n65.

203. Evans, *Luke*, 689.

204. Kilpatrick, "*Laoi* at Luke," 127; also see Ahn, *Reign of God*, 170 n65.

SAVIOR: VICTORY–PEACE–SALVATION 173

words, it cannot be used as a criterion for determining Luke's usage of the word.[205]

More importantly, the genitive/plural form "λαῶν" in 2:31 is used only once in Luke's writings. This kind of use cannot be considered the same as the nominative/plural use of λαός.[206] Among the New Testament writings, the same form is found only in Rev 7:9 and 11:9. In order to more fully identify the peoples at Luke 2:31, these occurrences might help us to analyze the identity of the term. We can find an important similarity between Luke 2:31–32 and Rev 7:9; 11:9 in terms of the use of λαῶν.

> "which have prepared in the presence of all peoples (τῶν λαῶν), a light for revelation to the Gentiles and for glory to your people Israel" (Luke 2:31–32)

> "there was a great multitude that no one could count, from every nation, from all tribes and peoples (λαῶν) and languages . . ." (Rev 7:9)

> "members of the peoples (τῶν λαῶν) and tribes and languages and nations . . ." (Rev 11:9)

It is noticeable that all the instances of λαῶν are related closely to the other nations. In Luke's Gospel, verse 32 specifies who the peoples are, mentioning that they are both the Gentiles and people of Israel.[207] Likewise, in Rev. 7:9 and 11:9, it is evident that the peoples include both Israel and people of other nations with different languages.

The phrase, πάντων τῶν λαῶν, furthermore, does not occur in the New Testament, except here at Luke 2:31. But it occurs three times in the LXX, 1 Kgs 8:53 (par. 8:12), Ode 13:31, and Zech 14:14. With the help of those occurrences, we may define the meaning of the phrase. First, πάντων τῶν λαῶν τῆς γῆς is used in 1 Kgs 8:53, which means all the peoples of the earth: "For you [Solomon] have separated them from

---

205. Marshall, *Luke*, 121. In contrast to Kilpatrick, Farris, *Hymns of Luke's Infancy Narratives*, 148, stresses that the term refers to the Gentiles, "not the tribes of Israel, who are mentioned in the OT texts, especially Isaiah 52:10."

206. The term λαός sometimes appears with the additional use of "all" (Luke 19:47; 20:6, 45; 21:38). Such a term, according to Evans (*Luke*, 689; italic original), becomes "a designation of the inhabitants of Jerusalem, a permanent audience, whose enthusiasm for Jesus is very forcefully expressed by they *hung on his words*." However, its number is always singular, in contrast to a plural number in Luke 2:31. Singular use should be not be equated with the use of plural on the grounds that its boundary is extended.

207. And this implies that the salvation is prepared in the presence of all peoples.

among all the people of the earth, to be your heritage." Although there is an additional phrase, τῆς γῆς, we can assume that these peoples are not limited only to Israelites. It can be interpreted as the Gentiles or as those who do not favour God. Second, this kind of point is also made in Zech. 14:14, πάντων τῶν λαῶν κυκλόθεν γῆς by adding the phrase πάντων τῶν λαῶν to κυκλόθεν γῆς. Here it is translated as all the surrounding peoples or nations. Again, the phrase is not interpreted purely as Israelites. But it is translated as different ethnic groups. As in the cases of the LXX, Luke's use of πάντων τῶν λαῶν cannot be regarded solely as Israelites.

Thus, as Farris rightly points out, "it seems best, therefore, to translate λαός as 'peoples,' that is, Israel and the Gentiles."[208] That the salvation is prepared in the presence of *all peoples* implies that both the Gentiles and Israel will be saved. This is also consistent with Luke's universalism indicated in 3:6: "and *all flesh* shall see the salvation of God."[209] Simeon's praise corresponds to Zechariah's praise in terms of salvation for the Gentiles, drawing the conclusion that both the Gentiles and the people of Israel, who favor Jesus (but who once hated him), will achieve salvation and peace through him in Luke's writings.

Peace and Salvation

Another issue I wish to highlight is peace and salvation expressed in Zechariah's praise. As indicated earlier, the way in which Jesus achieves salvation and peace is very different from that of the emperor. In Luke 1:77, Luke seems to centre on forgiveness of sins without any implication of national redemption in contrast to the emperor's salvation. While the emperor focuses on imperial redemption by overturning the current regime (or by removing his rivals with the help of his military *imperium*), it is hard to say that Jesus' salvation consists merely of national redemption when we talk about his salvation and peace. In Luke, Jesus' peace and salvation has nothing to do with deliverance from the Roman domination by force.

Jesus' salvation should be understood as "*redemption* from all *the enemies* that prevent them from serving him in 'holiness and

---

208. Farris, *Hymns of Luke's Infancy Narratives*, 148.

209. On the meaning of σάρξ as one having flesh and blood (or a person), see Matt 16:17; John 1:14; Rom 3:20; Gal 1:16; 2:16.

righteousness.'"[210] As in the accounts of the tax collectors, Luke sees Jesus as the one who brings peace and ultimately salvation to his people by forgiving their sins, because sins keep them away from God. In this respect, as Marshall rightly points out, the meaning of "knowledge of salvation" becomes more concrete by the additional expression of the phrase ἐν ἀφέσει ἁμαρτιῶν (v. 77; by forgiveness of their sins).[211] Again, the significance of this expression is linked directly to John the Baptist's preaching ("a baptism of repentance for the forgiveness of sins" at Luke 3:3).[212] Similarly, Rowe states, "The content of 1:77, that for which John is to prepare (ἑτοιμάσαι), fits exactly the purpose, action and effect of Jesus in the Gospel and in Acts, namely, σωτήρ and ἀφέσει ἁμαρτιῶν."[213] Luke stresses that Jesus offers his people both peace and salvation by focusing on forgiveness of their sins.

Moreover, the theme of salvation is also related to peace. A twofold statement in v. 79 stresses the peace that Jesus will bring: "to give light to those who sit in darkness and in the shadow of death, to guide our feet into the way of peace."[214] It is important to note that the way of peace in this verse can be understood as the outcome of salvation. The relationship between peace and salvation is again highlighted in other places. For example, according to Klostermann, Luke later in Acts relates peace to salvation directly; asserting that the way of peace is the same as the "way of salvation" of Acts 16:17.[215] As the elements of the imperial pattern, such as victory, peace, salvation, are actually all intertwined, Jesus' victory, peace and salvation are interrelated in Zechariah's song.

---

210. Farris, *Hymns of Luke's Infancy Narratives*, 137; italics mine; see above.

211. Marshall, *Luke*, 93. Lagrange, *Luc*, 61–61, discusses whether the word ἐν ἀφέσει is to be attached to salvation, knowledge, or to give. It is through forgiveness of sins that knowledge of salvation exists in any of the three cases. For the relationship between salvation and forgiveness of sins, see salvation of tax collectors.

212. See Farris, *Hymns of Luke's Infancy Narratives*, 139–40, maintaining that John is subordinate to the κύριος of v. 76, who is the ἀνατολὴ of v. 78 in connection with John's preaching at Luke 3:3, 8. For the discussion of the meaning of ἀνατολὴ, see Marshall, *Luke*, 94–95 and Farris, *Hymns of Luke's Infancy Narratives*, 140–41; Evans, *Luke*, 186–87; Goulder, *Luke*, 1:242.

213. Rowe, *Early Narrative Christology*, 70; also see above.

214. Brent, *Imperial Cult*, 95, attempts to relate those "seated in darkness and in the shadow of death" in Luke 1:79 to the members of the world described in Fabius' decree who 'would have gladly welcomed its destruction'(EJ, no.98 (a) line 8).

215. Klostermann, *Lukas*, 29.

Summary

As the assimilation theory shows, Luke applies Roman ideology (or imperial cult) to his presentation of Jesus' authority. On the basis of this theory, Luke uses several important political themes such as victory, peace, and salvation occurring in Luke–Acts. In doing so, the emperor's title, savior, has a significant role in identifying Luke's aim to highlight Jesus' authority and his identity as a true savior. However, this does not necessarily mean that Luke follows all the same values and contents of the emperor's title without any criticisms. In spite of some similarities, there are some marked differences between Jesus and the emperor. I have imported a basic concept of the contra-culture theory into Luke's Gospel in order to understand how Luke changes the methods of achieving victory and peace or how Luke differentiates Jesus from the emperor. With the help of this theory, it is possible, to some extent, to see the differences between the emperor's peace and Jesus' peace. Jesus' peace is not the same as that of the emperor: while the former rejects the use of violence, the latter makes use of his military *imperium* to obtain peace and security in the empire.

Furthermore, Jesus' salvation focuses particularly on forgiveness of sins of tax collectors, regarded as outcasts. By implicitly showing that the emperor's salvation does not reach those outcasts, Luke disgraces the emperor as a pseudo-savior. At the same time, Luke, heightening Jesus' universal dominion, portrays Jesus as a true savior who saves the tax collectors and offers them salvation. Therefore, the power/authority of the Lukan Jesus has been validated in his accounts.

In addition, I have taken an example of Zechariah's praise which bears the pattern of victory–peace–salvation. In his praise, the pattern is used for emphasizing Jesus' authority and his title, savior, as in other places. Luke views Jesus as the one who embraces even his enemies by forgiving their sins in contrast to the emperor who conquers them by force. Throughout Luke–Acts, Luke's description of Jesus centers on his identity as a savior and his authority to forgive sins.

Conclusion

In this study, I have attempted to put together hints of imperial authority in Luke's Gospel in order to argue, first, that Luke is not favorable towards Roman power and second, that he elevates Jesus' authority in connection with that of the emperor. Prior to the main discussion, in the *Introduction*, we have briefly discussed that the dichotomy between religion and politics was very unclear in the Roman Empire. There was no clear demarcation between religion and politics; rather, they were intertwined and overlapped. Misconception of their relationship can lead to the wrong conclusions both that the imperial cult was not religious in the Roman Empire, and that Jewish leaders and Herod were independent from Roman power. Luke, as one of the first-century writers, acknowledging the importance of social, cultural, and political values around him, becomes involved with the reality of the Roman Empire. His active engagement with secular history heightens his keen interest in the empire and the emperor. As the political leaders are heavily involved in the sphere of religion, Luke portrays Jesus as a significant religious, social, and political figure with authority. In this regard, the character of imperial authority should be taken into account in consideration of Luke's purposes in his Gospel.

Throughout this study, I have maintained that Luke strives to heighten Jesus' authority. In the beginning of his Gospel, he focuses on Jesus' superiority over John in the birth narratives, elevating Jesus' authority in comparison with John's charismatic authority by offering the different backgrounds (Jesus with Caesar and John with Herod). As shown, Luke uses the method of comparison and differentiation with several key figures. This similar parallelism reappears in the discussion of Luke's presentation of Jesus' authority in comparison with the emperor's authority (e.g., his moral *auctoritas* and titles) in the remaining chapters. Also, on the basis of Weber's categorization, Luke's portrayal of the Jewish leaders, Herod, and Pilate (holders of traditional authority and bureaucratic authority) is sketched out in Jesus' trial. His stance towards them provides us with his general attitude towards political power and the Roman Empire, which finally affects his description of the emperor's authority.

I have argued that Luke critiques both religious and political leaders in association with Jesus' death. What is noticeable in Jesus' trial is that Luke does not highlight Jesus' authority directly. Rather, he focuses his attention on the wrong accusations brought by the Jewish leaders and on the wrong verdict given by Pilate, a Roman governor delegated by the emperor. Luke demonstrates this by regarding them as those who are abusing their authority. To put it another way, Luke aims to devalue the authority of both the Jewish leaders and Pilate through the passion narrative. Their authority is not rooted in justice: first, the former wanted to kill Jesus, and second, the latter failed to give a just verdict despite his declaration of Jesus' innocence three times. In contrast to the emperor's emphasis on justice, Luke implicitly stresses that injustice was all too rife under his sovereignty. Pilate, as a Roman judge, failed to keep the Roman justice through the imperial judicial procedure, and he could not protect the innocent. Ironically, in this account Jesus' authority was not damaged at all even though he was crucified. Rather, his authority was vindicated by re-defining Pilate's authority as false.

Luke's emphasis on Jesus' authority in connection with his implicit critique of the emperor is also found in the tax-related accounts. One of the most important issues relating to the emperor's authority is expressed in Luke 2:1–2, 20:19–26, and 23:3, where the relationship between tax and Roman power is inherent. In order to answer the question about in what ways Luke describes him, I divided the emperor's authority/power into two realms, *imperium* and *auctoritas*. Augustus and his successors strived to restore morality with the focus on their moral *auctoritas*. However, in reality, the tax burden was very serious; various taxes, such as direct and indirect taxes, were exacted, and the tax payers suffered from them as a result. To make matters worse, the tax collectors exploited the oppressed. In this regard, Luke, aware that tax was related to the emperor's authority, implicitly connects the corruption of tax collectors with the failure of the emperor's claim to moral *auctoritas*. Based upon that the emperor, as a censor, even without the office, was ultimately responsible for immorality, Luke implicitly blames him for the tax collectors' wrongs. In contrast to the emperor's failure, it is implied that Jesus in Luke corrects their immorality through two stories, Levi and Zacchaeus. In spite of the emperor's attempt to restore morality, he could not restore such morality of tax collectors. Luke implicitly contrasts the emperor's failure or imperfection with Jesus' success, though this is not explicitly mentioned in the texts. In so doing, Luke tells us that Jesus' authority is superior to the emperor's moral *auctoritas*.

In order to advertise Jesus' authority, Luke often uses existing images as he does in the infancy narrative (Jesus–John). Through the use of several existing images, Luke strives to advertise who Jesus is in a more efficient way. By comparing with the emperor, Jesus' status in Luke could be easily acknowledged without further explanations to his audience, and accordingly, his status is elevated. Luke not only uses the existing images, but also moves on to differentiate the emperor's authority from Jesus' authority by showing his salvation activities. There are both continuity (assimilation theory) and discontinuity (contra-culture theory) between the emperor in the imperial cult and Jesus in Luke. He contrasts Jesus' authority with the emperor's authority in Luke 22:24–27 by focusing on the title "benefactor." When questioning the emperor's authority, Luke makes a grouping of the pagan kings called benefactors. As discussed, Luke depicts the benefactor-client system in a positive light, while expressing the pagan kings negatively. His positive portrayal of benefactor corresponds to his contemporaries' understanding of the title. For Luke, the problem lies not in the title, but with the holders of the title. Those who bear the title, from Luke's perspective, are not ideal benefactors due to their self-interest. In this regard, I have asserted that Luke differentiates false benefactors from true benefactors. For Luke, the pagan kings, including the emperor, are not true benefactors, on the grounds that they lack one of the main criteria for true benefactor, that is, service-oriented benefaction. In contrast to those kings, Luke reports that Jesus' benefaction is based upon service.

In a similar way, Luke critiques the emperor's authority by using another title, "savior." He re-interprets the basic patterns of the Roman propaganda, the so-called, victor/peace-bringer/savior. Luke, while stressing that Jesus' victory was not based upon coercive power, implicitly criticizes the emperor's coercive power rooted in his *imperium*. Luke expresses the relationship between Satan and the emperor's military *imperium* through several passages (e.g., Luke 4:1–13; 11:14–23; 8:26–39) in an indirect way. Unlike the emperor's use of his military *imperium*, Luke shows that Jesus rejected the use of the sword in several accounts, emphasizing that his peace had nothing to do with the use of violence.

Also, Luke's Jesus is viewed as a true savior through various tax-related accounts with the focus on repentance and forgiveness of sins.

He was not only the one who corrected tax collectors' wrongs, but also the one who saved them from evil. That is, Luke portrays Jesus as the one who successfully achieves victory and peace through his correction of their wrongdoings, not through the emperor's moral *auctoritas* or his military *imperium*. In this respect, Luke stresses that forgiveness of sins is linked directly to salvation (Luke 19:9). Jesus offers the tax collectors salvation by forgiving their sins. Zechariah's praise (Luke 1:68–79) functions as re-affirming Jesus as a true savior. Thus, Luke, questioning both the emperor's moral *auctoritas*/military *imperium* and his claim to savior/benefactor, validates Jesus' superiority over the emperor's authority in his Gospel.

Bibliography

Adair-Toteff, C. "Max Weber's Charisma." *JCS* 5 (2005) 189–204.
Ahn, Yong-Sung. *The Reign of God and Rome in Luke's Passion Narrative: An East Asian Global Perspective*. Biblical Interpretation Series 80. Leiden: Brill, 2006.
Alföldy, Geza. "Subject and Ruler, Subjects and Methods: An Attempt at a Conclusion." In *Subject and Ruler*, edited by A. Small, 254–61. Ann Arbor: Journal of Roman Archaeology, 1996.
Alter, Robert. *The Art of Biblical Narrative*. New York: Basic Books, 1981.
Ando, Clifford. *Imperial Ideology and Provincial Loyalty in the Roman Empire*. Classics and Contemporary Thought 6. Berkeley: University of California Press, 2000.
Ascough, Richard S. "Narrative Technique and Generic Designation: Crowd Senses in Luke–Acts and in Chariton." *CBQ* 58 (1996) 69–81.
Bagnall, Roger S., and Brian W. Frier. *The Demography of Roman Egypt*. Cambridge Studies in Population, Economy, and Society in Past Time 23. Cambridge: Cambridge University Press, 1994.
Barrett, C. K. *The Gospel according to St. John*. 2nd ed. Philadelphia: Westminster, 1978.
———. *Luke the Historian in Recent Study*. London: Epworth, 1961.
Bell, Catherine. *Ritual: Perspectives and Dimensions*. Oxford: Oxford University Press, 1997.
Benoit, Pierre. "L'enfance de Jean-Baptiste selon Luc 1." *NTS* 3(1956–57) 169–94.
Berry, John W. "Acculturation as Varieties of Adaptation." In *Acculturation: Theory, Models and Some New Findings*, edited by Amado M. Padilla, 9–25. AAAS Selected Symposium 39. Boulder, CO: Westview, 1980.
Bird, Michael F. "The Unity of Luke–Acts in Recent Discussion." *JSNT* 29 (2007) 425–48.
Blank, Josef. "Unity and Plurality in New Testament Ethics." In *Christian Ethics: Uniformity, Universality, Pluralism*, edited by J. Pohier and R. Mieth et al., 65-71. New York: Seabury, 1981.
Bleek, Friedrich. *Synoptische Erklarung der drei ersten Evangelien*. Leipzig: Engelmann, 1862.
Blok, Anton. "Variations in Patronage." *Sociologische Gids* 16 (1969) 365–78.
Blumenfeld, B. *The Political Paul: Justice, Democracy and Kingship in a Hellenistic Framework*. JSNTSup 210. Sheffield: Sheffield Academic, 2001.
Bock, Darrell L. *Luke*. 2 vols. Grand Rapids: Baker, 1994–1996.
———. "The Son of Man in Luke 5:24." *BBR* 1 (1991) 109–21.
Bond, Helen K. *Pontius Pilate in History and Interpretation*. SNTSMS 100. Cambridge: Cambridge University Press, 1998.
Borg, Marcus J. *Conflict, Holiness and Politics in the Teachings of Jesus*. Lewiston, NY: Mellen, 1984.

Borgman, Paul. *The Way according to Luke: Hearing the Whole Story of Luke–Acts.* Grand Rapids: Eerdmans, 2006.
Bourque, Nicole. "An Anthropologist's View of Ritual." In *Religion in Archaic and Republican Rome and Italy*, edited by Edward Bispham and Christopher Smith, 19–33. Edin-burgh: Edinburgh University Press, 2000.
Bousset, Wilhelm. *Kyrios Christos: A History of Belief in Christ from the Beginnings of Christianity to Irenaeus.* Translated by John E. Steely. Nashville: Abingdon, 1970.
Bowersock, G. W. *Augustus and the Greek World.* Oxford: Clarendon, 1965.
Brandon, S. G. C. *Jesus and the Zealots.* New York: Scribner, 1967.
Brent, Allen. *The Imperial Cult and the Development of Church Order: Concepts and Images of Authority in Paganism and Early Christianity before the Age of Cyprian.* Supplements to Vigiliae Christianae 45. Leiden: Brill, 1999.
Brown, David. *The Four Gospels: A Commentary, Critical, Experimental, and Practical.* Lon-don: Banner of Truth Trust, 1969.
Brown, Raymond E. *The Birth of the Messiah: A Commentary on the Infancy Narrative in Matthew and Luke.* New ed. London: Chapman, 1995.
———. *The Death of the Messiah.* 2 vols. London: Chapman, 1994.
Bruce, F. F. *Jesus and Christian Origins outside the New Testament.* London: Hodder & Stoughton, 1974
———. "Render to Caesar." In *Jesus and the Politics of His Day*, edited by Ernst Bammel and C. F. D. Moule, 249–64. Cambridge: Cambridge University Press, 1984.
Brunt, P. A. *Italian Manpower, 225 BC–AD 14.* Oxford: Clarendon, 1971, repr. 2004.
———. *Roman Imperial Themes.* Oxford: Clarendon, 1990.
Brunt, P. A., and J. M. Moor. *Res Gestae Divi Augusti: The Achievements of the Divine Augustus.* Oxford: Oxford University Press, 1967.
Bryan, Christopher. *Render to Caesar: Jesus, the Early Church, and the Roman Super-power.* Oxford: Oxford University Press, 2005.
Bultmann Rudolf. *The History of the Synoptic Tradition.* Translated by John Marsh. Oxford: Blackwell, 1963.
Burridge, Richard A. *Imitating Jesus: An Inclusive Approach to New Testament Ethics.* Grand Rapids: Eerdmans, 2007.
Cadbury, H. J. *The Making of Luke–Acts.* London: SPCK, 1958. 1st ed. 1927.
———. "The Titles of Jesus in Acts." In *The Beginnings of Christianity. Part I. The Acts of the Apostles. Volume V: Additional Notes to the Commentary*, edited by Kirsopp Lake and Henry J. Cadbury, 354–75. London: Macmillan, 1933.
Caird, C. B. *Saint Luke.* Philadelphia: Westminster, 1963.
Capponi, Livia. *Augustan Egypt: The Creation of a Roman Province.* Studies in Classics. London: Routledge, 2005.
Carter, Warren. *Matthew and Empire: Initial Explorations.* Harrisburg, PA: Trinity, 2001.
———. *Pontius Pilate: Portraits of a Roman Governor.* Collegeville, MN: Liturgical, 2003.
Cassidy, Richard J. *Jesus, Politics, and Society: A Study of Luke's Gospel.* 1978. Reprinted, Eugene, OR: Wipf & Stock, 2015.
———. "Luke's Audience, the Chief Priests, and the Motive for Jesus' Death." In *Political Issues in Luke–Acts*, edited by Richard J. Cassidy and Philip J. Scharper, 146–67. Maryknoll, NY: Orbis, 1983.
———. *Society and Politics in the Acts of the Apostles.* Maryknoll, NY: Orbis, 1987.

Clark, Andrew C. *Parallel Lives: The Relation of Paul to the Apostles in the Lucan Perspective*. Milton Keynes, UK: Paternoster, 2001.
Clark, K. Wills. *The Gentile Bias and Other Essays*. NovTSup 54. Leiden: Brill, 1980.
Cohn, H. *The Trial and Death of Jesus*. London: Weidenfeld & Nicholson, 1992.
Cole, A. *Mark*. Tyndale NT Commentaries. London: Tyndale, 1961.
Collins, Randall. *Weberian Sociological Theory*. Cambridge: Cambridge University Press, 1986.
Conzelmann, Hans. *The Theology of St. Luke*. Translated by Geoffrey Buswell. Philadelphia: Fortress, 1961.
Corbin-Reuschling, Wyndy. "Zacchaeus's Conversion: To Be or Not To Be a Tax Collector (Luke 19:1-10)." *Ex auditu* 25 (2009) 67–88
Coser, Lewis A. *Masters of Sociological Thought: Ideas in Historical and Social Context*. New York: Harcourt Brace Jovanovich, 1971.
Crossan, John D., and Jonathan L. Reed. *In Search of Paul: How Jesus' Apostle Opposed Rome's Empire with God's Kingdom*. San Francisco: HarperSanFrancisco, 2004.
D'Angelo, Mary Rose. "Abba and 'Father': Imperial Theology and the Jesus Traditions." *JBL* 111 (1992) 611–30.
Danker, Fredrick W. *Benefactor: Epigraphic Study of a Graeco-Roman and New Testament Semantic Field*. St Louis: Clayton, 1982.
———. *Jesus and the New Age: A Commentary on St. Luke's Gospel*. 2nd ed. Philadelphia: Fortress, 1988.
Darr, John A. *Herod the Fox: Audience Criticism and Lukan Characterization*. JSNTSup 163. Sheffield: Sheffield University Press, 1998.
Deissmann, Adolf. *Light from the Ancient East: The New Testament Illustrated by Recently Discovered Texts of the Greco-Roman World*. Rev. ed. London: Hodder & Stoughton, 1927.
Derrett, J. Duncan M. *Law in the New Testament*. 1970. Reprinted, Eugene, OR: Wipf & Stock, 2005.
———. "Luke's Perspective on Tribute to Caesar." In *Political Issues in Luke–Acts*, edited by Richard S. Cassidy and Philip J. Scharper, 38–48. Maryknoll, NY: Orbis, 1983.
de Ste. Croix, G. E. M. *The Class Struggle in the Ancient Greek World: From the Archaic Age to the Arab Conquests*. London: Duckworth, 1981.
Dibelius, Martin, and Hans Conzelmann. *The Pastoral Epistles*. Translated by Philip Buttolph and Adela Yarbro. Hermeneia. Philadelphia: Fortress, 1972.
Dolger, Franz Josef. "Der Heiland." *Antike und Christentum* 6 (1950) 241–72.
Doran, Robert. "The Pharisee and the Tax Collector: An Agonistic Story." *CBQ* 69 (2007) 259–70.
Dornseiff, F. "Σωτηρ." In *PW*, 2.3A.1:1211–21.
Dunn, James D. G. *Jesus Remembered*. Grand Rapids: Eerdmans, 2003.
Eck, Werner. *The Age of Augustus*. Translated by Deborah Luca Schneider. Malden, MA: Blackwell, 2003.
Eisenstadt, S. N., and L. Roniger. *Patrons, Clients and Friends: Interpersonal Relations and the Structure of Trust in Society*. Themes in the Social Sciences. Cambridge: Cambridge University Press, 1984.
Elise, Sharon. "Cultural and Structural Assimilation." In *International Encyclopedia of Sociology*. London: FD, 1995.
Elliott, John H. "Disgraced Yet Graced: The Gospel according to 1 Peter in the Key of Honor and Shame." *BTB* 25 (1995) 166–78. Reprinted in Elliott, *Conflict,*

Community, and Honor: 1 Peter in Social-Scientific Perspective, 51–86. Cascade Companions. Eugene, OR: Cascade Books, 2007.

———. *A Home for the Homeless: A Social-Scientific Criticism of 1 Peter, Its Situation and Strategy*. 2nd ed. 1990. Reprinted, Eugene, OR: Wipf & Stock, 2005.

———. "Patronage and Clientage." In *The Social Sciences and New Testament Interpretation*, edited by Richard L. Rohrbaugh, 142–56. Peabody, MA: Hendrickson, 1996).

———. *What Is Social-Scientific Criticism?* Guides to Biblical Scholarship. Minneapolis: Fortress, 1993.

Elliott, Neil. *The Arrogance of Nations: Reading Romans in the Shadow of Empire*. Paul in Critical Contexts. Minneapolis: Fortress, 2008.

Ellis, E. E. *The Gospel of Luke*. London: Nelson, 1966.

Esler, Philip Francis. *Community and Gospel in Luke–Acts: The Social and Political Motivations of Lucan Theology*. SNTSMS 57. Cambridge: Cambridge University Press, 1987.

Etzioni, A. *The Active Society: A Theory of Societal and Political Processes*. London: MacMillan, 1968.

Evans, C. F. *Saint. Luke*. London: SCM, 1990.

Evans, Elizabeth C. "Physiognomics in the Ancient World." In *Transactions of the American Philosophical Society* 59, Part 5. Philadelphia: American Philosophical Society,1969.

Farris, Stephen. *The Hymns of Luke's Infancy Narratives: Their Origin, Meaning and Significance*. JSNTSup 9. Sheffield: JSOT Press, 1985.

Finley, M. I. *The Ancient Economy*. London: Chatto & Windus, 1973.

Fisher, Nicholas R. E. "Roman Associations, Dinner Parties, and Clubs." In *Civilisation of the Ancient Mediterranean: Greece and Rome*, edited by Michael Grant and Rachel Kitzinger, 1199–225. New York: Scribner, 1988.

Fishwick, Duncan. *The Imperial Cult in the Latin West: Studies in the Ruler Cult in the Western Provinces of the Roman Empire*. 3 vols. Etudes préliminaires aux religions orientales dans l'Empire romain 108. Leiden: Brill, 1987–2005.

Fitzgerald, John T., ed. *Greco-Roman Perspectives on Friendship*. SBLRBS 34. Atlanta: Scholars, 1997.

Fitzmyer, Joseph A. *The Gospel according to Luke*. 2 vols. AB 28–28A. Garden City, NY: Doubleday, 1981-85.

Flender, Helmut. *St. Luke: Theologian of Redemptive History*. Translated by Reginald H. Fuller and Ilse Fuller. Philadelphia: Fortress, 1967.

Foerster, Werner, and Georg Fohrer. "σωτήρ." In *TDNT* 7:1003–23

Franklin, Eric. *Christ the Lord: A Study in the Purpose and Theology of Luke–Acts*. London: SPCK, 1975.

Freyne, Sean. *Galilee from Alexander the Great to Hadrian 323 B.C.E to 135 C.E.* Notre Dame: University of Notre Dame Press, 1980.

———. "The Herodian Period." In *Redemption and Resistance: The Messianic Hopes of Jews and Christians in Antiquity*, edited by Markus Bockmuehl and James Carleton, 29–43. London: T. & T. Clark, 2007.

———. *Jesus, a Jewish Galilean: A New Reading of the Jesus-Story*. London: T. & T. Clark, 2004.

Friedrichsen, Timothy A. "The Temple, a Pharisee, a Tax Collector, and the Kingdom of God: Re-reading a Jesus Parable (Luke 18:10–14a)." *JBL* 124 (2005) 89–119.

Friesen, Steven J. *Imperial Cults and the Apocalypse of John: Reading Revelation in the Ruins.* Oxford: Oxford University Press, 2001.

———. *Twice Neokoros: Ephesus, Asia and the Cult of the Flavian Imperial Family.* Religions in the Graeco-Roman World 116. Leiden: Brill, 1993.

Furnish, Victor P. *The Love Command in the New Testament.* Nashville: Abingdon, 1972.

Galinsky, Karl. *Augustan Culture: An Interpretive Introduction.* Princeton: Princeton University Press, 1996.

Garnsey, Peter, and Richard Saller. *The Roman Empire: Economy, Society and Culture.* Berkeley: University of California Press, 1987.

Garrison, Roman. *The Graeco-Roman Context of Early Christian Literature.* JSNTSup 137. Sheffield: Sheffield Academic, 1997.

Gellner, Ernst, and John Waterbury, eds. *Patrons and Clients in Mediterranean Societies.* London: Duckworth, 1977.

Gerard, Jean P. "Les riches dans la communaute lucanienne." *Ephemerides Theologicae Lovanienses* 71 (1995) 71–106.

Gibson, Jeffrey B. *The Temptations of Jesus in Early Christianity.* JSNTSup 112. Sheffield: Sheffield Academic, 1995.

Gilbert, Gary. "Roman Propaganda and Christian Identity in the Worldview of Luke–Acts." In *Contextualising Acts: Lukan Narrative and Greco-Roman Discourse*, edited by Todd Penner and Caroline Vander Stichele, 233–56. SBL Symposium Series 20. Atlanta: Society of Biblical Literature, 2003.

Goulder, M. D. *Luke: A New Paradigm.* 2 vols. JSNTSup 20. Sheffield: JSOT Press, 1989.

Gradel, Ittai. *Emperor Worship and Roman Religion.* Oxford: Clarendon, 2002.

Grant, F. C. *The Economic Background of the Gospels.* London: Oxford University Press, 1926.

Grant, Michael. *From Imperium to Auctoritas: A Historical Study of Aes Coinage in the Roman Empire 49 B.C.—A.D. 14.* Cambridge: Cambridge University Press, 1946. Reprinted, 1969.

———. *Roman Imperial Money.* London: Nelson, 1954.

Green, Joel B. *The Gospel of Luke.* NICNT. Grand Rapids: Eerdmans, 1997.

———. *The Theology of the Gospel of Luke.* New Testament Theology. Cambridge: Cambridge University Press, 1995.

Haenchen, Ernst. *The Acts of the Apostles.* Translated by Bernard Noble and Gerald Shinn. Oxford: Basil Blackwell, 1971.

———. *John 1: A Commentary on the Gospel of John Chapters 1–6.* Translated by Robert W. Funk. Hermeneia. Philadelphia: Fortress, 1984.

Hamel, Gildas H. *Poverty and Charity in Roman Palestine, First Three Centuries C.E.* Near Eastern Studies 23. Berkeley: University of California Press, 1990.

Hamm, Dennis. "Luke 19:8 Once Again: Does Zacchaeus Defend or Resolve?" *JBL* 107 (1988) 431–37.

———. "Zacchaeus Revisited Once More: A Story of Vindication or Conversion?" *Biblica* 2 (1991) 248–51.

Hands, A. R. *Charities and Social Aid in Greece and Rome.* Ithaca, NY: Cornell University Press, 1968.

Harland, Philip A. *Associations, Synagogues, and Congregations: Claiming a Place in Ancient Mediterranean Society.* Minneapolis: Fortress Press, 2003.

Harrison, J. R. "Paul and the Imperial Gospel at Thessaloniki." *JSNT* 25 (2002) 71–96.

Harrison, Stephanie. "The Case of the Pharisee and the Tax Collector: Justification and Social Location in Luke's Gospel." *CThM* 32 (2005) 99–111.

Hart, H. StJ. "The Coin of 'Render to Caesar . . . ' (A note on some aspects of Mark 12:13-17; Matt. 22:15-22; Luke 20:20-26)." In *Jesus and the Politics of His Day*, edited by Ernst Bammel and C. F. D. Moule, 241–48. Cambridge: Cambridge University Press, 1984.

Hays, Christopher M. *Luke's Wealth Ethics: A Study in Their Coherence and Character*. Tübingen: Mohr/Siebeck, 2010.

Hays, Richard B. "The Liberation of Israel in Luke–Acts: Intertextual Readings as Resistance." Paper presented at Fuller Theological Seminary, Pasadena, CA, Jan. 26, 2006.

———. *The Moral Vision of the New Testament—Community, Cross, New Creation: A Contemporary Introduction to New Testament Ethics*. San Francisco: HarperSanFrancisco, 1996.

Heichelheim, F. M. "Roman Syria." In *An Economic Survey of Ancient Rome*, edited by Tenney Frank. 6 vols. Baltimore: Johns Hopkins University Press, 1933–40.

Hemer, Colin J. *The Book of Acts in the Setting of Hellenistic History*. WUNT 49. Tübingen: Mohr/Siebeck, 1989.

Hoehner, Harold W. *Chronological Aspects of the Life of Christ*. Grand Rapids: Zondervan, 1977.

———. *Herod Antipas*. SNTSMS 17. Cambridge: Cambridge University Press, 1972.

———. "Why Did Pilate Hand Jesus over to Antipas?" In *The Trial of Jesus: Cambridge Studies in Honour of C. F. D. Moule*, edited by E. Bammel, 84–90. London: SCM, 1970.

Hoffman, Arthur Sullivant. *The Writing of Fiction*. New York: Norton, 1934.

Horrell, David G. "Domestic Space and Christian Meetings at Corinth: Imagining New Contexts and the Buildings East of the Theatre." *NTS* 50 (2004) 349–69.

———. *The Social Ethos of the Corinthian Correspondence*. Edinburgh: T. & T. Clark, 1996.

Horsley, Richard A. "Ethics and Exegesis: 'Love Your Enemies' and the Doctrine of Non-Violence." *JAAR* 54 (1986) 3–31.

———. *Jesus and Empire: The Kingdom of God and the New World Disorder*. Minneapolis: Fortress, 2003.

———. *Jesus and the Spiral of Violence: Jewish Resistance in Roman Palestine*. San Francisco: Harper & Row, 1987.

———, ed. *Paul and Empire: Religion and Power in Roman Imperial Society*. Harrisburg, PA: Trinity, 1997.

———, ed. *Paul and Politics: Ekklesia, Israel, Imperial, Interpretation: Essays in Honour of Krister Stendahl*. Harrisburg, PA.: Trinity, 2000.

———, ed. *Paul and the Roman Imperial Order*. Harrisburg, PA: Trinity, 2004.

Jervell, Jacob. *The Theology of the Acts of the Apostles*. New Testament Theology. Cambridge: Cambridge University Press, 1996.

Jewett, Robert. *Romans: A Commentary*. Hermeneia. Minneapolis: Fortress, 2007.

Johnson, Luke Timothy. *The Gospel of Luke*. SacPag 3. Collegeville, MN: Liturgical, 1991.

———. *The Writings of the New Testament: An Interpretation*. Philadelphia: Fortress, 1986.

Jones, A. M. H. *The Roman Economy: Studies in Ancient Economic and Administrative History*. Oxford: Basil Blackwell, 1974.
Jones, B. W. *The Emperor Domitian*. London: Routledge, 1992.
Kendall, D. *Sociology in Our Times*. 4th ed. Belmont, CA: Wadsworth, 2004.
Kennard, J. Spencer. *Render to God: A Study of the Tribute Passage*. Oxford: Oxford University Press, 1950.
Kertzer, David I. *Ritual, Politics, and Power*. New Haven: Yale University Press, 1988.
Kiernan, V. G. *Horace: Poetics and Politics*. New York: St. Martin's, 1999.
Kilgallen, John J. "Was Jesus Right to Eat with Sinners and Tax Collectors?" *Biblica* 93 (2012) 590–600.
Kilpatrick, G. D. "*Laoi* at Luke II 23 and Acts IV 25, 27." *JTS* 16 (1965) 127.
Kim, Seyoon. *Christ and Caesar: The Gospel and the Roman Empire in the Writings of Paul and Luke*. Grand Rapids: Eerdmans, 2006.
Kim, Young Yun, and William B. Gudykunst. *Cross-Cultural Adaptation: Current Approaches*. International and Intercultural Communication Annual 11. London: Sage, 1988.
Kingsbury, Jack Dean. *Conflict in Luke: Jesus, Authorities, Disciples*. Minneapolis: Fortress, 1991.
Klassen, William. "Love Your Enemies: Some Reflections on the Current Status of Research." In *The Love of Enemy and Nonretaliation in the New Testament*, edited by Willard M. Swartley, 1–31. Louisville: Westminster John Knox, 1992.
Klauck, Hans-Josef. "Die Armut der Junger in der Sicht des Lukas." In *Gemeinde, Amt, Sakrament: Neutestamentliche Perspektiven*, edited by Hans-Josef Klauck, 160–94. Wurzburg: Echter, 1989.
———. *The Religious Context of Early Christianity: A Guide to Graeco-Roman Religions*. Translated by Brian McNeil. London: T. & T. Clark, 2000.
Kloppenborg, John S. "Edwin Hatch, Churches and Collegia." In *Origins and Methods: Towards a New Understanding of Judaism and Christianity*, edited by B. H. Maclean, 212–38. JSNTSup 86. Sheffield: JSOT Press, 1993.
Klostermann, E. *Das Lukasevangelium*. Handbuch zum Neuen Testament 5. Tübingen: Mohr/Siebeck, 1929.
Knust, Jennifer W. "Paul and the Politics of Virtue and Vice." In *Paul and the Roman Imperial Order*, edited by Richard Horsley, 155–73. Harrisburg, PA: Trinity, 2004.
Kodell, J. "Luke's Use of *Laos*, 'People', especially in the Jerusalem Narrative (Lk. 19:28—24:53)." *CBQ* 31 (1969) 327–43.
Koester, Craig R. "The Saviour of the World (John 4:42)." *JBL* 109 (1990) 665–80.
Kreitzer, Larry J. *Striking New Images: Roman Imperial Coinage and the New Testament World*. JSNTSup 134. Sheffield: Sheffield University Press, 1996.
Kuhn, Heinz-Wolfgang. "Das Liebesgebot Jesu als Tora und als Evangelium: Zur Feindesliebe und zur christlichen und judischen Auslegung der Bergpredigt." In *Vom Urchristentum zu Jesus*, edited by Hubert Frankemolle and Karl Kertelge, 194–230. Freiburg: Herder, 1989.
Lagrange, M.-J. *L'Evangile selon St. Luc*. Paris: Lecoffre, 1948.
Latte, K. *Romische Religionsgeschichte*. Handbuch der Altertumswissenschaft 5.4. Munich: Beck, 1960.
Leaney, A. R. C. *A Commentary on the Gospel according to St. Luke*. Black's New Testament Commentaries. London: Black, 1958.

Leventman, Seymour, ed. *Counterculture and Social Transformation: Essays on Negativistic Themes in Sociological Theory*. Springfield, IL: Thomas, 1982.

Lietzmann, Hans. *Der Weltheiland: Eine Jenaer Rosenvorlesung mit Anmerkungen*. Bonn: Marcus & Weber, 1909.

Lintott, Andrew. *Imperium Romanum: Politics and Administration*. London: Routledge, 1993.

———. "What Was the 'Imperium Romanum'?" *Greece & Rome*, 2nd ser. 28 (1981) 53–67.

Loewe, William P. "Towards an Interpretation of Lk. 19:1–10." *CBQ* 36 (1974) 321–31.

Lohse, Eduard. "συνέδριον." In *TDNT* 7:860–71.

Loisy, Alfred. *L'Evangile selon Luc*. Paris: Nourry, 1924.

Lull, David J. "The Servant-Benefactor as a Model of Greatness (Luke 22:24-30)." *NovT* 28 (1986) 289–305.

MacMullen, Ramsay. *Roman Social Relations 50 B.C. to A.D. 284*. New Haven: Yale University Press, 1974.

Maddox, Robert. *The Purpose of Luke–Acts*. FRLANT 126. Göttingen: Vandenhoeck & Ruprecht, 1982.

Malherbe, Abraham J. "Christology in Luke–Acts 2." *RQ* 2 (1958) 115–127.

Malina, Bruce J. *The New Testament World: Insights from Cultural Anthropology*. London: SCM Press, 1981.

———. "Patron and Client: The Analogy behind Synoptic Theology." In *The Social World of Jesus*, 143–75. London: Routledge, 1996.

Malina, Bruce J., and Jerome H. Neyrey. "First-Century Personality: Dyadic, Not Individualistic." In *The Social World of Luke–Acts: Models for Interpretation* edited by Jerome H. Neyrey, 67–96. Peabody, MA: Hendrickson, 1991.

Marshall, I. Howard. *The Gospel of Luke: A Commentary on the Greek Text*. NIGTC 3. Exeter, UK: Paternoster, 1978.

———. *Luke: Historian and Theologian*. Exeter: Paternoster, 1970.

Marshall, Jonathan. *Jesus, Patrons, and Benefactors: Roman Palestine and the Gospel of Luke*. WUNT 2/259. Tübingen: Mohr/Siebeck, 2009.

Marwood, Martin A. *The Roman Cult of Salus*. British Archaeological Reports International Series 465. Oxford: B.A.R., 1988.

Mattingly, Harold. *Coins of the Roman Empire in the British Museum*. 5 vols. London: British Museum, 1923. Reprinted, 1966.

McComiskey, Douglas S. *Lukan Theology in the Light of the Gospel's Literary Structure*. Paternoster Biblical Monographs. Bletchley, UK: Paternoster, 2004.

Meeks, Wayne A. *The First Urban Christians: The Social World of the Apostle Paul*. New Haven: Yale University Press, 1983.

Meier, John P. *A Marginal Jew: Rethinking the Historical Jesus*. 3 vols. Anchor Bible Reference Library. Garden City, NY: Doubleday, 1991, 1994, 2001.

Mendez-Moratalla, Fernando. *The Paradigm of Conversion in Luke*. JSNTSup 252. London: T. & T. Clark, 2004.

Miles, Richard. "Communicating Culture, Identity and Power." In *Experiencing Rome: Culture, Identity and Power in the Roman Empire*, edited by Janet Huskinson, 29–62. London: Routledge, 2000.

Minear, Paul S. "Jesus' Audiences, according to Luke." *NovT* 16 (1974) 81–109.

———. "Luke's Use of the Birth Stories." In *Studies in Luke–Acts: Essays Presented in Honor of Paul Schubert*, edited by Leander E. Keck and J. Louis Martyn, 111–30. 1966. Reprinted, Philadelphia: Fortress, 1980.

———. "Notes on Luke 22:36." *NovT* 7 (1964) 128–34.

Mitchell, Alan C. *Anatolia, Land, Men, and Gods in Asia Minor I*. Oxford: Clarendon, 1993.

———. "Greet the Friends by Name: New Testament Evidence for the Greco-Roman *Topos* on Friendship." In *Greco-Roman Perspectives on Friendship*, edited by J. T. Fitzgerald, 225–62. SBLRBS 34. Atlanta: Scholars, 1997.

———. "Zacchaeus Revisited: Luke 19:8, as a Defence." *Biblica* 71 (1990) 153–76.

Mommsen, Theodor. *Romisches Strafrecht*. Systematisches Handbuch der deutschen Rechtswissenschaft 1.4. Leipzig: Dunker & Humbolt, 1899.

Moralee, Jason W. "For Salvation's Sake (*Hyper Soterias*): Ideology, Society, and Religion in the Dedications for Salvation from the Roman and Late Antique Near East, 100 BC to AD 800." PhD diss., University of California at Los Angeles, 2002.

Morris, Leon. *The Gospel according to St. Luke: An Introduction and Commentary*. Grand Rapids: Eerdmans, 1974.

Moxnes, Halvor. *The Economy of the Kingdom: Social Conflict and Economic Relations in Luke's Gospel*. Overtures to Biblical Theology. 1988. Reprinted, Eugene, OR: Wipf & Stock, 2004.

———. "Patron-Client Relations and the New Community in Luke–Acts." In *The Social World of Luke–Acts: Models for Interpretation*, edited by Jerome H. Neyrey, 241–68. Peabody, MA: Hendrickson, 1991.

Neagoe, Alexandru. *The Trial of the Gospel: An Apologetic Reading of Luke's Trial Narratives*. SNTSMS 116. Cambridge: Cambridge University Press, 2002.

Neale, David A. *None but the Sinners: Religious Categories in the Gospel of Luke*. JSNTSup 58. Sheffield: Sheffield Academic, 1991.

Nelson, Peter K. "The Flow of Thought in Luke 22:24–27." *JSNT* 43 (1991) 113–23.

———. *Leadership and Discipleship: A Study of Luke 22:24-30*. SBLDS 138. Atlanta: Scholars, 1994.

Neufeld, Edmund K. "The Gospel in the Gospels: Answering the Question 'What Must I Do To Be Saved?'" *JETS* 51(2008) 267–96.

Neyrey, Jerome H. "God, Benefactor and Patron: The Major Cultural Model for Interpreting the Deity in Greco-Roman Antiquity." *JSNT* 27 (2005) 465–92

———.*The Passion according to Luke: A Redaction Study of Luke's Soteriology*. 1985. Reprinted, Eugene, OR: Wipf & Stock, 2007.

Nilsson, Martin P. *Greek Piety*. Translated by Herbert Jennings Rose. Oxford: Clarendon, 1948.

———. *A History of Greek Religion*. 2nd ed. New York: Norton, 1964.

Nock, Arthur Darby. "Deification and Julian." *JRS* 47 (1957) 115–23 = (1972), vol. 2 833–46.

———. *Essays on Religion in the Ancient World*. 2 vols. Edited by Zeph Stewart. Cambridge: Harvard University Press, 1972.

———. "Soter and Euergetes." In *Essays on Religion in the Ancient World*, edited by Zeph Stewart, 2:720–35. 2 vols. Oxford: Oxford University Press, 1972. Originally in *The Joy of Study: Papers on the New Testament and Related Subjects Presented to Honour Frederick Clifton Grant*, edited by S. E. Johnson. New York: Macmillan, 1951.

Nolland, John. *Luke*. 3 vols. Word Biblical Commentary 35 A, B, C. Dallas: Word, 1989, 1993.

North, J. A. *Roman Religion*. Greece & Rome: New Surveys in the Classics 30. Oxford: Oxford University Press, 2000.

Oakes, Peter. *Philippians: From People to Letter*. SNTSMS 110. Cambridge: Cambridge University Press, 2001.

———, ed. *Rome in the Bible and the Early Church*. Grand Rapids: Baker, 2002.

———. "A State of Tension: Rome in the NT." In *The Gospel of Matthew in Its Roman Imperial Context*, edited by John Riches and David C. Sim, 75–90. JSNTSup 276. London: T. & T. Clark, 2005.

Oakman, Douglas E. *Jesus and the Economic Questions of His Day*. Studies in the Bible and Early Christianity 8. Lewiston, NY: Mellen, 1986.

O'Fearghail, Fearghus. *The Introduction to Luke–Acts, A Study of the Role of Luke 1,1— 4,44 in the Composition of Luke's Two-Volume Work*. AnBib 126. Rome: Pontifical Biblical Institute Press, 1991.

O'Hanlon, John. "The Story of Zacchaeus and the Lukan Ethic." *JSNT* (1981) 2–26.

Okorie, A. M. "The Characterisation of the Tax Collectors in the Gospel of Luke." *CThM* 22 (1995) 27–32.

O'Neil, Edward N. "Plutarch on Friendship." In *Greco-Roman Perspectives on Friendship*, edited by John T. Fitzgerald, 105–22. Resources for Biblical Study 34. Atlanta: Scholars, 1997.

Otto, Walter. "Augustus Soter." *Hermes* 45 (1910) 448–60.

Parsons, Mikeal C. *Body and Character in Luke and Acts*. Grand Rapids: Baker, 2006.

———. *Luke: Storyteller, Interpreter, Evangelist*. Peabody, MA: Hendrickson, 2007.

———. "Short in Stature: Luke's Physical Description of Zacchaeus." *NTS* 47 (2001) 50–57.

Pearson, Brook W. R. "The Lukan Censuses, Revisited." in *CBQ* (1999) 262–82.

Perkins, Pheme. "Taxes in the New Testament." *JRE* 12 (1984) 182–200.

Perrin, Norman. *Rediscovering the Teachings of Jesus*. New York: Harper & Row, 1967.

Pesch, Rudolf. *Das Markusevangelium*. Vols. 1–2. Herders theologischer Kommentar zum Neuen Testament 2. Freiburg: Herder, 1977.

Petracca, V. *Gott oder das Geld: Die Besitzethik des Lukas*. Texte und Arbeiten zum neutestamentlichen Zeitalter 39. Tübingen: Francke, 2003.

Piper, John. *Love Your Enemies: Jesus' Love Command in the Synoptic Gospels and in the Early Christian Paraenesis: A Hsitory of the Tradition and Interpretation of Its Uses*. SNTSMS 38.Cambridge: Cambridge University Press, 1979.

Piper, Otto A. "God's Good News: The Passion Story according to Mark." *Interpretation* 9 (1955) 165–82.

Plummer, A. *A Critical and Exegetical Commentary on the Gospel according to St. Luke*. 10th ed. ICC 28. NY: Scribner, 1914.

Porter, Stanley E. "The Reasons for the Lukan Census." In *Paul, Luke and the Graeco-Roman World: Essays in Honour of Alexander J. M. Wedderburn*, edited by A. Christophersen et. al., 165–88. JSNTSup 217. London: Sheffield Academic, 2002.

Powell, Mark A. "Salvation in Luke–Acts." *Word and World* 12/1 (1992) 5–10.

———. *What Is Narrative Criticism?* Guides to Biblical Scholarship. Minnea-polis: Fortress, 1990.

Price, S. R. F. "Gods and Emperors: The Greek Language of the Roman Imperial Cult." *JHS* 104 (1984) 79–95.

———. *Rituals and Power: The Roman Imperial Cult in Asia Minor.* Cambridge: Cambridge University Press, 1984.
Ramsay, W. M. "Luke's Narrative of the Birth of Christ." *Exp* 4 (1912) 385–407, 481–501.
Rehak, P. *Imperium and Cosmos: Augustus and the Northern Campus Martius*, edited by John G. Younger. Madison: University of Wisconsin Press, 2006.
Rich, John. "Patronage and Interstate Relations in the Roman Republic." In *Patronage in Ancient Society*, edited by Andrew Wallace-Hadrill, 117–35. London: Routledge, 1990.
Richardson, J. S. "*Imperium Romanum*: Empire and the Language of Power." *JRS* 81 (1991) 1–9.
Riches J., and David C. Sim, eds. *The Gospel of Matthew in Its Roman Imperial.* JSNTSup 276. London: T. & T. Clark, 2005.
Robbins, Vernon K. "Luke–Acts: A Mixed Population Seeks a Home in the Roman Empire." In *Images of Empire*, edited by Loveday Alexander, 201–21. JSOTSup 122. Sheffield: JSOT Press, 1991.
Robinson, J. A. T. *Re-dating the New Testament.* Philadelphia: Westminster, 1976.
Rousseau, John J., and Rami Arav. *Jesus and His World: An Archaeological and Cultural Dictionary.* Minneapolis: Fortress, 1996.
Rowe, C. Kavin. *Early Narrative Christology: The Lord in the Gospel of Luke.* Grand Rapids: Baker Academic, 2009.
———. "Luke–Acts and the Imperial Cult: A Way through the Conundrum?" *JSNT* 27 (2005) 279–300.
———. *World Upside Down: Reading Acts in the Graeco-Roman Age.* Oxford: Oxford University Press, 2010.
Russell, D. A. *Plutarch.* 2nd ed. London: Bristol Classics, 2001.
Sahlins, Marshall. *Stone-Age Economics.* Chicago: Aldine-Atherton, 1972.
Saller, Richard P. "Patronage and Friendship in Early Imperial Rome: Drawing the Distinction." In *Patronage in Ancient Society*, edited by Wallace-Hadrill, 49–62. London: Routledge, 1990.
———. *Personal Patronage under the Early Empire.* Cambridge: Cambridge University Press, 1982.
Salmon, E. T. *A History of the Roman World from 39 BC to AD 138.* 3rd edn. London: Methuen, 1957.
Sanders, E. P. *Jesus and Judaism.* Philadelphia: Fortress, 1985.
———. *Judaism: Practice and Belief, 63 B.C.E-66 C.E.* Philadelphia: Trinity Press International, 1992.
Sanders, Jack T. *The Jews in Luke–Acts.* Philadelphia: Fortress, 1987.
Sandmel, Samuel. "Parallelomania." *JBL* 81 (1962) 1–13.
Schalit, A. *König Herodes: Der Mann und sein Werk.* Berlin: de Gruyter, 1969.
Schmidt, Steffen W. et. al., eds. *Friends, Followers and Factions: A Reader in Political Clientelism.* Berkeley: University of California Press, 1977.
Schmidt, Thomas E. "Taxes." In *Dictionary of Jesus and the Gospels*, edited by Joel B. Green and Scot McKnight, 804–7. Downers Grove, IL: InterVarsity, 1992.
Schneider, G. "Gott und Christus als Kyrios nach der Apostelgeschichte." In *Begegnung mit dem Wort*, edited by J. Zmijewski and E. Nellessen, 161–74. Bonn: Hansstein, 1980.

———. "The Political Charge against Jesus (Luke 23:2)." In *Jesus and the Politics of His Day*, edited by Ernst Bammel and C. F. D. Moule, 403–14. Cambridge: Cambridge University Press, 1984.
Schottroff, Luise. "Non-Violence and the Love of One's Enemies." In *Essays on the Love Commandment*, edited by Luise Schottroff et. al., 9–39. Translated by Reginald H. Fuller and Ilse Fuller. Philadelphia: Fortress, 1978.
Schurmann, H. *Jesu Abschiedsrede: Lk. 22, 21–38*. Munster: Aschendorff, 1957.
———. *Das Lukasevangelium (Kommentar zu 1:1—9:50)*. Herders Theologischer Kommentar zum Neuen Testament, 3/1. Freiburg: Herder, 1969.
Schwartz, Daniel R. "Pontius Pilate." In *ABD*, 5:395–401.
Sherwin-White, A. N. *Roman Society and Roman Law in the New Testament*. Grand Rapids: Baker, 1963.
Shriver, Donald W., Jr. *An Ethics for Enemies: Forgiveness in Politics*. Oxford: Oxford University Press, 1995.
Slingerland, Dixon. "The Composition of Acts: Some Redaction-Critical Observations." *JAAR* 56 (1998) 99–133.
Smallwood, E. Mary. *The Jews under Roman Rule: from Pompey to Diocletian*. SJLA 20. Leiden: Brill, 1976.
Smith, Mark D. "Of Jesus and Quirinius." *CBQ* 62 (2000) 278–93.
Stenschke, C. W. *Luke's Portrait of Gentiles Prior to Their Coming to Faith*. Wissenschaftliche Untersuchungen zum Neuen Testament 108. Tübingen: Mohr/Siebeck, 1999.
Sutherland, C. H. V. *Coinage in Roman Imperial Policy: 31 B.C.—A.D. 68*. London: Methuen, 1951 = *Roman Imperial Coinage*, vol. 1 (31 BC–AD 69). Rev. ed. London: Spink, 1984.
Swartley, Willard M. *Covenant of Peace: The Missing Peace in New Testament Theology and Ethics*. Grand Rapids: Eerdmans, 2006.
———, ed. *The Love of Enemy and Non-Retaliation in the New Testament*. Louisville: Westminster John Knox, 1992.
———. "War and Peace in the New Testament." In *ANRW* 2.26.3, 2298-408.
Talbert, Charles H. *Literary Pattern, Theological Themes, and the Genre of Luke Acts*. SBLMS 20. Cambridge, MA: Society of Biblical Literature, 1974.
Tannehill, Robert C. *The Narrative Unity of Luke–Acts: A Literary Interpretation: Volume 1: The Gospel of Luke*. Philadelphia: Fortress, 1986.
———. *The Narrative Unity of Luke–Acts: A Literary Interpretation: Volume 2: The Acts of The Apostles*. Minneapolis: Fortress, 1994.
———. "The Story of Zacchaeus as Rhetoric: Luke 19:1-10." *Semeia* 64 (1994) 201–21.
Theissen, Gerd. *The Gospels in Context: Social and Political History in the Synoptic Tradition*. Minneapolis: Fortress, 1991.
———. "Non-Violence and Love of Our Enemies (Matthew 5:38-48; Luke 6:27-38)." In *Social Reality and the Early Christians: Theology, Ethics and the World of the New Testament*, 115–57. Translated by Margaret Kohl. Minneapolis: Fortress, 1992.
———. "The Political Dimension of Jesus' Activities." In *The Social Setting of Jesus and the Gospels*, edited by Wolfgang Stegemann et. al., 225–250. Minneapolis: Fortress Press, 2002.
———. *The Social Setting of Pauline Christianity*. Edited and translated by John H. Schutz. Edinburgh: T. & T. Clark, 1982.

Turner, H. E. W. "The Chronological Framework of the Ministry." In *Historicity and Chronology in the New Testament*, edited by D. E. Nineham et al., 59–74. London: SPCK, 1965.
Turner, Nigel. *Grammatical Insights into the New Testament*. Edinburgh: T. & T. Clark, 1965.
———. *Syntax (A Grammar of NT Greek)*. Vol. 3. Edited by J. H. Moulton. Edinburgh: T. & T. Clark, 1963.
Tyson, Joseph B. *The Death of Jesus in Luke–Acts*. Columbia: University of South Carolina Press, 1986.
Walaskay, Paul W. *"And so We Came to Rome": The Political Perspective of St. Luke*. SNTSMS 49. Cambridge: Cambridge University Press, 1983.
Walker, William O. "Jesus and the Tax Collectors." *JBL* 97 (1978) 221–38.
Wallace, Daniel B. *Greek Grammar Beyond the Basics: An Exegetical Syntax of the New Testament*. Grand Rapids: Zondervan, 1996.
Wallace-Hadrill, Andrew. "Image and Authority in the Coinage of Augustus." *JRS* 76 (1986) 66–87.
———. *Patronage in Ancient Society*. London: Routledge, 1990.
Walton, Steve. "The State They Were In: Luke's View of the Roman Empire." In *Rome in the Bible and the Early Church*, edited by Peter Oakes, 1–41. Grand Rapids: Baker, 2002.
Weatherly, Jon A. *Jewish Responsibility for the Death of Jesus in Luke–Acts*. JSNTSup 106. Sheffield: Sheffield Academic, 1994.
Weber, Max. "Der Beruf zur Politik." In *Soziologie: Weltgeschichtliche Analysen. Politik*, edited by J. Winckelmann, 167–85. 3rd ed. Stuttgart: Kroner, 1964.
———. *Economy and Society: An Outline of Interpretive Sociology*. Edited by Guenther Roth and Claus Wittich. Berkeley: University of California Press, 1978.
———. *The Theory of Social and Economic Organisation*. Translated by A. R. Henderson and Talcott Parsons. New York: MacMillan, 1964.
———. "The Three Types of Legitimate Rule." Translated by Hans Gerth. *Berkeley Publications in Society and Institutions* 4 (1955) 1–11.
———. *Wirtschaft und Gesellschaft: Grundriss der verstehenden Soziologie*. Edited by Johannes Winckelmann. 5th ed. Tübingen: Mohr/Siebeck, 1976. Online: http://www.textlog.de/weber_wirtschaft.html. *Economy and Society: An Outline of Interpretive Sociology*. Edited by Guenther Roth and Claus Wittich. Berkeley: University of California Press, 1978.
Weinstock, Stefan. "Pax and the 'Ara Pacis.'" *JRS* 50 (1960) 44–58.
Wells, Colin M. *The Roman Empire*. London: Fontana, 1984.
Wendland, Paul. "Σωτήρ." *ZNW* 5 (1904) 335–53.
Wengst, Klaus. *Pax Romana and the Peace of Jesus Christ*. Translated by John Bowden. London: SCM, 1987.
White, John L. *The Apostle of God: Paul and the Promise of Abraham*. Peabody, MA: Hendrickson, 1999.
White, Richard C. "A Good Word for Zacchaeus: Exegetical Comment on Luke 19:1–10." *LThQ* 14 (1979) 89–96.
Wilson, Stephen G. *The Gentiles and the Gentile Mission in Luke–Acts*. SNTSMS 23. Cambridge: Cambridge University Press, 1973.
Winter, Bruce W. "Acts and Roman Religion: B. The Imperial Cult." In *The Book of Acts in Its Graeco-Roman Setting*, edited by David W. J. Gill and Conrad Gempf,

93–103. The Book of Acts in Its First Century Setting 2. Grand Rapids: Eerdmans, 1994.

———. *Seek the Welfare of the City: Christians as Benefactors and Citizens.* Grand Rapids: Eerdmans, 1994.

Winter, Paul. "The Treatment of This Source by the Third Evangelist in Luke XXI–XXIV." *ST* 8 (1955) 138–72.

———. *On the Trial of Jesus.* Studia Judaica 1. Berlin: de Gruyter, 1961.

Witherington, Ben, III. "Salvation and Health in Christian Antiquity: The Soteriology of Luke-Acts in Its First Century Setting." In *Witness to the Gospel: The Theology of Acts*, edited by I. Howard Marshall and David Peterson, 145–66. Grand Rapids: Eerdmans, 1998.

Wright, N. T. "God and Caesar: Then and Now." In *The Character of Wisdom: Essays in Honor of Wesley Carr*, edited by Martyn Percy and Stephen Lowe, 157–71. London: Ashgate, 2004.

———. *Jesus and the Victory of God.* Christian Origins and the Question of God 2. London: SPCK, 1996.

———. "Paul and Caesar: A New Reading of Romans." In *A Royal Priesthood? The Use of the Bible Ethically and Politically: A Dialogue with Oliver O'Donovan*, edited by Craig Bartholomew et. al., 173–93. Scripture and Hermeneutics Series 3. Grand Rapids: Zondervan, 2002.

Yamazaki-Ransom, Kazuhiko. *The Roman Empire in Luke's Narrative.* JSNTSup 404. London: T. & T. Clark, 2010.

Yinger, J. Milton. "Toward a Theory of Assimilation and Dissimilation." *ERS* 4 (1981) 249–64.

Zahn, Theodor. *Das Evangelium des Lucas.* Kommentar zum Neuen Testament 3. Leipzig: Deichert, 1913.

Zanker, Paul. *The Power of Images in the Age of Augustus.* Translated by Alan Shapiro. Jerome Lectures, 16th ser Ann Arbor: University of Michigan Press, 1988.

www.ingramcontent.com/pod-product-compliance
Lightning Source LLC
Chambersburg PA
CBHW070328230426
43663CB00011B/2251